Eric Hobsbawm was a Fellow of the British Academy American Academy of Arts and Sciences. Before retirement at Birkbeck College, University of London, and after retirem New School for Social Research in New York. His previ include *The Age of Extremes*, *The Age of Revolution* and *The Age of Empire*. He died at the age of ninety-five in October 2012.

Also by Eric Hobsbawm

Fractured Times

Culture and Society in the Twentieth Century

Eric Hobsbawm

ABACUS

First published in Great Britain in 2013 by Little, Brown
This paperback edition published in 2014 by Abacus

A CIP catalogue record for this book
is available from the British Library.

ISBN 978-0-349-13909-8

Typeset in Baskerville by M Rules
Printed and bound in Great Britain by
Clays Ltd, St Ives plc

Papers used by Abacus are from well-managed forests
and other responsible sources.

MIX
Paper from
responsible sources
FSC® C104740

Abacus
An imprint of
Little, Brown Book Group
100 Victoria Embankment
London EC4Y 0DY

An Hachette UK Company
www.hachette.co.uk

www.littlebrown.co.uk

Contents

PART III: UNCERTAINTIES, SCIENCE, RELIGION

PART IV: FROM ART TO MYTH

Acknowledgements

I would like to express my gratitude to the Salzburg Festival, and especially its President Mrs Helga Rabl-Stadler and to Prof Heinrich Fischer of Salzburg University, to the *London Review of Books* where several of the chapters first appeared, to Rosalind Kelly, Lucy Dow and Zöe Sutherland who assisted in the research and editing and to Christine Shuttleworth for excellent translations. I also apologise to Marlene for concentrating more intensely than I should have done on the work on this book.

Preface

And we are here as on a darkling plain
Swept with confused alarms of struggle and flight,
Where ignorant armies clash by night.

Matthew Arnold, 'Dover Beach'

This is a book about what happened to the art and culture of bourgeois society after that society had vanished with the generation after 1914, never to return. It is about one aspect of the all-embracing seismic change humanity has been living through since the Middle Ages ended suddenly in the 1950s for 80 per cent of the globe, and about the 1960s, when the rules and conventions that had governed human relations visibly frayed for the rest. It is consequently also a book about an era of history that has lost its bearings, and which in the early years of the new millennium looks forward with more troubled perplexity than I recall in a long lifetime, guideless and mapless, to an unrecognisable future. Having thought and written from time to time as a historian about the curious intertwining of social reality and art, towards the end of the last century I found myself being asked to talk about it (sceptically) by the organisers of the annual Salzburg Festival, a notable survival of 'The World of Yesterday' of Stefan Zweig, who was very much associated with it. These Salzburg lectures form the starting point of the present book, written between 1964 and 2012. More than half of its content has never been published before, at least in English.

It begins with an incredulous fanfare on twentieth-century manifestos. Chapters 2–5 are realistic reflections on the situation of the arts at the start of the new millennium. They cannot be understood unless we plunge back into the lost world of yesterday. Chapters 6–12 are about this world, essentially shaped in nineteenth-century Europe, which created not only the basic canon of 'classics', especially in music, opera, ballet and drama, but also in many countries the basic language of modern literature. My examples are mainly taken from the region that forms my own cultural background – geographically central Europe, linguistically German – but they also pay attention to the crucial 'Indian summer' or 'belle époque' of that culture in the last decades before 1914. It ends with a consideration of its heritage.

Few pages are more familiar today than Karl Marx's prophetic description of the economic and social consequences of Western capitalist industrialisation. But as in the nineteenth century European capitalism established its domination over a globe it was destined to transform by conquest, technical superiority and the globalisation of its economy, it also carried with it a powerful prestigious cargo of beliefs and values, which it naturally assumed superior to others. Let us call these the 'European bourgeois civilisation' that never recovered from the First World War. The arts and sciences were as central as belief in progress and education to this self-confident world-view, and indeed were the spiritual core that replaced traditional religion. I was born and brought up in this 'bourgeois civilisation', dramatically symbolised by the great ring of mid-century public buildings surrounding the old medieval and imperial centre of Vienna: the Stock Exchange, the university, the Burgtheater, the monumental City Hall, the classical Parliament, the titanic museums of art history and natural history facing each other and, of course, the heart of every self-respecting nineteenth-century bourgeois city, the Grand Opera. These were the places where 'cultured people' worshipped at the altars of culture and the arts. A nineteenth-century church was added in the background only as a belated concession to the link between Church and emperor.

Novel as it was, this cultural scene was deeply rooted in the old princely, royal and ecclesiastical cultures before the French Revolution, that is to say, in the world of power and extreme wealth, the quintessential patrons of the high arts and displays. It still survives to a significant extent through this association of traditional prestige and financial power, demonstrated in public show, but no longer hedged by the socially accepted aura of birth or spiritual authority. This may be one reason why it has survived the relative decline of Europe to remain the quintessential expression anywhere in the world of a culture combining power and free spending with high social prestige. To this extent the high arts, like champagne, remain Eurocentric even on a globalised planet.

This section of the book concludes with some reflections on the heritage of this period and the problems it faces.

How could the twentieth century confront the breakdown of traditional bourgeois society and the values that held it together? This is the subject of the eight chapters of the third section of the book, a set of intellectual and counter-intellectual reactions to the end of an era. Among other matters these consider the impact of the twentieth-century sciences on a civilisation that, however devoted to progress, could not understand them and was undermined by them; the curious dialectics of public religion in an era of accelerating secularisation, and of arts that had lost their old bearings but failed to find new ones either through their own 'modernist' or 'avant-garde' search for progress in competition with technology or through alliance with power or, finally, via a disillusioned and resentful submission to the market.

What went wrong for bourgeois civilisation? While it was based on an all-destroying, all-transforming mode of production, its actual operations, institutions, political and value systems were designed by and for a minority, though one that could and would expand. It was (and still remains today) meritocratic, that is to say neither egalitarian nor democratic. Until the end of the nineteenth century the 'bourgeoisie' or upper-middle class still meant quite small groups of people. In 1875 even in well-schooled Germany only about 100,000 children went to the humanist gymnasia (grammar or secondary schools) and very few of these made it to the final examination, the Abitur. No more than some 16,000 studied at universities. Even on the eve of the Second World War, Germany, France and Britain, three of the largest, most developed and educated countries, with a total population of 150 million, contained no more than 150,000 or so university students between them or one tenth of 1 per cent of their joint populations. The spectacular expansion of secondary and, above all, university education after 1945 has multiplied the number of the educated, that is to say, those largely trained in the nineteenth-century cultures taught in schools, but not necessarily the number at ease in these cultures.

Obviously the danger to this system had to come from the great majority outside these elites. They might look forward to a progressive but egalitarian and democratic society without or after capitalism like the socialists, but they adopted many of the values of bourgeois 'modernity' and to that extent did not provide any specific alternative. Indeed, culturally the object of the 'politically conscious' social-democratic militant was to give the worker free access to these values and the socialist local authorities provided it. Paradoxically the genuine developments of subaltern culture at this time, such as the world of professional football and its public, were apt to be seen as politically irrelevant and immature diversions. So far as I know, the unusual passion for football of the Viennese proletariat in the Vienna of my childhood was taken for granted, but had no association whatever with the equally passionate attachment of their voters to the Social Democratic Party.

The basic argument of the papers combined in this book is

that the logic of both capitalist development and bourgeois civilisation itself were bound to destroy its foundation, a society and institutions run by a progressive elite minority, tolerated, perhaps even approved of, by the majority, at least so long as the system guaranteed stability, peace and public order and the modest expectations of the poor. It could not resist the combined triple blow of the twentieth-century revolution in science and technology, which transformed old ways of earning a living before destroying them, of the mass consumer society generated by the explosion in the potential of the Western economies, and the decisive entry of the masses on the political scene as customers as well as voters. The twentieth century, or more precisely its second half, was that of the common Western man and, though to a lesser extent, woman. The twenty-first century has globalised the phenomenon. It has also demonstrated the defects of the political systems identifying democracy with effective universal suffrage and representative government, especially given the fact that politics and the structure of governance have remained immune to globalisation and have indeed been reinforced by the almost universal transformation of the globe into a collection of sovereign 'nation states'. Moreover, the ruling or at least hegemonic elites, old or new, have no idea of what to do, or, if they claim to have, lack the necessary power to act.

Culturally the century of common men and women has been far more positive, even as it has reduced the public for classical bourgeois high culture to a niche for the elderly, the snobbish or the prestige-hunting rich. By 1960 classical music provided barely 2 per cent of the recording output, essentially of works composed before the twentieth century – for the musical avant-garde never acquired a significant public. Indeed, the combination of novel technology and mass consumption has not only created the general cultural landscape in which we live but also generated its greatest and most original artistic achievement: the moving picture. Hence the hegemony of the democratised USA in the twentieth-century global media village, its originality in new forms of artistic creation – in writing style, musical, theatrical, mixing the educated and living subaltern traditions – but also the scale of its power to corrupt. The development of societies in which a techno-industrialised economy has drenched our lives in universal, constant and omnipresent experiences of information and cultural production – of sound, image, word, memory and symbols – is historically unprecedented. It has totally transformed our ways of apprehending reality and art production, especially by ending the traditional privileged status of 'the arts' in the old bourgeois society, that is to say their function as measures of good and bad, as carriers of value: of truth, beauty and catharsis.

They may continue to be valid for the public of the Wigmore Hall, but they are incompatible with the basic assumption of a dislocated market society, namely that 'my satisfaction' is the only object of experience, however achieved. In Jeremy Bentham's phrase (or rather John Stuart Mill's) 'push-pin is as good as poetry'. It patently is not, if only because it underestimates the extent to which the solipsism of consumer society has been melded with the rituals of collective participation and self-display, both official and unofficial, that have come to characterise our show-business states and civil societies. Except that while bourgeois society thought it knew what culture was about (as T. S. Eliot put it, 'In the room the women come and go, / Talking of Michaelangelo'), we no longer have the words or concepts for the very different character of this dimension of our experience. Even the question 'Is this art?' is likely to be asked only by those who cannot accept that the classical bourgeois concept of 'the arts', though carefully preserved in its mausoleums, is no longer alive. It reached the end of its road as early as the First World War with Dada, Marcel Duchamp's urinal and Malevich's black square. Of course art did not then end, as it was supposed to. Nor, alas, did the society of which 'the arts' were an integral part. However, we no longer understand or know how to deal with the present creative flood drowning the globe in image, sound and words, which is almost certain to become uncontrollable in both space and cyberspace.

I hope the present book can help to bring more clarity to this discussion.

1

Manifestos

Most of the participants here have written manifestos. I have no manifestos to propound and I don't think I have ever drafted a document under that name, although I have drafted equivalent texts. However, I've been reading documents called manifestos for the best part of a century and I suppose this gives me some credibility as a commentator on a manifesto marathon. I started my intellectual life at school in Berlin at the age of fifteen with one manifesto – Marx and Engels's *Communist Manifesto*. I have a press-photograph of me in my eighties reading the Italian daily newspaper *Il Manifesto*, which is, I think, the last European paper to describe itself as communist. Because my parents were married in the Zurich of the First World War among Lenin and the Dadaists of the Cabaret Voltaire, I would like to think that a Dadaist Manifesto issued a loud fart at the moment of my conception, but unfortunately the first Dadaist Manifesto was recited three months before this could have happened.

Actually, systematic manifesto-readers are a twentieth-century species. There had been plenty of such collective statements, mainly religious and political, in earlier centuries, but they went under different labels: petitions, charters, appeals and so on. There were the great declarations – the Declaration of Independence of the USA, the Declaration of the Rights of Man – but typically they are statements of very official governments and organisations, like the Declaration of Human Rights of 1948. Most manifestos belong to the last century.

How will manifestos survive the twenty-first century? Political parties and movements are not what they were in the last century and they were, after all, one of the two great producers of manifestos. The arts were the other. Again, with the rise of the business society and MBA jargon, they have been largely replaced by that appalling invention, the 'mission statement'. None of the mission statements I have come across says anything worth saying, unless you are a fan of badly written platitudes. You can't walk more than a few yards through the undergrowth of print without stubbing your toe on some example, almost universally vapid in sentiment, telling you the equivalent of 'Have a nice day' and 'Your call is important to us'.

Still, manifestos are competing quite successfully with mission statements. There are almost twenty million potential clicks under this heading on Google, and this leaves plenty, even if you exclude Manifesto Records and its various products. I can't say they all live up to the dictionary definition, which is 'a public declaration of principles, policies or intentions, specially of a political nature'. Or of any other nature. They include a breast-feeding manifesto, a wildlife gardening manifesto, a manifesto for the hills, which deals with livestock in the Scots highlands, and a rather tempting manifesto for a new walking culture by Wrights and Sites with plenty of references to the Dadaists, the Situationists, André Breton and Brecht, but, rather surprisingly, none to the champion of urban walkers, Walter Benjamin. And, of course, they include all the manifestos of this marathon.

I haven't had a chance to hear much of this weekend's manifestos, but one thing that strikes me about them is that so many of them are individual statements and not, like almost all manifestos in the past, group statements, representing some collective 'we', whether formally organised or not. Certainly that is the case of all the political manifestos I can think of. They always speak in the plural and aim to win supporters (also in the plural). That is also traditionally the case of manifestos in the arts, which have become popular since the Futurists introduced the word into the world of art in 1909, thanks to Marinetti's Italian gift of the rhetorical gab. In doing so they beat the French to it by a few years. I am sure the Cubists would have liked to invent the M-word, but they were not very political at that time and better at thinking in paint than in words. I am of course thinking of avant-gardes that recognise themselves as such at the time, not of labels and schools that are created retrospectively like 'post-Impressionism', or are invented by critics and, increasingly, by dealers like 'Abstract Expressionism'. I am thinking of genuine groups of people, sometimes built round a person or a periodical, however short-lived, conscious of what they are against as well as what they think they have in common: Dadaists, Surrealists, De Stijl, LEF or the Independent Group round which Pop Art emerged in Britain in the 1950s. Or, for that matter, the original photographers' collective, Magnum. If you like, they are all campaigning bodies.

I'm not sure what purely individual manifestos are there for, other than one person's fears for the present and hopes for the future, which they may or may not hope is shared by others. How is this to be realised? Is it primarily by self-cultivation and shared experience, as Vivienne Westwood tells us in her attractive manifesto? How else? The Futurists invented public self-advertisement. It is a sign of our disintegrating and chaotic society that media publicity is today the first thing that comes into a potential manifestant's mind rather than the traditional way of collective action. Of course individuals may also use a manifesto to advertise, and so to claim priority for, some personal innovation, as in Jeff Noon's Literary Manifesto in 2001 (*Guardian*, 10 January 2000). There is also the terrorist manifesto pioneered by the Unabomber in 1995, which advertises an individual attempt to change society, in this case by sending incendiary bombs to selected enemies, but I'm not sure whether this belongs to the field of politics or conceptual art. But there's yet another purely individual manifesto or ego trip that has nobody in mind but the solipsist who issues it. The extreme example of this is that extraordinary document, Yves Klein's *Chelsea Hotel Manifesto of 1961*. Klein, you may remember, had built a career on painting a single colour, an immediately recognisable dark blue. Nothing else: on square and oblong canvases, on anything three-dimensional, mostly sponges but also on models whom he got to roll in the paint. The manifesto explains that it was because he was haunted by the blue sky – though Klein's blue is as un-cerulean a colour as I have ever seen. As he lay on the beach in Nice, he tells us, 'I began to feel hatred for the birds which flew back and forth across my blue cloudless sky, because they tried to bore holes in my greatest and most beautiful work. Birds must be eliminated.'

I don't have to tell you that Klein found critics to explain his profundity and dealers to sell him to the punters. He has been given the sort of immortality he deserved by the Gagosian Gallery, which has copyrighted his manifesto.

This brings me to the content of the manifestos of my lifetime. The first thing that strikes me, looking back on them, is that the real interest of these documents is not in what they actually call for. Most of that tends to be obvious, even platitudinous – and large landfill sites could be made to overflow with such stuff, or it is destined for rapid obsolescence. That is true even of the great and inspiring *Communist Manifesto*, which remains so alive that in the last ten years it has been rediscovered by the capitalists themselves, in the absence, in the West, of a left with serious political significance. The reason we read it today is the same one that made me read it when I was fifteen: it is the wonderful, irresistible style and verve of the text. But chiefly it is the soaring analytical vision of world change in the first few pages. Most of what the manifesto actually recommended is of purely historical interest, and most readers skip it except for the clarion call at the end – the one about the workers having nothing to lose except their chains, they have a world to win. Workers of all countries unite. Unfortunately this is also well past its sell-by date.

Of course that is the trouble about any writings concerning the future: it is unknowable. We know what we don't like about the present and why, which is why all manifestos are best at denunciation. As for the future, we have only the certainty that what we do will have unintended consequences.

If all this is true of so permanent a text as the Communist Manifesto, it is even more true of manifestos in the creative arts. For a lot of artists, as an American jazz player once told me in a nightclub, 'Words are not my instrument.' Even where they are, as among poets, even the very bright ones, creation doesn't follow the path of 'I think and then I write', but a much less controllable one. That, if I may say so, is the trouble with conceptual art. Intellectually the concepts in conceptual art are usually uninteresting, unless they can be read as jokes, like Duchamp's urinal or, to my mind much more fun, the works of Paul Klee.

So reading most manifestos in the arts for their intended meaning is a frustrating experience except maybe as a performance. And even then they are better as wit and jokes than in the oratorical mode. This is probably why Dada, that style for stand-up comics, is still the standby of so many manifestos today: its humour is both funny and black and, like Surrealism, it doesn't call for interpretations but for the imagination to play, which is, after all, the foundation of all creative work. And anyway the test of the pudding is not the description of the dish on the restaurant menu, however flowery, but the eating.

This is where the creators in the arts have been more successful than their manifestos. In my *Age of Extremes* I wrote: 'Why brilliant fashion designers, a notoriously non-analytic breed, sometimes succeed in anticipating the shape of things to come better than professional predictors, is one of the most obscure questions in history and, for the historian of the arts, one of the most central.' I still don't know the answer. Looking back at the arts in the last decade before 1914, we can see that much about them anticipated the breakdown of bourgeois civilisation after that date. The Pop Art of the 1950s and 1960s acknowledged the implications of the Fordist economy and mass consumer society and, in doing so, the abdication of the old visual work of art. Who knows, a historian writing fifty years hence may say the same about what is happening in the arts, or what goes by the name of art, in our moment of capitalist crisis and may retreat for the rich civilisations of the West. Like the remarkable quasi-documentary film *Man on Wire*, but much more uneasily, the arts walk the tightrope between soul and market, between individual and collective creation, even between recognisable and identifiable human creative products and their engulfment by technology and the all-embracing noise of the internet. On the whole late capitalism has provided a good living for more creative people than ever before, but it has fortunately not made them satisfied either with their situation or with society. What anticipations will the historian of 2060 read into the cultural productions of the past thirty years? I don't know and can't know, but there'll be a few manifestos issued on the way.

Part I

THE PREDICAMENT OF 'HIGH CULTURE' TODAY

2

Where Are the Arts Going?

Actually it is inappropriate to ask a historian what culture will look like in the new millennium. We are experts on the past. We are not concerned with the future, and certainly not with the future of the arts, which are experiencing the most revolutionary era of their long history. But since we cannot rely on the professional prophets, in spite of the gigantic sums being expended by governments and businesses on their prognoses, a historian may venture into the field of futurology. After all, despite all upheavals, past, present and future do form an indivisible continuum.

What characterises the arts in our century is their dependence on, and their transformation by, the historically unique technological revolution, particularly the technologies of communication and reproduction. For the second force that has revolutionised culture, that of the mass consumer society, is unthinkable without the technological revolution, for example without film, without radio, without television, without portable sound in your shirt pocket. But it is precisely this that allows few general predictions on the future of art as such. The old visual arts, such as painting and sculpture, have until recently remained pure handicraft; they have simply not been part of industrialisation – hence, incidentally, the crisis in which they find themselves today. Literature, on the other hand, adjusted itself to mechanical reproduction half a millennium ago, in the days of Gutenberg. The poem is intended neither as a work for public performance (as was once the case with the epic, which therefore died out after the invention of printing), nor – as for example in Chinese classical literature – as a work of calligraphy. It is simply a unit mechanically assembled from alphabetical symbols. Where, when and how we receive it, on paper, on screen or elsewhere, is not entirely unimportant, but it is a secondary matter.

Music, meanwhile, has in the twentieth century, and for the first time in history, broken through the wall of purely physical communication between instrument and ear. The overwhelming majority of sounds and noises that we hear as a cultural experience today reach us indirectly – mechanically reproduced or transmitted from a distance. So each of the Muses has had a different experience of Walter Benjamin's age of reproduction, and faces the future in a different way.

So let me begin with a brief overview of the individual areas of culture. As a writer, I may be permitted to look first at literature.

I will begin with the realisation that (in contrast to the early twentieth century) humanity in the twenty-first century will no longer consist mainly of illiterates. Today there are already only two parts of the world where the majority of people are illiterate: southern Asia (India, Pakistan and the surrounding regions) and Africa. Formal education means books and readers. A mere 5 per cent rise in literacy means an increase of fifty million potential readers, at least of textbooks. What is more, since the middle of our century most of the population in the so-called 'developed' nations can expect to receive secondary education, and in the last third of the century a significant percentage of the age groups in question receives higher education (in England today the proportion is around a third). So the audience for literature of all kinds has multiplied. And with it, incidentally, the whole 'educated public' to which all the arts of Western high culture have been addressed since the eighteenth century. In absolute figures this new audience for literature continues to rise steeply. Even the actual mass media are aimed at it.

The film *The English Patient*, for example, shows the hero reading Herodotus, and straight away masses of British and Americans buy this old Greek historian, having previously at best known only his name.

Such democratisation of written material must necessarily – as in the nineteenth century – lead to fragmentation through the rise of old and new vernacular literatures and – also as in the nineteenth century – to a golden age for translators. For how, other than through translations, could Shakespeare and Dickens, Balzac and the great Russians become the common property of the international bourgeois culture? This is still partly true in our own times. A John le Carré becomes a bestseller, because he is regularly translated into thirty to fifty languages. But the position is today fundamentally different in two respects.

First, as we know, the word has for some time been in retreat from the image, and the written and printed word from that spoken on the screen. Comic strips and picture books with minimal text are now by no means aimed only at beginners still learning to spell. What carries much more weight, however, is the retreat of the printed in the face of the spoken and illustrated news. The press, the main medium of Habermas's 'public sphere' in the nineteenth and well into the twentieth centuries, will hardly be able to maintain this position in the twenty-first century. But second, today's global economy and global culture need a global language to supplement the local language, and not only for an insignificant elite in terms of numbers, but for broader strata of the population. Today English is this global language, and will probably remain so in the twenty-first century. An international specialist literature in English is already developing. And this new English-Esperanto has as little to do with the English literary language as the church Latin of the Middle Ages has to do with Virgil and Cicero.

But all this cannot stop the quantitative rise of literature, that is, of words in type – not even that of *belles lettres*. In fact I would almost like to maintain that – despite all pessimistic prognoses – the traditional main medium of literature, the printed book, will hold its own without great difficulty, with a few exceptions, such as the great reference books, lexicons, dictionaries, etc., the darlings of the internet. First, there is nothing easier and more practical to read than the small, portable and clearly printed pocket book invented by Aldus Manutius in Venice in the sixteenth century – much easier and more practical than the print of computer text, which again is incomparably easier to read than the flickering text on the screen. Which is something that can be confirmed by anyone who spends an hour reading the same text first in printed form and then on the computer screen. Even the ebook does not rest its claim on superior readability, but on greater storage capacity and no turning of pages.

Second, printed paper is, as yet, more durable than technologically more advanced media. The first edition of *The Sorrows of Young Werther* is still legible today, but thirty-year-old computer texts are not necessarily so, either because – like old photocopies and films – they have only a limited life, or because the technology becomes out of date so quickly that the latest computers simply cannot read them any more. The triumphal progress of the computer will not kill off the book just as the cinema, the radio, the television and other technological innovations have failed to do so.

The second fine art that is doing well today is architecture, and this will continue in the twenty-first century. For humanity cannot live without buildings. Paintings are a luxury, but houses are a necessity. Who designs and builds buildings, where, how, with what materials, in what style, whether as architect, engineer or computer – all this will probably change, but not the need to create buildings. Indeed, one can even say that in the course of the twentieth century the architect, particularly the architect of great public buildings, has become the ruler of the world of the fine arts. He – generally it is still a he – finds the most suitable, that is, the most costly and impressive, expression for the megalomania of wealth and power, and also that of nationalisms. (After all, the Basque region has just commissioned an international star to produce a national symbol, namely an unconventional art museum in Bilbao, which will house another national symbol, Picasso's *Guernica*, although actually Picasso did not paint it as an example of Basque regional art.)

That this trend will continue into the next century is fairly certain. Today Kuala Lumpur and Shanghai are already proving their prospective entitlement to economic world-class status with new record heights for skyscrapers, and Germany, reunited, is transforming its new capital into a gigantic building site. But what sort of buildings will become symbols of the twenty-first century? One thing is certain: they will be large ones. In the age of the masses they are less likely to be the seats of government, or even those of the great international corporations, even if these continue to lend their names to skyscrapers. Almost certainly, they will be buildings or building complexes open to the public. Before the bourgeois age they were, at least in the West, the churches. In the nineteenth century they were typically, at least in the cities, the opera houses, the cathedrals of the bourgeoisie, and the railway stations, the cathedrals of progress by technology. (It would be worth studying one day why, in the second half of the twentieth century, monumentality stopped being a feature of railway stations and their successors, the airports. Perhaps it will return tomorrow.) At the end of our millennium there are three types of building or complex that are suitable as new symbols of the public sphere: first, the large sport and performance arenas and stadiums; second, the international hotel; and third, the most recent of these developments, the gigantic closed buildings of the new shopping and entertainment centres. If I had to bet on one of these horses, it would be the arenas and stadiums. But if you ask me how long the fashion will last that has been rampant since the building of the Sydney Opera House, namely of designing these buildings in unexpected and fantastic forms, I can give you no answer.

What about music? At the end of the twentieth century we are living in a world saturated with music. Sounds accompany us everywhere, and particularly when we are waiting in closed spaces – whether on the telephone, on an aircraft or at the hairdresser's. The consumer society seems to consider silence a crime. So music has nothing to fear in the twenty-first century. Admittedly it will sound quite different by comparison with the twentieth century. It has already been fundamentally revolutionised by electronics, which means that it is already largely independent of the inventive talent and technical skill of the artistic individual. The music of the twenty-first century will be mainly produced, and will reach our ears, without much human input.

But what will we actually be listening to? Classical music basically lives on a dead repertoire. Of the sixty or so operas performed by the Vienna State Opera in 1996/7, only one was by a composer born in the twentieth century, and things are not much better in the concert hall. In addition, the potential concert audience, which even in a city of more than a million inhabitants at best consists of about twenty thousand elderly ladies and gentlemen, is hardly replenishing itself. This cannot go on indefinitely. Indeed, as long as the repertoire remains frozen in time, not even the huge new audience of indirect listeners to music can rescue the classical music business. How many recordings of the Jupiter Symphony, of Schubert's *Winterreise*, or the *Missa Solemnis* can the market find room for? Since the Second World War this market has been saved three times by technological innovations, that is, by the successive moves to long-playing records, to cassettes and to CDs. The technological revolution continues, but the computer and the internet are practically destroying copyright as well as the producer's monopoly, and will therefore probably have a negative effect on sales. All of this in no way means the end of classical music, but with some degree of certainty it does mean a change in its role in cultural life, and with total certainty a change in its social structure.

A certain exhaustion can also be observed today even in commercial mass music, an area that has been so lively, dynamic and creative in this century.

I will mention only one indication. In July, for example, a survey of rock-music fans and experts showed that almost all of the one hundred 'best rock records of all time' came from the 1960s, and practically none from the last two decades. But so far, pop music has succeeded over and over again in reinvigorating itself, and should be able to do so in the new century too.

So there will be singing and swinging in the twenty-first century just as in the twentieth, even if sometimes in unexpected forms.

Where the visual arts are concerned, things look different. Sculpture is scraping a miserable existence at the edge of culture, for it has been abandoned in the course of this century by both public and private life as a means of recording reality or human-shaped symbolism. Just compare the cemetery of today with its nineteenth-century counterpart, decked with monuments. In the 1870s of the Third Republic, more than 210 monuments were erected in Paris, that is, an average of three per year. A third of all these statues disappeared during the Second World War, and the massacre of statues, as is well known, continued merrily on aesthetic grounds under André Malraux. Moreover, after the Second World War, at least outside the Soviet area, few new war memorials were built, partly because the names of the new dead could be engraved on the bases of the First World War memorials. The old allegories and symbols have vanished too. In short, sculpture has lost its main market. It has tried to save itself, perhaps by analogy with architecture, by gigantism in public spaces – big is impressive, whatever the shape – and with the help of a few serious talents; with what success 2050 will judge better than we can.

The basis of the Western visual arts – in contrast, for example, to the Islamic arts – is the representation of reality. Fundamentally, figurative art has thus suffered since the mid-nineteenth century from the competition of photography, which achieves its main traditional task, the representation of the impression of the senses on the human eye, more easily, more cheaply and far more precisely. This, I believe, explains the rise of the avant-garde since the Impressionists, that is, of a painting beyond the capabilities of the camera: whether through new techniques of representation, through Expressionism, through fantasy and vision, and ultimately through abstraction, the rejection of representationalism. This search for alternatives was modified by the cycle of fashion into an endless search for the new, which of course, by analogy with science and technology, was considered to be better, more progressive, more modern. This 'shock of the new' (Robert Hughes) has lost its artistic legitimacy since the 1950s, for reasons that I do not have time to examine more closely here. In addition, modern technology today also produces abstract, or at least purely decorative, art just as well as manual craft. Painting thus finds itself in what is to my mind a desperate crisis; which does not mean that there will be no more good, or even outstanding, painters. It is probably not by chance that the Turner Prize, conferred on the best young British artists of the year, has found fewer painters among the candidates in the last ten years. This year (1997) there are none at all among the four candidates in the final round of this competition. Painting is also disregarded at the Venice Biennale.

So what are the artists doing? They are making so-called 'installations' and videos, although these are less interesting than the work of stage designers and advertising specialists. They play with often scandalous *objets trouvés*. They have ideas, sometimes bad ones. The visual arts of the 1990s are moving from art back to the idea: only humans have ideas, in contrast to the lens or the computer. Art is no longer what I can do and produce creatively, but what I am thinking. 'Conceptual art' is ultimately derived from Marcel Duchamp. And, like Duchamp, with his ground-breaking exhibition of a public urinal as 'readymade art', such fashions do not aim to extend the field of fine art, but to destroy it. They are declarations of war on fine art, or rather on the 'work of art', the creation of a single artist, an icon intended to be admired and revered by the observer, and to be judged by critics according to aesthetic criteria of beauty. Indeed, what art critic does this today? Who today still uses the word 'beauty' without irony in critical discourse? Only mathematicians, chess players, sports reporters, admirers of human beauty, whether in appearance or voice, who are able without difficulty to come to a consensus on 'beauty' or lack of beauty. Art critics cannot do this.

What seems significant to me now is that, after three-quarters of a century, visual artists are returning to the mood of the Dadaist years, that is, to the apocalyptic avant-gardes of the years around 1917–23, which wanted not to modernise art as such, but to liquidate it. I believe they have somehow recognised that our traditional concept of art is now really on the way out. It still applies to the old manually created art, which has petrified into classicism. But it simply no longer applies to the world of sensory impressions and feelings that today inundate mankind.

And this for two reasons. First, because this inundation can simply no longer be analysed into a disconnected series of personal artistic creations. Even haute couture is today no longer understood as the playground of brilliant individual creators, of a Balenciaga, a Dior, a Gianni Versace, whose great works, commissioned as one-off pieces by rich patrons, inspire and thus dominate the fashion of the masses. The big names have become commercials for the global firms in the industry of general adornment of the human body. The house of Dior lives not on creations for rich ladies, but on mass sales of the cosmetics and ready-to-wear clothing ennobled by its name. This industry, like all those that serve a humanity no longer under the duress of the physical subsistence level, has a creative element, but it is not and cannot be creation in the sense of the old vocabulary of the autonomous artistic individual who aspires to genius. Indeed, in the new vocabulary of offers of employment, 'creative' now hardly means more than work of a not exclusively routine nature.

Second, we live in a world of consumer civilisation, in which the (preferably immediate) fulfilment of all human wishes is supposed to determine the structure of life. Is there a hierarchy among the possibilities of wish fulfilment? Can there be one? Is there any sense at all in singling out one or other source of this delight and examining it separately? Drugs and rock music, as we know, have gone together since the 1960s. The experience of English youth at their so-called raves does not consist separately of music and dancing, drinking, drugs and sex, of one's own clothing – adornment of the body at the height of current fashion – and that of the mass of others at these Orphic festivals, but of all these together, at this and no other moment. And it is precisely these connections that today form the typical cultural experience for most people.

The old bourgeois society was the age of separatism in the arts and high culture. As religion was once, art was 'something higher', or a step towards something higher: that is, 'culture'. The enjoyment of art led to spiritual improvement and was a kind of devotional activity, whether in private, like reading, or in public, in the theatre, the concert hall, the museum, or in the acknowledged sites of world culture, such as the Pyramids or the Pantheon. It was sharply distinguished from everyday life and from mere 'entertainment', at least until one day 'entertainment' was promoted to become culture, for example, Johann Strauss conducted by Carlos Kleiber, rather than Johann Strauss played at a Viennese wine tavern, or the Hollywood B-film promoted to the status of art by the critics of Paris. This kind of artistic experience of course still exists, as is proved by, among other things, our own participation in the Salzburg Festival. But first, it is not culturally accessible to everyone, and second it is, at least for the younger generation, no longer the typical cultural experience. The wall between culture and life, between reverence and consumption, between work and leisure, between body and spirit, is being knocked down. In other words, 'culture' in the critically evaluative bourgeois sense of the word is giving way to 'culture' in the purely descriptive anthropological sense.

At the end of the twentieth century the work of art not only became lost in the spate of words, sounds and images in the universal environment that once would have been called 'art', but also vanished in this dissolution of the aesthetic experience in the sphere where it is impossible to distinguish between feelings that have developed within us and those that have been brought in from outside. In these circumstances, how can we speak of art?

How much passion for a piece of music or a picture today rests on association – not on the song being beautiful, but on its being 'our song'? We cannot say, and the role of the living arts, or even their continued existence in the twenty-first century, will remain unclear until we can do so.

3

A Century of Cultural Symbiosis?

The historian leaves futurology to others. But he has an advantage over the futurologist. History helps him, if not to predict the future, then to recognise the historically new in the present – and thus perhaps to throw light on the future. So I will begin my contribution to the festival dialogues with a glance at the past.

Does anyone today remember the old saying, 'When someone goes on a journey, he has a story to tell'? It comes from a time when travel was still something quite unusual. In 1935, when my friend, the wonderful French Hellenist Jean-Pierre Vernant, aged twenty, discovered Greece for the first time with rucksack and two companions, the Greek villagers rang the bells as soon as the strangers came into view, and vied with each other to offer them hospitality. For the arrival of a stranger brought them something new – after all, there were hardly ever any – and did honour to the village.[1] What is the picture today? In the mid-1990s, nine to ten million foreigners visited Greece, which meant that in the holiday season there were as many foreigners there as Greeks. Since October 1999, according to official figures, our globe has supported more than six billion inhabitants. The number of all tourists at home and abroad is reliably estimated to have reached over five billion by 1998. (That many of these people travelled more than once a year only underlines the unprecedented geographical mobility in which we presently live.) And just one more figure about the mobility of humanity. It is not impossible that the American population census for this year will establish that more than half of the thirty-four million inhabitants of the state of California come not from the United States, but from Latin America, Asia and Africa. If this is not the case now, it certainly will be in a few years.

What does this mobility mean for the world in the twenty-first century, and not least for culture? This is my theme today. I would like to ask you to think about it. Unfortunately this is not only a problem for academics, creators of culture and consumers of that culture, but also a controversial, one could even say explosive, question for politicians. Not least for politicians in this beautiful country, but not by a long way only for these. For everywhere, along with the billions of travellers, epidemics travel too – from Aids to xenophobia.

There are three fairly diverse forms of human mobility. First of all, the normal national and international traffic, that is, travel for both business and pleasure – regular commuting aside; second, emigration and immigration, whether deliberate or enforced. But third, since the late twentieth century there has been a completely new phenomenon, which one might perhaps call transnationality: that is, people for whom the crossing of borders is of little importance, since their existence is not tied to any particular place or country. A few decades ago there were hardly more than a dozen such transnational people, probably all known in Salzburg, as most of them were stars of the world of music, the most international of all arts. Today they are numbered at least in tens of thousands, and in the new century there will be millions of them. An important part of business travel probably already falls within the realm of transnationality.

Although for many people, perhaps even for most tourists, cultural experience is an important motive for travel – for even Disneyland and the exoticism of the tropics are part of culture – this area is not very rewarding in terms of my topic. Tourism is becoming increasingly important in the global economy – by the end of the century it already accounted for 12 per cent of all jobs – but culturally it has not resulted in much that is new. Europe has long become used to mass tourism. In fact at the end of the twentieth century this trend was already so advanced that measures were taken to monitor and restrict access to the great cultural locations and events; today this is already common practice, for example, with important international art exhibitions.

The new century will necessarily lead to further monitoring and restrictions, if only because the masses of visitors are physically unmanageable for the locations, whether these are Florence and Venice or ski pistes and mountain peaks. In contrast to worldwide environmental problems, such localised pollution is comparatively easily dealt with. And the locals have long become used to the masses of tourists. As a group, they do not belong to our actual lives, even if our economy depends on them. They do not stay long. We complain about them, but only as one complains about the daily nuisances of a mass society – the flood of lorries on the motorways, the difficulty of finding parking spots, the crowded underground trains. Of course there are also types of tourist that no one would want, such as the English football hooligans; and since short trips over long distances are always getting easier, it is unfortunately likely that certain destinations in this century, such as Ibiza, will be increasingly sought out by (mostly youthful) barbarians. But this too is nothing new in itself: the great port cities have for centuries prepared their Reeperbahns and other sailors' quarters for such invasions.

On the other hand there is at least one kind of tourism that brings in not only money, but also other advantages, to locals, and is therefore enthusiastically encouraged, particularly in culturally remote areas. And especially since these are increasingly colonised by middle-class second homes. Hence the growth by leaps and bounds of specifically cultural tourism in recent decades, which will certainly continue in the new century. Today there are already at least thirteen hundred cultural festivals in Europe. My family has a small house in the border area between England and Wales. In the course of the summer we have within our reach, across a few dozen kilometres in various directions, a small classical music festival, an important literary festival and a well-known jazz festival, which attract an international, or at least Anglo-American, public to the area. These visitors discover, among other things, several Michelin-starred restaurants in a nearby small historic town. This pattern will probably develop further in the new century, but without bringing us much that is unexpected. So there is not much to be said about the cultural effects of tourism in the twenty-first century.

The new species of global business traveller is probably more interesting, for it leads us into the new world of globalisation. Since we are here dealing with several hundred thousand people, it has already created two quite original cultural directions: that is, the worldwide (and almost exclusively anglophone) daily newspaper – I am thinking here of the *Herald Tribune* – and the peculiar clutch of international hotel television programmes. The interesting thing about these media is not just that they are aimed at a global audience, or at least at an audience that may be in Moscow today and in Mexico tomorrow, and so need global weather reports and can be alerted (for example, weekly in the *Financial Times*) to cultural offerings throughout the world. As every hotel guest knows, they are a mixture of global, national and local information, such as television programmes, with personally selected entertainment shows, which means, above all, films. Literature is practically absent; the other visual arts exist only at the extreme margins; and, except in the context of films, music in the international hotel is there chiefly as a background, if at all. It is already typical of today's experience of music that the occasions on which one concentrates on hearing and making music – such as going to a concert or singing in the bathtub – form only a tiny fraction of the music we daily absorb. In addition, today most people's musical experience by means of modern technology, and surely soon via the internet, is almost 100 per cent privately accessible and therefore not dependent on public media.

The world culture of the global hotel guest is probably hardly cause for enthusiasm. But I do not believe that it pre-empts the world culture of the twenty-first century. On the one hand, CNN proves that today it still addresses itself primarily to an untypical public, that is, the still almost exclusively masculine, adult business executive travelling on his own. Today he is part of a single, Americanised, global professional style, in terms of business, culture and even language. So the CNN culture represents only a fraction of the new world culture.

On the other hand, the media are at an intermediate technological stage and thus, like industry in the era of Henry Ford (and incidentally of McDonald's), still in the age of standardisation: that is, the very limited choice determined by an ever smaller number of global – that is, culturally Americanised – corporations. What is offered to us at present is, if only for technological reasons, merely the common denominator of many diverse cultures. And this is merely a very limited, sometimes an extremely small, part of cultural life. In a few years, thanks to digital technology and the internet, this will look noticeably different.

For it is already clear today that globalisation does not simply sweep away regional, national and other cultures, but combines with them in a peculiar way. Here are two examples. In a corner of Ecuador live a community of Indians who have somehow become embedded into the modern global economy as weavers and dealers in textiles. Decades ago one could encounter these Indians with their packs everywhere in the cities of Latin America – sometimes they even got as far as New York. The Otavaleños were and are easily recognisable: the women in their dark blue skirts, the men in ponchos, with long braided hair.

In the course of the last decades they have become rich. They are among the richest people in Ecuador, which means that they can afford the goods on offer in the modern Western consumer society. But the extraordinary thing is that they have not become Americanised; on the contrary, they, so to speak, 'Otavalenise' the influence of the United States. The adolescents wear jeans and Reebok trainers like their Californian counterparts, but at the same time the hats of their forefathers and their hair in the traditional long plaits. The women drive Cherokee jeeps, but are dressed in traditional costume. Here globalisation has not brought assimilation but, at least in this new Indian bourgeoisie, new opportunities to underline what is specific to the old culture, such as customs and language.

My second example of this sort of syncretism comes from a report by the British writer Ian Buruma from Lhasa, the capital of faraway Tibet. This, according to Buruma, is a city whose soundtrack is dominated both by Indian and Chinese pop music and by the rattle of machine-guns from the American videos marvelled at by young Tibetans in the video arcades. Buruma describes a Tibetan nightspot. I quote:

> The decor looks somehow Tibetan, the curtains white and lined with red, blue and green stripes. The songs are both Tibetan and Chinese ... some of the artists wear traditional Tibetan costume ... Excerpts from Hollywood films are shown on video screens, including something from *Titanic* and the destruction of Atlanta from *Gone With the Wind*, as well as the usual scenes from Tibet that probably come from promotional videos for tourists: folk dancing, grazing yaks,

monks blowing horns [and the like]. On the wall hangs the
Mona Lisa, next to her a plastic head of a Bodhisattva.[2]

It is often assumed that globalisation involves the assimilation
of the world to a single predominant pattern, in practice a
Western or, more precisely, an American one. This is probably
true of the technologically governed sides of life – airports,
modern office design, football stadiums. But we can already
determine that culturally it leads to a heterogeneous world of
cultural confusion, coexistence or even perhaps a world of syn-
cretisms. Can the outlines of the future be read in the small
towns of Ecuador and the nightspots of Lhasa? But why not?

And this brings me to the question of the enormous mass
migrations that currently inundate all parts of the world: those
that resist them, such as the European Union, China and
Japan, as well as those that try to assimilate them, such as
North America and Australia. The greater the gap between the
lands of unimaginable wealth and peace and those of poverty,
the more gigantic the streams of humanity that flow from one
to the other. And, in contrast to the time before the global
catastrophes of the twentieth century in which only a few,
almost exclusively European peoples had learned that there
were countries somewhere whose streets, as it was said, were
paved with gold, today there is no place so remote where this
fact is not known. What are the cultural consequences of this
redistribution of humanity?

This mass migration is in one respect quite new, for it takes
place in an era in which humankind no longer lives under the
constraints of time and distance. In other words, emigrants no
longer face an either-or, a long-term or even a lifelong separation from their homes, as was the case until late into the
twentieth century. In our own times even the longest journeys
are measured not in days, and still less in weeks or months, but
in hours; telephone, that is oral, communications in minutes;
and written communications via email in seconds. Emigrants

thus remain in constant contact with home, return regularly, indeed increasingly lead a double life, active in their country of origin and their new country alike. We all know such cases. Of course there is no difference in principle between such an international double life and similar double lives within a country – for example, that of an Italian professor who lives in Turin and works in Naples. But what interests me here is that such a life today takes place on at least two sides of borders, of states, of languages, of cultures – and also of classes. So what is the significance of such a simultaneous life in a minimum of two cultures?

First of all, it weakens the status of the hegemonic or ruling cultures – particularly since these, with the passing of illiteracy, are losing their monopoly of public written language. The old mass migration in practice meant in the first generation minimal assimilation and the practical coexistence of the two cultures (practical in the second generation) in the hope of complete assimilation to the hegemonic culture of the country of immigration. Apart from this, the two cultures hardly influenced each other. The classical example is Hollywood, as is well known an almost 100 per cent creation of Jewish immigrants from central and eastern Europe, who incidentally developed a dynamic high culture of their own in New York – the first American productions of Ibsen were in Yiddish. But a noticeable Jewish influence, or any influence at all from mass immigration (perhaps with the exception of the Irish), is simply not to be found in the films of Hollywood's golden decades. The image of America that they offer is 100 per cent Anglo. Even the names of actors were as far as possible systematically anglicised, except in cases of exotic specialities. Conversely, the millions of Italians resident in the USA, or returning to Italy, had little or no influence on Italian culture. In addition, the culture of immigrants was doubly isolated, since as a result of permanent separation from their old homes they had no live contact with their old world. The so-called 'long-distance nationalism' of the modern national diasporas thus mostly still exists in a past that is no longer there. The Irish Republic's struggle for independence from the United Kingdom was over eighty years ago, but the American Irish were in the thick of it to the very end and enthusiastically supported the IRA. And the situation is still clearer with the émigré Croats, Ukrainians, Latvians and so on, who were for a long time allowed no contact at all with their homelands.

Today, however, immigrants live in three worlds: in their own, in that of the country of immigration, and in the global world, which is made the common property of humanity by technology and the modern capitalistic consumer and media society. But the natives of the countries of reception, including the second and third generations of immigrants, also live in a world of unlimited variety: that is, in countries where speakers of the other ninety languages to be found in London's primary schools are now part of everyday life, above all in the big cities.

This asymmetry lies at the root of the question, so highly politicised today (especially in the anglophone world), of so-called multiculturality: that is, the *public* recognition of *all* cultural groups making themselves known as such. For it is only their own concerns that are of importance to each group. As long as the state places no obstacles in the way of Islam, for the British Muslim the situation of British Jews, Hindus, Catholics or Buddhists is irrelevant. But not for teachers in English schools with children from Nigeria, the Caribbean, India, Greek and Turkish Cyprus, Bangladesh, Kosovo and Vietnam, and just as little for the BBC programme planners. But I would rather not venture further into the thicket of the discussion of cultural identities. That all these cultures are influenced by the English one is nothing new. What is new is that the various cultures that, thanks to mass migration, exist in every country also influence and stimulate the culture of the reception country, and that the elements of global culture penetrate all the others.

This is most easily observed in pop and dance music, since

here, in contrast to classical music, nothing hinders the assimilation of unorthodox or unfamiliar elements. I am thinking here
of the contribution of the Latin American – that is, mainly
Caribbean – immigrants to the United States. But equally interesting is the new reception of the old immigrant cultures in the
American blockbuster film, which is aimed not at a niche
market of immigrants, but at the general Hollywood public.
To name only one example: the genre of the glamorising Mafia
film has existed really only since the 1970s, and would have
been unthinkable earlier. (Incidentally, Italian-Americans themselves would have indignantly rejected it as defamatory.) In the
British cinema, immigration from South Asia plays a similar
part; admittedly, at least so far, we are here speaking largely of a
cinema aimed at intellectuals.

Can such a combination also be discerned in traditional high
culture? Certainly in literature, and quite particularly in the
novel. As usual, older immigrants are the first to have their say:
an important component of North American literature today is
the genre of the consciously Jewish-American novel (Saul
Bellow, Philip Roth). But the American life of the more recent
immigrants from Asia, the Jews of the twenty-first century, is
already making its appearance in the literature of the USA.

But the best current example of such coexistence and min-
gling of worlds is cuisine, which is becoming internationalised in
every country. According to Buruma, one can even order pizza
in the restaurants of distant Lhasa. Indigenous cuisines persist – indeed, they sometimes have to do so for religious
reasons – but both immigration and universal holiday travel
turn their diversity into an everyday experience. In fact they
enable a worldwide Darwinist struggle for culinary existence,
from which so far two victors seem to be emerging: a globalised
form of Chinese cuisine, and Italian cooking. In cultural terms
the triumphal procession of the espresso and the pizza (with
help from scampi) can be compared only with the hegemony of
the Italian baroque opera. In addition, modern technology

29

delivers mango and papaya to every supermarket; the globalisation of production creates the supermarket in which they are daily to be found; and, thanks to the economic hegemony of the United States, the entire globe consumes Coca-Cola, hamburgers and fried chicken.

But particularly characteristic of our age – and so, we may assume, of the new century – is the specific influence of certain immigrant groups in the reception countries. Some of those present here will probably think of the Turks in Germany and the North Africans in France. As an Englishman, I think of South Asia. From a culinary point of view, since the end of the British Empire India has conquered England through South Asian immigration. The number of Indian restaurants (incidentally largely monopolised by immigrants from a certain province in Bangladesh) has risen from a few hundred to sixty to eighty thousand – which means that the English themselves have been converted. New menus, unknown in South Asia, have even been invented for the English taste. There are practically no British, however xenophobic, for whom words such as samosa, chicken tikka masala and vindaloo have not become as familiar as fish and chips – probably even more so since fish has become a luxury dish. A similar case is the so-called Mexican cuisine in the United States, a barbaric mutation of which, Tex-Mex, has already existed for some time in the south-western states.

So in culinary terms too we continue to live not in one but in several worlds at the same time. For the curse of the Tower of Babel has up to the present day made a single world culture an impossibility. On the contrary, the progress of wealth and general formal education will perhaps call into question the present global monopoly of the English language. Today probably 90 per cent of all text on the internet is written in English – and not only because Americans and English are so strongly represented among internet users. But when the 1100 million Chinese, the 500 million Hindi speakers and the 350 million

Spanish speakers outside the USA use the net even half as much, then the virtual monopoly not only of the English language, but also of the western European alphabet, will be over.

And yet cultures will remain more than supermarkets where we provide for ourselves according to our personal tastes. First, the syncretic global culture of the modern consumer society and the entertainment industry is probably part of all our lives. But second, in the post-industrial age of information, the school – that is, secondary and tertiary education and beyond – is more decisive than ever before, and forms, both nationally and worldwide, a unifying element, not only in technology, but also in the formation of classes. In the borderless marketplace of the internet, group-specific subcultures, even the smallest, can form a cultural scene and a medium that interests no one else – let us say perhaps transsexual neo-Nazis, or Islamic admirers of Caspar David Friedrich – but a system of education that decides who in society will attain wealth and civil power cannot be determined by postmodern jokes. What is needed is a usable educational programme aimed at the community of educable youth, not only within a country or a cultural circle, but also worldwide. This guarantees, at least within a particular area of intellectual cultures, a certain universalism both of information and of cultural values, a sort of basic stock of things that an 'educated person' should know. That the names of Beethoven, Picasso and the *Mona Lisa* will disappear from the list of general knowledge in the twenty-first century is thus highly unlikely. Of course this basic stock of 'general knowledge' will no longer be as regional as it was fifty years ago. Travel to Machu Picchu, Angkor Wat, Isfahan and the southern Indian temple cities will be as much a part of education as visiting Venice and Florence. But whether there will be many new world classics in the old arts – literature, painting and music – is a question I would not like to engage in here.

But does this new, complicated, multidimensional globe, in constant motion and constant combination, bring the hope of human fraternisation, from which our age of xenophobia seems so far removed? I do not know. But I believe the answer is perhaps to be found in the football stadiums of the world. For the most global of all sports is at the same time the most national. For the majority of humanity today, it is eleven young men on a football pitch who embody 'the nation', the state, 'our people', and not politicians, constitutions and military deployments. Apparently these national teams are made up of national citizens. But we all know that these sports millionaires appear in a national context for only a few days each year. In their main occupation they are highly paid, transnational mercenaries, almost all employed in other countries. The teams daily acclaimed by a national public are a motley assemblage from God knows how many nations and races, in other words from the acknowledged best players from all over the world. In the most successful national clubs there are sometimes hardly more than two or three native players. And this is logical, even for the racists among the football fans, for they too want a victorious club even if it is no longer racially pure.

Happy the land that, like France, has opened up to immigration and does not question the ethnicity of its citizens. Happy the land that is proud to be able to choose for its national team among Africans and Afro-Caribbeans, Berbers, Celts, Basques and the sons of eastern European and Iberian immigrants. Happy, not only because this has enabled it to win the World Cup, but because today the French – not the intellectuals and the principal opponents of racism, but the masses, who after all invented and still embody the word 'chauvinism' – have declared their best player, the son of Muslim immigrants from Algeria, Zinedine Zidane, to be quite simply the 'greatest Frenchman'. This is admittedly not far removed from the old ideal of the brotherhood of all nations, but it is even further from the viewpoint of neo-Nazi thugs in Germany and that of the governor of Carinthia. And if people are not judged by their skin colour, their language, their religion and the like, but by their talents and achievement, then there is reason for hope. And there is reason for hope, for the course of historical development leads in the direction of Zidane and not in that of Jörg Haider.[3]

4

Why Hold Festivals in the Twenty-First Century?

The question 'Why hold festivals in the twenty-first century?' should not be confused with the question 'Have festivals a future in the twenty-first century?' They obviously have. Festivals are multiplying like rabbits. Their number has been soaring since the 1970s and nothing suggests that this growth has come to an end. In North America alone there are apparently 2500 of the species. Jazz festivals number at least 250 in thirty-three countries. Their number increases every year. In Britain, the country about which I am better informed than elsewhere, there are 221 music festivals this year (2006), whereas three years ago there were only 120. And this is true not only of music-oriented festivals, but also of other cultural and art events, including genres already in existence since the 1930s, such as film festivals and the literary or book festivals that have been escalating in recent years and that, incidentally, mostly have their musical side too. Festivals are today as globalised as football championships.

In itself, this is hardly surprising. Festivals have become a firm component of the economically ever more important complex of the entertainment industry, and particularly of cultural tourism, which is rapidly expanding, at least in the prosperous societies of the so-called 'developed' world. Nothing is easier now than long journeys. There is plenty of money around, compared with the first fifty years of the Salzburg Festival, and there is also a cultural audience swollen by the enormous expansion of higher education. This year, an English travel agency specialising in cultural tourism offered this audience about 150 such tours in thirty-six countries, specifically including twenty-seven tours to music festivals. In short, there is a great deal of money to be made these days in the culture business.

But what such statistics mean is by no means obvious. For artistic creation does not depend on profit-seeking. Festivals, although embedded in the larger economic system, are, like opera, not basically rational enterprises in economic terms. They cannot exist purely on ticket sales, even at luxury prices, any more than the Olympic Games or the football World Cup. Like opera, festivals, particularly costly ones, are hardly possible without public or private subsidies and commercial sponsorship. Incidentally they are also different in principle from the great sports festivals of today, not only because these, unlike the 'song and chariot-fight' of Schiller's poem 'The Cranes of Ibycus', have no consciously cultural aspect, but also because they are not competitions in which there are winners and losers.

Economic analysis does not therefore take us very far. I believe we must adopt a different approach to the problem – for example a geographical one. Let us begin with the increasingly evident localisation of these regularly recurring cultural festivals, mainly – so far – outside the actual centres of cultural production in late capitalism: that is, the cities and national capitals. The list of the best-known modern festivals includes neither London nor New York, Washington nor Los Angeles, neither Paris nor Rome nor Moscow. A dynamic entrepreneur of my acquaintance, who founded a very successful literary festival in Hay-on-Wye, a provincial British backwater, today has a stable of such festivals, from Mantua in Italy and Segovia in Spain to Paraty in Brazil and Cartagena in Colombia. But his attempt to export the same formula to London backfired. Festivals flourish particularly in medium-sized and small towns, even in the open countryside, like some of the successful pop music festivals, or the Glimmerglass opera festival [in Cooperstown, New York]. For cultural initiatives, and festivals in particular, require a certain communal spirit, which means not only a sense of common interests and feelings, but even – as at pop festivals – of public collective self-expression, which can emerge in the superhuman dimensions of the megalopolis only in exceptional circumstances.

For enjoyment of art is not a purely private experience, but a social one, sometimes even a political one, especially in the case of planned public performances in purpose-built settings such as theatres. It was for this reason that culture was the actual scene of the education process of the new cultural and civic elites in the lands of the aristocratic monarchy. It was in the literal sense, and not only in the sense of Habermas, a 'public sphere', even if not yet, as in bourgeois countries, one that was constitutionally recognised, but it was still effective, simply because it, as it were, undermined from the inside the authority of rulers and of birthright, without first confronting them politically. It is not by chance that in the nineteenth century theatre or opera performances gave rise to political demonstrations or even, as in Belgium in 1830, to revolutions, or that schools of a consciously national – that is, politically patriotic – nature developed in music.

The genealogy of today's festivals begins with the discovery of the stage as the cultural-political and social expression of a new elite that is self-assured and bourgeois, or rather recruited according to education and ability instead of birth. Italy is probably the classic example of this development. Nowhere is it as clearly manifested as in the country where, as Verdi said, 'The theatre is the real seat of Italian music,' and where no fewer than 613 new theatres were built in the fifty years from 1815: that is, twelve or thirteen a year. In this building fever, private entrepreneurs played hardly any role. Although this flood of theatres was controlled while for various reasons also being supported by the authorities – for example by the Habsburg monarchy in Lombardy and the Veneto – and it adopted the court tradition even in the architecture of the theatres, it was still potentially subversive. And not only because the Italian princely courts supported culture to a lesser extent than their (incidentally much more numerous) German counterparts. In Italy the initiative mostly came from circles and groups of citizens and patricians of a city who competed in theatre-building with other cities in the region. In the new urban image, the building, deliberately built for splendour, a worldly temple of the intellect, usually confronted the divine temple of the Church. And the culture that it propagated was a wholly national one. Before the 1848 revolution almost eight hundred opera productions had already been mounted on the peninsula, practically all of them from the brand-new Italian repertoire of the young composers. This was twice as many as in the preceding twenty-five years. The citizens of Viterbo and Senigallia, of Ancona and Parma, learned to be Italians through the stage – which, in Italy, meant the opera.

What has this historical digression, which I owe to the historian Carlotta Sorba, to do with the future of festivals? Modern festivals too have often been created from similar initiatives – today probably motivated by economics, but not without local patriotism – for example the Rossini opera festival in Pesaro or, still under the banner of Benjamin Britten, the Aldeburgh Festival. But many festivals, especially the internationally known ones such as Salzburg, depend only to a small extent on a stable, local audience, but rely mainly on newcomers, at best, and, like the old summer holiday resorts, on regular visitors. Here the appeal of the locality or the landscape does play a certain role, which Salzburg has brilliantly exploited from the start with scenery and Mozartkugeln. But many festivals, particularly since the rise of youth cultures, are today organised, localised celebrations by the lovers of a specific musical style, such as heavy metal, or an instrument, such as the guitar, or of technology, in the case of electronic music festivals. They are an expression of strong but worldwide communities of interests and predilections, whose members like to meet face to face from time to time.

This is particularly important in the arts anchored in youth culture, such as rock. Here the experience largely consists in the collective self-expression of the participants, and the interactive element in the festival – in other words, the interplay between the artists and the mass audience – is decisive. In the festivals of the old or the new elite culture, this is less important. There is chamber music in the classical and jazz repertoires, but not in punk rock or heavy metal.

One other thing links these new types of festival with the Italian operatic explosion in the nineteenth century: as yet, they have no classics. As today in the cinema and on the commercial stage, something new was expected at the theatre and the concert hall, whether or not performed by well-known and admired artists. It is true, admittedly, that in the course of time every living art creates its classic works or classic artists, who enter the habitual repertoire, such as the three or four of Donizetti's seventy-five or so operas that are still performed, or the classic films available on DVD. This is also the case with rock. But the situation becomes serious when a style or a genre dries up, or loses contact with the broader public, and all that remains is a dead repertoire of classics, or an avant-garde alien to the masses. Since the First World War this has been the situation of Western classical music, and since the 1960s it has been the situation of jazz. The attempt to revive both by means of revolutionary flight from tradition misfired. The public allowed itself to be provoked, but not converted. This year's programme at the Verbier Music Festival includes, with the exception of jazz concerts, works by fifty-six dead and at best half a dozen living composers, but no full-length works by the latter, and altogether, with the exception of the Russians, hardly any works from the second half of the last century. In attending a world-renowned music festival, one has no expectation of adventure.

On the other hand, this year the one hundred thousand or so who attended during the four days of the Roskilde Festival – a festival mainly of rock and pop music – were able to hear 170 bands from all over the world, both well known and unknown, but almost all of them new, unexpected and original. These then are journeys of discovery. Anyone who is curious can even find out 'if Frank Zappa, Vivaldi and John Coltrane have something in common' – I am quoting a band that calls itself the Anarchist Evening Entertainment. So while classical forms of music stagnate, non-classical ones are striking out on new paths.

Thus, in the age of globalisation, the foundation WOMAD (World of Music and Dance), originally an initiative of two young Englishmen, is systematically dedicating itself to so-called world music, that is, to the link between the musical traditions of the world. This year, WOMAD music festivals are taking place in England, Australia, New Zealand, Sicily, Spain, the Canaries, South Korea and Sri Lanka, and – to mention only the programme in the ancient amphitheatre of Taormina – artists from Burundi, Jamaica, South Africa, Korea, Sicily, China, the Cape Verde islands, Great Britain and Ireland are appearing. As so often, behind these journeys of discovery lies a cultural or subversive, even a political, impulse. Convincing proof of this could be found in the heyday since 1960 of Brazilian music, which has now of course become world famous. But this is not part of the present discussion.

With initiatives of this kind, the question 'why' provides its own answer. We live in a time of cultural expansion and alteration. What characterises the new festivals is not so much innovation and a break with the past, but above all the discovery of developing forms of artistic communication and the aesthetic experience, often through the emergence of new, self-organised groups of the public. Whether these will become a regular component of the general cultural assets of the cultured audience cannot be predicted. What is important is that the recognised – as it were, 'official' – high culture (incidentally almost exclusively formed on European models) should not cut itself off institutionally from as yet unrecognised tendencies of development in the arts and nations. In the twenty-first century, festivals, old or new, which remain open to new paths, can play a more important part in the cultural life of our globalising world, in its state of continual upheaval, than they have done in the past century. Indeed, when one considers that it is practically only since the Second World War that festivals have begun to proliferate, the twenty-first century can be considered the actual heyday of this form of cultural experience. Certainly festivals will play a more modest role in this respect than the internet, but the internet is still so young – at most a dozen years old – and its influence on the development of the arts in the twenty-first century is not yet foreseeable.

But the artistic experience, like all forms of human communication, is more than 'virtual'. So there will certainly still be room for actual events in actual locations where one can somehow continue to dream of the fusion of community, art and *genius loci*, of audience and artists. And where the dream will occasionally, for a moment, become reality.

But what about the traditional classical-music and drama festivals? Do we still need them? That is, are they necessary for the survival of Western classical music of the seventeenth to the twentieth centuries? This wonderful heritage must be preserved. It would be tragic if it should be effectively lost, or found refuge solely in a few university faculties, like the great tradition of epic poetry. There is no doubt that these two art forms are in a bad way. Growth certainly does not always mean a boom in the arts in question. The rise in music festivals is among other things also an expression of the crisis in classical music, whose fossilised repertoire and ageing public are no longer kept afloat by the technological progress of the recording industry. With jazz, whose musicians have long been dependent on the cycle of jazz festivals, the situation is similar. How does this field defend itself from the drop in income? The regular audience of the big cities or of normal concert tours is no longer enough. Only a very small part of the new generations, even of cultured young people, can summon up enthusiasm for symphonies. A formula has to be found that will bring together the scattered minorities worldwide in financially solvent masses. In the age of globalisation, festivals are such a formula. As far as classical music is concerned, this is probably the most compelling answer to the question 'Why hold festivals in the twenty-first century?'

But we may well ask: how great is their contribution to the rescue operation? This is as yet by no means clear. Compared with the potential of the internet, it is probably modest. And yes, let us be quite honest: would global culture collapse if, let us say, in the next five years *Traviata* and *Aida*, *Tosca* and *Bohème*, even *Figaro* and *The Magic Flute*, were performed just half as many times on the world's stages as before?

Of course the most famous festivals will continue to flourish, as showplaces of prestige and luxury tourism; for, thank goodness, the classical Western cultural tradition is still valued even in other parts of the world as a sign of modernisation, and, like a woman's diamonds, as a status symbol even in today's business life, particularly when it is exclusive. Large corporations are becoming patrons of the arts, like the princes of the past, many of whom of course in their time began as bankers, for example, the Medici.

Indeed, the end of communism has probably strengthened

them, since it has released to the West from the socialist states – the last flourishing habitat of classical music – a flood of important talents, which are cheap in terms of the international dollar currency. Let us hope we can also assume that the Russian *nouveaux riches* who would like to become established in the West include billionaires willing to finance the westward triumphal progress of Russian artists and culture. Not all Moscow billionaires specialise in the purchase of footballers. And who knows, the wealthy Indians and Chinese are perhaps already on the path that has been well trodden by the Japanese.

So we should not worry too much about the material future of Salzburg and similar festivals. But what will be their future as cultural sites if we do not succeed in grafting new stock onto the withering stem of the Western musical tradition? Is it possible that Salzburg will eventually turn into a sort of Spanish Riding School, where exercises that are hardly understood today by anyone, and which interest only a small number of people, are still to be seen publicly as historical exotica? Probably not in the foreseeable future. But for how much longer can we still hope to preserve the few, endlessly repeated, guaranteed bankable operas by means of ever more desperate antics on the parts of the directors and set designers? The question must remain open – but whatever the answer may prove to be, it is not a pleasant one.

Please forgive these sceptical words, spoken as a prelude to this festival. And please forget these worries about the future, at least for a few days, in the festival hall, as I too will forget them. For the next few weeks, the wonderful present of the 2006 Salzburg Festival will be enough for us all.

5

Politics and Culture in the New Century

Let me begin with an incident that illustrates the constant, but often obscure, relations between politics and culture today. Sometime in April 2002 the boss of a large and ambitious French corporation, which had transformed itself from running-water supplies to an international giant of films, music and media under the deliberately meaningless name of Vivendi, sacked the chairman of his French pay-TV channel, Canal-Plus. As French presidential elections were impending, all leading candidates joined in execrating him. So did a large and eminent selection of French actors, producers and directors. For M. Messier, as a logical businessman, was guided by his bottom line, and Canal-Plus was losing money. Unfortunately for him, Canal-Plus enjoyed its franchise in France on condition that a percentage of its income went as subsidy to French film production. Without this subsidy, there would be very little film production in France. And, from the point of view of a specific

French culture, or at least cultural production in the French language, this is a matter of some substance. In other words, unless the only culture that is to be produced is the one that is viable by the criteria of the market – that is, today, a largely globalised market – there must be other ways of ensuring the production of what could not otherwise compete in this market. And politics is the obvious engine of redistribution, though not the sole one.

Here we have two players in the game of 'culture' and politics at the beginning of the twenty-first century: politics and the market. They decide how cultural goods and services are to be financed – essentially by the market, or by subsidy. Politics comes in as an obvious source of, or refuser of, subsidies. But there is a third player who decides what can, ought or ought not to be produced. Let us call him or it 'the moral mechanism', both in the negative sense of that which defines and discourages the impermissible, and in the positive sense of imposing the desirable. This is essentially a matter of politics (i.e. political power). For the market in principle decides only what makes or fails to make money, not what one ought or ought not to sell. I shall say almost nothing about political or moral correctness, though its force is not confined to authoritarian states, churches and other institutions imposing a rigid and exclusive orthodoxy. These are fortunately today less common than they were in most of the last century. The extremes of orthodoxy are probably behind us although one of the most lunatic examples, that of the Taliban in Afghanistan, who banned and where possible destroyed both images and secular music, has only just disappeared. Nevertheless, expressing 'politically incorrect' opinions about a number of familiar topics or political issues is not free of risk, and some subjects are still, or again, utterly beyond public debate in a number of very democratic countries.

These, then, are the three players in our game: the market, political power, and the moral imperative. Let us, as the politicians always say when they claim to have been misquoted, 'get them into perspective'.

The best way of doing so is to compare the relationship of politics with culture – that is to say (for the purpose of this lecture), the arts and humanities – with the relationship of politics with the natural sciences. There are two differences. First, in the case of fundamental research in the sciences, the market has never been, and even today is not, a viable alternative to non-profit financing. This is not only because some of the central fields of scientific research in the twentieth century were so expensive that no private funding would have ever considered them as potential profit-makers – nuclear physics, for instance – but because the fundamental dynamo of progress has been *pure* and not applied research. And the results of pure research, still less its financial results, cannot be specified in advance. This does not mean that pure research, undertaken for strictly non-profit motives, may not spin off some very nice big earners, but that is a very different question.

Second, the natural sciences must operate without censorship or political correctness, or they don't operate at all. No government that funds nuclear research can afford to care a damn what the Koran or the Mahabharata or Marxism-Leninism has to say about the nature of matter, or the fact that 30 per cent of the voters in the USA may believe that the world was created in seven days. And why can they not afford to care? Because, since the early twentieth century, fundamental research in the natural sciences has been essential to the holders of political power in a way that the arts and humanities have not. It has been essential for war. To put the matter with brutal simplicity: Hitler learned the hard way that he lost little by driving out Jewish musicians and actors. However, it proved fatal to have driven out Jewish mathematicians and physicists.

I will add just one small supplementary observation. Being indispensable does not give natural scientists any special power in politics. Though power cannot afford to refuse to pay for them, and even Soviet Russia had to give them more freedom to do their own thing than anyone else, atomic scientists in both the USA and the USSR discovered that governments do not take notice of their wishes any more than they do those of conductors and painters.

So, where then do culture and the arts stand in relation to both politics and the market at present? The major issue at stake between them today, at least in democratic countries, is funding: that is to say, the funding of activities that are neither so cheap as not to require any, or so saleable that they can be left to the business calculations of the market. The problem lies somewhere in the space between two groups that require no subsidy: those poets who need only some paper and do not expect to earn a living by the sale or rental of their products, and the zillionaire pop musicians. It is most obvious where the cost of production is high and its object is uncommercial – as in building large new museums and art galleries – or where the market demand for an expensive product is limited, as in serious theatre and opera. As it happens, the Western world has become so much richer over the past decades that the source of subsidies, public and private, has ballooned – just think of the Lottery money – while the rewards of the market have also risen steeply. General prosperity has also made it possible for cultural niche markets to flourish modestly, based on such minority interests as, say, the desire for historically accurate performance of baroque music.

On the other hand, the problem becomes more urgent when expectations outrun reality, or have to be reduced to fit in with reality. Take a look at Berlin, with its three major opera houses, after half a century of competitive subsidies in East and West: the annual sum for culture that the Bonn government paid into West Berlin before German reunification was 550 million D-mark. Take a look at the classical music scene everywhere. It has been kept going for decades essentially by the rising general prosperity, but above all by technology: by the rise of new media like in-car entertainment and the Walkman, and the need periodically to replace private record collections, by LPs, tapes and

CDs. The present crisis of the recording industry simply brings home to us the narrowness of the core public for live classical music; for New York it has been estimated at no more than some twenty thousand people.

How, then, do culture, politics and the market interact? So far as political decision-makers are concerned, at least in democratic states, culture is simply not very important in domestic affairs, as demonstrated by the amount spent by the US Federal government on the arts and humanities as against that on the sciences. Internationally, however, culture can be a serious matter, especially when it becomes symbolic of national or state identity: hence the campaigns, bitterly fought on both sides, for and against the return of the Elgin marbles or against the sale abroad of some archive or artefact defined as a national treasure. The French case shows that the media for the communication of culture are probably the most politically explosive, notably language and alphabet, and, of course, the educational institutions through which most citizens acquire knowledge of the established arts. These are the zones in which political considerations are most likely to confront market forces, when issues of the arts arise.

Even so, while culture does not rate highly in home politics, nevertheless, it has some importance. Politicians may be sensitive to voters' strong views on matters of taste and morality, but, speaking nationally, much less so than they would have been in the past. And, of course, by tradition the arts and high culture have great prestige. They indicate high status socially and internationally and are cherished by the elites of states. In the USA, which lacks a national hierarchy of public honours, giving to the culture, more even than giving to education, has by tradition been the way in which the super-rich reach the top of the social tree. Being on the board of the Metropolitan – opera or museum – is what really establishes a billionaire socially in New York. In most other developed states the arts retain their historic claims for *public* assistance. Given the enormous explosion of cultural tourism, the arts can also now sell themselves to politicians as a national or regional economic asset, which loosens the fiscal purse strings. Recently Barcelona and Bilbao in Spain have been dramatically successful in this endeavour. Culture will therefore remain something on which governments and politicians have views, to which they give public honour and on which they are prepared to spend some money – preferably not taxpayers' money.

From the point of view of the market, the only interesting culture is the product or service that makes money. But let us not be anachronistic. In the cultural fields the contemporary concept of 'the market' – an undiscriminating, globalising search for maximum profit – is quite novel. Until a few decades ago the arts, even for those who made profits from them as investors or entrepreneurs, were not like other products. Dealing in art, publishing books, financing new plays or organising the international tours of a great orchestra were *not* undertaken because they could be shown to be more profitable than selling women's lingerie. Duveen or Kahnweiler, Knopf or Gallimard would not have gone into the hardware business if it had been more lucrative than art dealing or book publishing. What is more, the concept of a single universal rate of profit to which all enterprise must conform is a recent product of the globalised free market, as is the concept that the sole alternative to going out of business is unlimited growth.

Writing books is what I am least ignorant about, so you will excuse me if I take my examples from literature. The past quarter of a century has seen a gigantic process of concentration and takeover. Hardly any imprints are not owned by some media or other corporation. The oldest surviving private house, John Murray, which published Byron, has finally been taken over. No longer are trade publishers, ideally buttressed by long backlists, happy to make a modest rate of profit – certainly far less than what corporation accountants insist on today – on fairly modest outlays. An American one used to tell me on his return from the Frankfurt Book Fair: 'What I've spent on a year's supply of foreign titles amounts to no more than the cost of a couple of luxury cars.' Conversely, another friend, who never tried to write a blockbuster, and only once had a novel made into a film, made a modest living for years by writing a regular succession of intelligent novels for a few thousand regular readers – until one day his publisher refused his next novel, saying he now needed something that promised bigger returns. Plainly, this has not necessarily been bad for literature as a whole. The number of book titles published in this country keeps increasing, and there is no reason to believe that the percentage of good ones has fallen. In some countries, including Britain, the sale of books continues to rise, although this is not typical.

Unhappy as my friend's experience is, in the new situation entrepreneurs have discovered that more money is to be made out of culture than anyone except Hollywood moguls previously thought, all the more so as the real dynamo of economic progress has been in something that is an essential element in the arts, namely the revolution in the *communication* of information, image and sound. On the other hand, not only the entrepreneurs of the arts but the primary producers have also learned the rules of the maximising game. A small minority in some of the arts, as in professional sports, have grasped in the past two or three decades that there is really big, even enormous money to be made. Hence the rise of the agent as against the publisher, or film company, or recording company, and, for the more modest, the appearance of the Authors' Licensing and Copyright Society, which now extracts Xerox reproduction rights for writers as the Performing Right Society has long done for musicians.

In the decades since the 1970s, as the wealth of the developed world has soared into the stratosphere, the resources available for financing culture and the arts have therefore grown explosively, although distribution has become considerably more unequal. Most of this new global wealth has gone into the private sector, but obviously its growth has also benefited the public revenues. Much of this vast rise in private wealth has gone to a small segment of the ultra-rich, including some who have shown themselves willing to subsidise good causes on a virtually cosmic scale, such as George Soros, Bill Gates and Ted Turner. Admittedly private munificence, whether by individuals, corporations or foundations, is comparatively rare outside the USA, and art enjoys only a modest proportion of it, except in the form of a spectacular price inflation in the market for the fine arts that very rich people buy. In any case, at least outside the USA, other sectors almost certainly contribute more to them than the rich, even if they don't mean to, as witness the distribution of Lottery money in the UK.

Indeed, this is true also in other fields of deliberate giving. The British voluntary sector drew more than a third of its income from the general public, less than 5 per cent from business donations, and more than twice as much from government contracts as from the combined gifts of business and charitable trusts. I would guess that public subsidy to the arts in most countries is still far more important than private subsidy. As for the private sector, leaving aside a few individuals with special interests in the arts, the major means of distributing private profit, directly and indirectly, for the benefit of the arts is the enormous and (except in times of economic depression) continuous growth of advertising. The biggest private Maecenases (or, as the jargon has it, 'sponsors') today are probably the advertising budgets of the big commercial brand names, global and national, in addition to, of course, the industries of entertainment, the media and communication, which may properly be regarded as being in the culture business themselves. Nevertheless, there is an awful lot of loose change lying around in the market that can be spent on sponsoring the arts, and, like the universities, people in the arts are learning to scoop some of it up.

So the arts are currently far from being starved of resources. If anything, the opposite is the case. At the lower end of the scale of distribution, the number and munificence of cultural prizes continue to grow strikingly. At the top end we can probably say that more museums, opera houses and other cultural locations have been built or rebuilt in the Western world in the past thirty years than at any time since the great nineteenth-century boom in such building. The problem is rather who and what to put into them. There is a double, perhaps even a triple, problem. Some of the activities that take place inside them are simply petering out. Take opera – as distinct from ballet and stage musicals, both of which are still live genres. Virtually none of the operas in the regular repertoire is much younger than eighty years old and virtually none was written by a composer born after 1914. Nobody lives by writing operas any more, as people did in the nineteenth century and as professional play-wrights still do. Overwhelmingly, operatic production, like Shakespearean play production, consists of attempts to freshen up eminent graves by putting different sets of flowers on them. Certain of the creative arts – notably some of the visual ones, since modernism ran out of steam – have virtually given up the ghost. As for what is called 'conceptual art', a century and a half of painters' manifestos demonstrate that the intellectual field of concepts is not one in which even great creative artists necessarily excel. And in any case, creators who set out to defy the public also restrict the demand for their work. To put it crudely, there is insufficient high-culture art, especially contemporary work, that people in large numbers want to see and hear.

Consider Tate Modern. For historical reasons there is just not enough non-British modern art to fill a real Museum of Modern Art like the New York MoMA – so Tate Modern is in fact largely an empty space. Fortunately the truly box-office sector of the art gallery business is the display of temporary travelling exhibitions, preferably international blockbusters, and Tate Modern is establishing itself as an important location for these. Still, it is an expensive way of providing yet another exhibition venue. Or take the living performance of classical (Western) music, which in any case appeals to only a very small number of the population – a fraction of those who account for the 2 per cent of record sales, which is all the market-driven recording industry devotes to classical music. Even that sector is notoriously reluctant to fill large concert halls to hear sounds too unlike the familiar ones of the pre-1914 classics. And the acceptable classic repertoire is limited. The large, labour-intensive Philharmonic, as well as other orchestras that do not also double as opera-pit bands, are kept going on the symphonies and concertos. In spite of the efforts of Shostakovich, Vaughan Williams and Martinu, symphonies have ceased to be a primary interest of composers since the Great War. It is hard to imagine what the large orchestras would do without the basic stock of the music that attracts the broad public, which consists, I would guess, of no more than between one hundred and two hundred pieces, covering the past two and a half centuries.

Of course niche markets, such as those for contemporary innovative music, have developed alternative or supplementary mechanisms for survival, notably, since the Second World War and especially since the 1960s: the circuit of specialist music festivals. In this they are like the market for that even smaller minority than the lovers of classical music, the lovers of jazz. Both markets have naturally benefited from the growing prosperity of the lovers of these sounds. Nevertheless it is safe to say that the enormous traditional infrastructure built for the arts in and since the nineteenth century – possibly with the exception of the commercial theatre – could categorically not be maintained without substantial public subsidy or private patronage, or a combination of both. Consider what has happened to the music halls of London, or the vast number of often enormous cinemas or 'picture palaces' that were built in Britain between the wars for an art that lived entirely by the laws of the market. Most of them simply ceased to exist, or were turned into something else like bingo halls, when the demand for them went. It is political decision that has let post offices go while preserving churches (as distinct from chapels) and museums; equally it allowed the Holborn Hippodrome to disappear but built municipal theatres in the provinces.

I want to stress that this is a special problem of some forms of the visual and musical arts, rather than a general problem. I have discussed the reasons for this elsewhere – notably in Chapter 15 of this book – and it does not apply to either literature or architecture among the older arts, or to the basic mass arts developed in the last century, those based on the moving photograph and the mechanical reproduction of sound. However, even for these, subsidies or special arrangements favouring them may be essential. This is patently true for architects, since it is primarily non-profit-seeking patronage that finances the works that bring them prestige and make them remembered. But it has also been true of the film industry of every country other than India and perhaps Japan, faced with the global monopoly of Hollywood.

Even a good deal of literature, especially the classics, remains in print, and much good new writing is published that would never pass the profit threshold set by the accountants, because of non-market decisions. In post-communist eastern Europe, serious academic writing has survived largely because of the magnificent efforts of George Soros's foundations. In the West, the choice of books to be studied for school and university examinations determines the fortunes of lucky writers, and of their publishers' backlists. Indeed, at least in the English-speaking world, the vastly expanded institutions of higher education have incidentally acted as a form of concealed subsidy for creative talent in the arts with insufficient appeal in the market: the painters who earn the main part of their living as art-college teachers; the writers whose salary comes from teaching literature or 'creative writing'; the more peripatetic poets, writers, musicians and other pillars of culture 'in residence' for a term or two. No wonder that, since the 1950s, an entirely new branch of fiction has emerged in Britain and the USA, the 'campus novel' about the fortunes not of students but of dons. Kingsley Amis's *Lucky Jim* is probably the first, and certainly the funniest, work in this genre.

Very well, then. Public subsidy and/or private patronage are an essential component of the cultural scene, and likely to continue. And since there is no shortage of cash in the Western world, and pluralism means that no single body, even within one country, decides on what is and is not subsidised, does anything more need to be said on the subject? I think it does, for three reasons. First, we have seen in eastern Europe what can happen when a massive system of subsidising the arts and culture simply collapses, being replaced by a market society or, at best, by states too poor to maintain more than a fraction of their former support. Ask the great Russian opera and ballet units, and the Hermitage Museum! It is not going to happen in the UK but even in prosperous countries governments, especially tax-cutting ones, have limited funds to allocate to culture. David Hockney and Damien Hirst have just demanded more museums. But on what grounds can we demand priority for building more museums rather than other public amenities? Especially since Bilbao and Libeskind's works show that the attraction of new museums lies in the building itself rather than what is in it?

Second, we are seeing today how the world economy in the form of obligatory free trade can reinforce the domination of one globally established industry, with which national cultural productions in other countries are unable to compete. The film industries of Europe are the obvious examples, but as I speak to you, we face a similar conflict in English-language literature. The Booker Prize has been taken over by a corporation that insists that it should henceforth be open to American authors who have not hitherto competed. Behind the US authors there is the muscle of the US publishing and media. Does that mean that, as with the US film industry, it will henceforth be looking primarily at the domestic North American market, at the expense of writers from, and for the smaller anglophone communities in, Britain and the Commonwealth, who have hitherto benefited from the willingness of the less provincial British public to welcome their work? Some of the Booker Prize judges, past and present, are worried. Even those who don't share their fears can see why. What is more, in a world where the spokesmen for nations, old and new, big, little and minimal, demand space for their culture, the political dangers of subsidy are real. In my own field of history the past thirty years have been the golden age of building historical museums, heritage sites, theme parks and spectacles, but also of the public construction of fictitious national or group histories.

There is a third reason for reflection. Until the end of the last century, technological progress has, on the whole, been good for the arts – at least for those arts that did not, like painting, stick to the pre-capitalist, artisan, economy, which produces one-off, unrepeatable objects, sold singly and valued for their irreproduceability. It has created or made possible the new arts that were and still are central to our civilisation – those of the moving camera and sound reproduction. Its capacity to emancipate performance from physical presence has brought the arts to a public measured in hundreds of millions. In spite of the pessimists' fears, it has destroyed neither the old nor the new arts. Books have survived the invention of films and television, and they continue to flourish. Films have survived the introduction of videos and DVDs, which now form a financial pillar of the movie industry. Even traditional easel portraits in oils, the first genre to be challenged by technology in the shape of the photograph, have survived to decorate twenty-first-century boardrooms and the classier private homes.

And yet, in the era of cyber-civilisation, which we have just begun to enter, this may no longer be true. To take an obvious point, it looks like undermining the most elementary requirement of cultural continuity in Western culture (it does not apply to the same extent in some other cultures): the conservation of its material products. Some of you may be aware of the battle that is now being waged within the world of librarians, for and against those who, given the exponential growth of printed material, want to replace as much of it as possible by less space-filling media. But not only have some of them – photographic ones, and perhaps the material of disks – a far shorter shelf-life than paper, but technological progress is now so fast as to produce its own obsolescence. Material recorded on computer disks ten years ago may have become virtually unreadable by the computers of 2002, and quite often the computer languages in which they were written and the devices capable of reading them have long since gone out of production. This may well affect the publication of writing for restricted and special communities – in my field at least, where monographs are now increasingly published online. Even more troubled are the profit-makers in the music business, who discover that the foundations of the record industry seem to be crumbling. Technology and ingenuity have now made it possible for any child with a computer to download an unlimited quantity of recorded music without paying a penny. Again, the internet has become both an addition to, and a replacement for, other cultural activities; some surveys suggest that more time is spent by the common reader online than with books and periodicals. I do not say these problems cannot be overcome, nor do I want to make your flesh creep. I merely note that developments in the cyber-age are so fast, so dramatic and so unforeseeable compared with the old established ways of looking at cultural funding.

These matters are important not only for people who decide on distributing money to the arts, but for all of us. We live in a society changing so rapidly and unpredictably that almost nothing that we have inherited can any longer be taken for granted. The older among us have been brought up in the framework of a culture made by and for the nineteenth-century bourgeoisie, which established the institutions and set the public and private standards for the conventional arts: the buildings, the concept of what goes on inside them, the tradition of what people do and how they feel in the presence of 'the arts', the nature of the public itself. Patently this model of culture is still alive, and the enormous numerical expansion of cultural tourism even seems to reinforce it. In any case we who come to festivals like Aldeburgh continue to represent it. And yet, it is today only one part – perhaps an increasingly diminishing part – of the cultural experience. Since all of us have lived through half a century of television and rock music, this must include even a large contingent of the admirable Wigmore Hall's rather senior audiences. And it is disintegrating. How much of it can be preserved? For whom should it be preserved? How much of it ought to be allowed to sink or swim without the public lifebelt?

I have no answer to these questions, except the obvious observation that the interests of culture can no more be left to the free market than the interests of society. But no questions can be answered until they are asked, and I hope I have helped in the asking.

Part II

THE CULTURE OF THE BOURGEOIS WORLD

6

Enlightenment and Achievement:
The Emancipation of Jewish
Talent since 1800

My subject tonight, unlike most historical work in the field of Jewish history, deals not with the impact of the outside world – almost invariably vast – on the Jews – almost invariably a small minority of the population – but with the opposite, namely the impact of the Jews on the rest of humanity. And, in particular, with the explosive transformation of this impact in the nine- teenth and twentieth centuries, that is to say since the emancipation and, I would add, self-emancipation of the Jews began in the late eighteenth century.

My basic thesis is simple and old-fashioned. It has been well put in the last lines of Arnold Paucker's *Erfahrungen und Erinnerungen*. Like him, 'I write these words at a time when it has become fashionable to call into question even the *Aufklaerung* [the Enlightenment], that is to say that progress which alone offered us Jews a life worthy of human beings' (my translation). And, I would add, progress that made it possible for Jews to make the second major contribution to world civilisation since their original invention of a tribal monotheism that gave universalist ideas to the founders of Christianity and Islam. Let me put it another way. The history of the world between the expulsion of the Jews from Palestine in the first century AD and the nineteenth century is one of Jewish self-segregation as well as imposed segregation. They lived within the wider society of gentiles, whose languages they adopted as their own and whose cuisine they adapted to their ritual requirements; but only rarely and intermittently were they able – and, what is equally to the point, willing – to participate in the cultural and intellectual life of these wider societies. Consequently their original contribution to this life was marginal, though their contribution as intermediaries between various intellectual cultures, notably between the Islamic and the Western Christian worlds in the (European) Middle Ages, was very significant. And this even in fields in which, since emancipation, the Jewish contribution has been absolutely enormous.

Consider a field of outstanding Jewish achievements: mathematics. So far as I am aware no significant developments in modern mathematics are specifically associated with Jewish names until the nineteenth century. Nor – and once again I speak as a layman ready to be corrected – do we find that Jewish mathematicians working in their own intellectual environment had made major advances that were discovered by the wider mathematical world only much later, as in the case of the Indian ones whose work of the fourteenth to sixteenth centuries, written in the Malayalam language, remained unknown until the second half of the twentieth century. For that matter, consider chess, the excessive practice of which was actively discouraged by Jewish religious authority in general and by Maimonides in particular as a distraction from the study of the law. No wonder the first Jewish chess-player to gain a wider reputation was the Frenchman Aaron Alexandre (1766–1850) whose life coincided with the emancipation.

It may well be that the fourteenth to the eighteenth centuries, by the Western calendar, saw the peak of this segregation or ghettoisation, both imposed and self-imposed, reinforced, after 1492, by the expulsion of non-converting Jews from the Spanish dominions, including, of course, those in Italy and elsewhere. This diminished the occasions for social and intellectual contact with non-Jews, other than those arising out of the professional activities that linked them to the gentile world. Indeed, it is difficult to think of Jews during that period who were in a position to have informal intellectual contact with educated gentiles outside the only major urban Jewish population remaining in the West, the largely Sephardic emigrant community of Amsterdam. Remember that most Jews were either confined to ghettos or excluded from settlement in large cities until well into the nineteenth century.

It has been well observed that in those days 'the outside world did not overly occupy the Jewish mind'.[1] Indeed, the elaborate codification of the practices of orthodoxy that constituted the Jewish religion in the compendia of the time, notably the *Shulchan Aruch* reinforced segregation, and the traditional form of Jewish intellectual activity, the homiletic exposition of the Bible and the Talmud and their application to the contingencies of Jewish life, left little scope for anything else. What is more, rabbinical authority banned philosophy, science and other branches of knowledge of non-Jewish origin,[2] including, in darkest Volhynia, even foreign languages.[3] The gap between the intellectual worlds is best indicated by the fact that the (rare) pioneers of emancipation among Eastern Jewry felt they needed to translate into Hebrew works evidently available to any educated person in the gentile print culture, such as Euclid and works on trigonometry as well as books on geography and ethnography.[4]

The contrast between the situation before and after the era of emancipation is startling. After many centuries during which the intellectual and cultural history of the world, let alone its political history, could be written with little reference to the contribution of any Jews acceptable as such to the orthodox, other than perhaps Maimonides, we almost immediately enter the modern era when Jewish names are disproportionately represented in it. It is as though the lid had been removed from a pressure cooker of talents. Yet the almost immediate prominence of such names – Heine, Mendelssohn Bartholdy, Ricardo, Marx, Disraeli – and the flourishing emancipated milieu of wealthy educated Jews in a few favoured cities, notably Berlin, should not mislead us. At the end of the Napoleonic Wars the great bulk of Ashkenazi Jews remained unintegrated in gentile society, probably even in Germany, except – a very recent development – administratively as subjects with civil surnames. Even top families had some way to go: all her life Karl Marx's mother did not feel entirely at home in high German, and the first two generations of the Rothschilds corresponded with one another in Judendeutsch in the Hebrew script. The Jews of the central European hinterlands of the Habsburg Empire remained unaffected by emancipation until the 1840s at the earliest, when immigration into cities became possible, and those of Galicia and the *shtetls* in Russia not until very much later. It has been said of American Jews that 'until well into the 20th century the majority of the immigrants could recall, or had come directly from, a traditional Jewish society' governed by 'the discipline imposed by the *halacha*'.[5] The bulk of the Sephardim also remained in their traditional segregated state. Indeed, except for such small enclaves as the refugee communities in France and the Netherlands, and the ancient communities in northern Italy and the Midi of France, I doubt whether we can find any places before the French Revolution where the totality of Jews, and not merely the elite, were integrated into surrounding society: for example, they habitually spoke the local vernacular of the gentiles among themselves.

The process of Jewish emancipation therefore resembles not so much a suddenly gushing fountain as a tiny stream rapidly turning into a massive river. I have grouped together the mathematicians, physicists and chemists listed in the respective articles of the *Encyclopaedia Judaica* by birth dates. Only *one* in all these three groups was born before 1800, thirty-one were born in the first half of the nineteenth century, and 162 in the second half. (The analogous curve for medicine, the intellectual field in which pre-emancipation Jews were already established in the wider world, is less dramatic.) I need hardly add that at this stage we are concerned overwhelmingly with the Ashkenazi wing of Jewry, which formed a large and growing majority of the world's Jewish population, and were involved in particular with its increasing mega-urbanisation. The number of Jews in Vienna, for instance, jumped from less than 4000 in 1848 to 175,000 on the eve of the First World War.

Not that we should underestimate the demonstration effect, or even the actual impact, of small elites of the wealthy and educated – say, the 405 Jewish families in early nineteenth-century Berlin.[6] Pre-democratic liberal societies were constructed for such groups. Thus the Italian Jews, though representing 0.1 per cent of the population might, under the restrictive Italian electoral law, amount to 10 per cent of the electorate; the election of Cavour in the kingdom of Savoy in 1851 was ensured by the votes of the Turin Jewish community. This may help to explain the rapid emergence of Jews on the public scene in western and central Europe. So far as I am aware, Jews hardly appear either in the French Revolution or among its European sympathisers, except, as one might expect, in the bourgeois milieu of the Netherlands. In contrast, by the time of the 1830 revolutions, the Jewish presence in politics was impossible to overlook in France (especially in the Midi), in Germany and in northern Italy, notably around Mazzini, whose secretary was Jewish, as were several of his activists and financiers. By 1848 the prominence of Jews had become quite startling. One Jew became a minister in the new French revolutionary government (Crémieux); another (Daniel Manin) became the leader of revolutionary Venice. Three Jews sat prominently in the Prussian Constituent Assembly, four in the Frankfurt Parliament. It was a Jew who, after the latter's dissolution, saved its Great Seal, which was returned to the Federal Republic a few years ago by his British descendant. In Vienna it was Jewish university students who launched the call for the March revolution, and Jews provided eight out of the twenty-nine signatures on the Manifesto of Vienna Writers. In Poland, only a few years after Metternich's list of subversives in Austrian Poland contained no obvious Jewish names, Jews expressed enthusiasm for Polish freedom, and a rabbi, elected to the imperial Reichstag, sat with the Polish faction. In pre-democratic Europe, politics, even revolutionary politics, belonged to a small squadron of the educated.

There was no doubt in the minds of emancipators that two changes were essential if it was to proceed: a degree of *secularisation* and *education* in, as well as *the habitual use* of, the national language, preferably, but not necessarily, an accepted language of written culture – think of the enthusiastically Magyarised Jews of Hungary. By secularisation I mean not necessarily the abandonment of the Jewish faith (though among the emancipated there was a rush to conversion, whether sincere or pragmatic), but the reduction of religion from an unremitting, omnipresent and all-embracing framework of life to something that, however important, filled only part of it. This kind of secularisation ought to include the intermarriage or partnership of educated Jewish women with gentiles, which was to play a relatively major role both in culture and later in (left-wing) politics. The relation of women's emancipation to Jewish emancipation is a very significant subject, but unfortunately I have neither the time nor, to be honest, the qualifications for discussing it tonight.

Primary education, necessarily in the vernacular, did not become universal until the last third of the nineteenth century, although almost universal literacy could be assumed in large parts of Germany by mid-century. After 1811 it would have been technically difficult for a Jewish boy in Germany to avoid the public educational system, and it was certainly no longer virtually compulsory to learn the Hebrew letters in a religious establishment as it continued to be in the East. West of the borders of Russian and Austrian Poland, the *cheder* was no longer a competitor to the secular school. Secondary education remained highly restricted throughout, ranging from a mid-century minimum of less than 0.1 per cent (Italy) to a maximum (Prussia) of less than 2 per cent of the relevant age group (from ten to nineteen), while university education was even more circumscribed. As it happens, this maximised the chances of the children of disproportionately prosperous small communities such as the Jews, especially given the high status that learning enjoyed among them. That is why the Jewish share in Prussian higher education was at its maximum in the 1870s. It declined thereafter, as higher education began its general expansion.[7]

To speak, read and write the same language as educated non-Jews was the precondition of joining modern civilisation, and the most immediate means of desegregation. However, the passion of emancipated Jews for the national languages and cultures of their gentile countries was all the more intense, because in so many cases they were not joining, as it were, long-established clubs but clubs of which they could see themselves almost as founder members. They were emancipated at the time of the creation of German, Hungarian and Polish classic literature and the various national schools of music. What could be closer to the cutting edge of German literature than the milieu of Rahel Varnhagen in early nineteenth-century Berlin? As Theodor Fontane wrote about one impassioned Jewish emancipator: 'Only in the region he inhabits do we find a genuine interest in German literature' ('Ein wirkliches Interesse fur deutsche Literatur hat nur die(se) Karl Emil Franzos Gegend').[8] In much the same way, two or three generations later, emancipated

Russian-Jewish intellectuals fell, in Jabotinsky's words, 'madly, shamefully in love with Russian culture'. Only in the multilingual Levant did the absence of national-linguistic cultures make language change less crucial. There, thanks to the new Alliance Israelite Universelle of 1860, modernising Jews received their education in French, while continuing to speak, but no longer to write, in Judeo-Spanish, Arabic or Turkish.

However, of all the emancipatory languages, German was by far the most crucial, for two reasons. Throughout half of Europe – from Berlin as far as the depths of Greater Russia, from Scandinavia to the Adriatic, and into the remotest Balkans – the road from backwardness to progress, from provincialism to the wider world, was paved with German letters. We tend to forget that this was once so. German was the gateway to modernity. On the occasion of the centenary of the birth of Schiller, the poet who was the classical voice of moral and political freedom for the common readers of German in the nineteenth century, Karl Emil Franzos, wrote a story, 'Schiller in Barnow', that illustrates this wonderfully well. In this story a small, ill-printed volume of Schiller's poems becomes the medium through which a Dominican monk, a young Ruthenian village schoolmaster and a poor Jewish boy from a *shtetl* in what the author bitterly calls 'Demi-Asia' ('Halb-Asien') find the liberation offered by the nineteenth-century version of education and modern culture.[9] The story culminates in the reading of the 'Ode to Joy'. In the darkest East, Schiller was even translated into Hebrew. This emancipatory role of German explains why the city fathers of the most Jewish centre in Galicia, the town of Brody, which was 76 per cent Jewish, insisted that German had to be the language of instruction in their schools. In 1880 they even fought – and won – their case in the imperial court in Vienna on the grounds, patently implausible, that this was a Landesübliche, a language (of common use) in Galicia.

It was not. Almost all Eastern Jews spoke Yiddish, a German dialect, the relic of a past bond with the wider society, but now –

like Sephardic Spanish since 1492 – a badge of linguistic separation. A priori, one might have expected Yiddish to coexist as
an oral medium with the written national language, as other
German dialects did and as Schwyzerdütsch still does, but,
unlike these, it was a barrier to joining the modern world that
had to be removed: linguistically and, as the language of the
most obscurantist communities, ideologically. Wearing 'German
jackets', as well as speaking Polish or German, was the mark of
the small band of early pioneers of emancipation in Warsaw.[10]
In any case the children of Yiddish-speaking immigrants in
German schools found themselves handicapped by their gram-
matical usages, being correct enough in Yiddish but making
mistakes in written German. Wealthier Jews, parvenus into an
established society, were even more likely to abandon visible
and audible marks of their origins. Characteristically, in Arthur
Schnitzler's novel *Der Weg ins Freie*, that wonderfully perceptive
account of the nuances of Jewish assimilation in *fin de siècle*
Vienna, old Ehrenberg, the rich businessman, renounces the
old German Liberal hope of Viennese Jews in his wife's salon
with a deliberate relapse, in the presence of gentile 'society', into
semi-Yiddish: 'vor die Jours im Haus Ehrenberg is mir mieß'.[11]

The division between non-assimilated, Yiddish-speaking
Ostjuden and assimilated Westjuden thus became, and
remained, fundamental until both perished in the same holocaust.[12] Though no doubt familiar in educated conversation,
this division seems first to have been formally made in the
Bukowina from the 1870s,[13] where a proud, extraordinarily distinguished and educated middle class encountered the first
stirrings (by the doubters of Germanisation) towards giving Jews
a national status through their own national language – Yiddish.
For emancipated Jews in Mitteleuropa, 'Ostjuden' defined what
they were not, and did not want to be: people so visibly different as almost to constitute a different species. After listening to
the adults' conversation as a young boy in Vienna, I remember
asking an older relative, 'What sort of names do these Ostjuden

have?' – to her patent embarrassment, since she knew that our family, the Grüns and Koritschoners, had come straight to Vienna from Austrian Poland, just as such distinguished figures in German Jewry as Rudolf Mosse, Heinrich Graetz, Emmanuel Lasker and Arthur Ruppin had come directly from Prussian Poland.

And yet it was the mass migration of the Ostjuden from the late nineteenth century onwards that marked and helped to transform the impact of Jews on the modern world. While there is obvious continuity, the Jewish impact on the gentile world in the twentieth century is not comparable to that in the nineteenth. When the liberal-bourgeois century ushered in the twentieth, it would mirror the title of an important new book, *The Jewish Century*.[14] The American Jewish community became the largest by far in the Western diaspora. Unlike any other diaspora in the developed countries, it was overwhelmingly composed of poor Ostjuden and far too vast to fit into the existing, acculturated, German-Jewish framework in the USA. It also remained rather culturally marginalised, except perhaps in jurisprudence, until after the Second World War.[15] The modernisation of the Jews in Poland and Russia through massive political consciousness, reinforced by the Russian Revolution, transformed the nature of Jewish emancipation, including the Zionist version. So did the enormous expansion of educated non-manual jobs, notably, in the second half of the last century, in higher education. So did Fascism, the foundation of Israel and the dramatic decline of Western anti-Semitic discrimination after 1945. The sheer scale of the Jewish cultural presence would have been inconceivable before the First or even the Second World War. So, obviously, would the sheer size of the identity-conscious, disproportionately book-buying Jewish public, which clearly affected the shape of the literary mass market for Jewish themes, first in the Weimar Republic and later elsewhere. A distinction between the two periods must therefore be made.

From the start, the contribution of emancipated Jews to their host societies had been disproportionately large but, by the very nature of emancipation, it was culturally unspecific: they wanted to be simply unhyphenated French, Italian, German and English. Conversely, even allowing for widespread anti-Semitic feelings, in their liberal phase these societies also welcomed a prosperous and educated minority that reinforced their political, cultural and national values.[16] Consider, until the Second World War, the field of popular show business in which Jews really were dominant: operetta and musicals in both Europe and the USA, theatre, and later the movies, or, for that matter commercial popular song on both sides of the Atlantic. In the nineteenth century Offenbach was French, Strauss was Austrian. Even in the twentieth century Irving Berlin was American. In the totally Jewish-controlled Hollywood of the great period you will search in vain for anything other than what Zukor, Loew and Mayer considered 100 per cent white American values, or even for stars with names hinting at an immigrant origin. In the public life of united Italy the 0.1 per cent of Jews played a far larger role than in any other state: seventeen of them sat in the Senate or rose to be prime ministers or ministers, even generals.[17] Yet they were so indistinguishable from other Italians that not until after 1945 do we find historians drawing attention to their extraordinary over-representation.

This was also the case in the high arts. Jewish composers produced German and French music. In some ways this is still so with Jewish musicians and virtuoso performers, whose conquest of the orchestra pits and concert halls were the first signs of emancipation in the benighted East. The great twentieth-century Jewish violinists and pianists reinforced the repertoire of Western classical music, unlike the modest gypsy fiddlers, the black jazz and Latin American musicians, who extended its reach. A handful of nineteenth-century London Irish writers (Wilde, Shaw, Yeats) have left a larger, recognisably 'Irish' mark on English literature than Jewish writers left on any nineteenth-century European literature. On the other hand, in the 'modernist' period the Jewish contribution to vernacular literatures and the visual arts became much more identifiable as well as influential. This was perhaps because modernist innovation in these fields made them more attractive to a group uncertain of its situation in the world, as well as to emancipated newcomers, especially from the East. Equally, it may have been because the crisis of nineteenth-century society moved gentile perceptions closer to the unfixed situation of Jewry. It was the twentieth century that imbued Western culture with ideas derived from the very consciously Jewish father of psychoanalysis. A Jew becomes central in James Joyce's *Ulysses*, as Thomas Mann becomes preoccupied with such themes and Kafka makes his enormous and posthumous impact on the twentieth century. Conversely, as we are being moved by the generally American, but perhaps global, meanings of Arthur Miller's *Death of a Salesman*, we barely notice, as David Mamet has reminded us, how recognisably Jewish is the experience on which it is based.

In the visual arts, one or two distinguished figures who happened to be Jews (Liebermann, Pissarro) gave way to a cosmopolitan twentieth-century diaspora in which Jews were not only more numerous – *c.* 20 per cent of the 'artists' biographies' in the catalogue of the great Berlin/Moscow 1900–1905 Exhibition appear to be Jewish – but also more prominent (Modigliani, Pascin, Marcoussis, Chagall, Soutine, Epstein, Lipchitz, Lissitzky, Zadkine), and sometimes more recognisably Jewish. Recently, Americanised mass-media culture has even introduced Yiddish locutions and idioms into current gentile journalists' English. Today most anglophone gentiles understand the word 'chutzpah' as hardly anyone except Jews did forty years ago.

Since there is very little scope for national and cultural coloration in the modern natural sciences, the same situation could not be the case in these fields, which became increasingly remote from common sense as well as incomprehensible to the layman in the twentieth century. The contribution of Jews in this area increased dramatically after 1914, as the record of the relevant Nobel prizes demonstrates. However, only the ideologies of the radical right could link the two as 'Jewish science'. The social and human sciences offered greater scope; indeed, for obvious reasons, the nature, structure and transformations of society in an era of radical historical change attracted emancipated Jews disproportionately almost from the beginning, both in practice and in theory – starting with the Saint Simonians and Marx. This fits in with that understandable Jewish proclivity to support movements for revolutionary global transformation, which is so striking in the epoch of the Marx-inspired socialist and communist movements. Indeed, one might say that the western Jews of the early nineteenth century received emancipation from an ideology not associated with them, while the eastern Ashkenazim largely emancipated themselves through a universalist revolutionary ideology that was closely associated with them. This is true even of the original Zionism, so deeply penetrated by Marxism, that actually built the original state of Israel. Correspondingly, in the twentieth century, certain fields developed (such as, in certain regions of Europe, sociology and, in particular, psychoanalysis) that sometimes seemed as disproportionately populated by Jews as, say, the international club of violin virtuosos. But what characterised these sciences, like all the others to which Jews contributed so signally, was not genetic association, but lack of fixity, and therefore innovation. It has been rightly said that, in Britain, 'the greatest impact of the exiles [from central Europe] was probably in the newer, more cross-disciplinary fields (art history, psychology, sociology, criminology, nuclear physics, biochemistry), and the most rapidly changing professions (film, photography, architecture, broadcasting) rather than in those long established'.[18] Einstein has become the best-known face of twentieth-century science not because he was a Jew, but because he could become the icon of a science in revolution in a century of constant intellectual upheaval.

This brings me to a final question in this bird's-eye view of the Jewish contribution to the wider world of Western culture and knowledge. Why has it been so much more marked in some regions than in others? Consider the difference between the serious Nobel science prizes of the UK, Russia, Israel and South Africa. Of the seventy-four British prizes, eleven were won by Jews, but, with one possible exception, none of them was British-born. Of the eleven Russian prizes won since 1917, six or seven are Jewish, presumably all natives of the region. Until 2004 no Nobel science prizes had been won by Israeli researchers in any country, although Israel has one of the highest outputs per capita of scientific papers. The year 2004, however, produced two, one native-born and one Hungarian-born. On the other hand, since Israel became independent, two or perhaps three have been won by members of the modest Lithuanian-Jewish population of South Africa (*c.* 150,000), though all outside that continent. How are we to explain such striking differences?

Here we can only speculate. In the sciences clearly the enormous increase in the research professions is crucial. Let us remember that the total number of university teachers in Prussia, even in 1913, was under two thousand; the number of public secondary teachers in Germany was little more than 4200.[19] Does not the exiguous number of academic posts in the field help to explain the surprising absence of Jews from the list of eminent conventional academic economic theorists before the Second World War (with the notable exception of Ricardo)? Conversely, the fact that chemistry is the field in which Jews chiefly won Nobel prizes before 1918 is surely connected with the fact that it was the one in which academically trained specialists were first employed in substantial numbers – the three big German chemical companies alone employed about a thousand.[20] The only one of my seven paternal uncles who achieved a professional career before 1914 did so as a chemist.

But these are superficial criteria, though not negligible ones.

Patently, without both the opening of academia in the USA to the Jews after 1948 and its vast expansion, the enormous wave of home-grown US Nobels after 1970 would have been impossible.[21] A more important factor, I suggest, is segregation, whether of the pre-emancipation kind or by territorial/genetic nationalism. This may explain the relatively rather disappointing contribution of Israel, considering the relatively vast size of its Jewish population. It would seem that living among and addressing the gentiles is a stimulus for the higher creative efforts, as it is for jokes, films and pop music. In this respect it is still much better to come from Brooklyn than Tel Aviv.

On the other hand, where Jews are given equal rights, at least in theory, a certain degree of uneasiness in the relationship between them and non-Jews has proved historically useful. This was clearly the case in Germany and the Habsburg Empire, as well as in the USA, until well after the Second World War. It was certainly so in the first half of the twentieth century in Russia/the USSR[22] and overseas, in South Africa and Argentina. The substantial support by Jews of other groups suffering official racial discrimination, as in South Africa and the USA, is surely a symptom of such uneasiness. It is not found in all Jewish communities. I would suggest that even in the countries of the fullest toleration – France in the Third Republic, western Austria under Franz Joseph, the Hungary of mass Magyar assimilation – the times of maximum stimulus for Jewish talent may have been those when the Jews became conscious of the limits of assimilation – the *fin-de-siècle* moment of Proust, who came to maturity in the Dreyfus decade, the era of Schoenberg, Mahler, Freud, Schnitzler and Karl Kraus. Is it possible for diaspora Jews to be so integrated as to lose that stimulus? It has been argued from time to time that this was the case of the established Anglo-Jewish community in the nineteenth century. In the UK, certainly, Jews were less than prominent in the leadership or on the intellectual scene of the socialist and social-revolutionary movements or less rebellious than they were elsewhere – certainly less so than east of the Rhine and north of the Alps. I am unqualified to come to a conclusion one way or another. Whatever may have been the case up to the days of Hitler and the Holocaust, it is no longer so.

But what of the future? The paradox of the era since 1945 is that the greatest tragedy in Jewish history has had two utterly different consequences. On the one hand it has concentrated a substantial minority of the global Jewish population in one nation state: Israel, which was itself once upon a time the child of Jewish emancipation, with the drive to enter the same world as the rest of humanity. It has shrunk the diaspora, dramatically so in the Islamic regions. On the other hand, in most parts of the world it has been followed by an era of almost unlimited public acceptance of Jews, by the virtual disappearance of the anti-Semitism and discrimination of my youth, and by unparalleled and unprecedented Jewish achievement in the fields of culture, intellect and public affairs. There is no historic precedent for the triumph of the *Aufklärung* in the post-Holocaust diaspora. Nevertheless, there are those who wish to withdraw from it into the old segregation of religious ultra-orthodoxy and the new segregation of a separate ethnic-genetic state-community. If they were to succeed, I do not think it would be good for either the Jews or the world.

7

The Jews and Germany

Most of world history until the late eighteenth century could be written without more than marginal reference to the Jews, except as a small people who pioneered the monotheistic world religions, a debt acknowledged by Islam, but creating endless problems for Christianity, or, rather, for the Jews unlucky enough to live under Christian rulers. Practically all the intellectual history of the Western world, and all that of the great cultures of the East, could be written without more than a few footnotes about the direct Jewish contribution to them, though not without paying considerable attention to the role of Jews as intermediaries and cultural brokers, notably between the classic Mediterranean heritage, Islam and the medieval West. This is rather surprising when we consider the extraordinary prominence in twentieth-century cultural, intellectual and public life of members of this tiny group of people, which, even at its demographic peak before the Holocaust, formed less than 1 per cent of the world population.

Since most public life was closed to them, their absence from it before the French Revolution was perhaps to be expected. Yet it is also clear that Jewish intellectual activity for most of the last two millennia, perhaps with the exception of the Hellenistic era, was overwhelmingly inward looking. Only the occasional sage, in the many centuries between Philo the Jew and Spinoza, appeared to be seriously concerned with non-Jewish thinking, and these individuals, like Maimonides, were, not fortuitously, apt to be born in the open civilisation of Muslim Spain. The great rabbis, whose commentaries on the sacred texts, in all their Babylonian subtlety, still form the main subject in the Talmudic academies, were not interested in the views of unbelievers. With the possible exception of medicine, where acknowledged Jewish expertise crossed communal frontiers, Jewish learning and intellectual effort focused on holy matters. Is not the Yiddish word for place of worship, the synagogue, the old German word for school?

It is evident that an enormous oilfield of talent was waiting to be tapped by the most admirable of all human movements, the Enlightenment of the eighteenth century, which, among its many other beneficial achievements, brought about the emancipation of the Jews. When we consider that, for almost a century after Joseph II, the Toleranzedikte of 1781–2 was virtually confined to the small Jewish communities of western and west-central Europe, and that Jews had hardly begun to make their mark in some of the major fields of their subsequent intellectual achievement, the size of the contribution that Jews began to make to nineteenth-century history is quite extraordinary. Who could write world history without paying attention to Ricardo and Marx, both products of the first half-century of emancipation?

For understandable reasons, most writers on Jewish history,

predominantly Jews themselves, tend to concentrate on the impact of the outside world on their people rather than the other way round. Even Peter Pulzer's excellent 'political history of a minority' does not quite escape from such introversion. The two Jews whose impact on German politics was the greatest, the founders of the German labour movement, Marx and Lassalle, barely appear (there are precisely three references to Lassalle, one of which concerns his father), and the author is clearly ill at ease with the 'disparity between the large number of Jews prominent in the Wilhelmine Socialdemocratic party's leadership and debates and the slower growth of its electoral following among Jews', preferring to concentrate on the latter.

Nevertheless, his perceptive, though sometimes over-detailed analysis avoids most of the temptations of Jewish historical separatism. His work is part of what is perhaps the last survivor of the German-Jewish Liberal tradition, the group of historians associated with the Leo Baeck Institute in London. It has all the quiet, low-key strength and balance of the work that has issued from this admirable institution under the auspices of scholars like Arnold Paucker and Werner Mosse. Like his colleagues, Pulzer understands what has since Hitler become almost incomprehensible, namely why German Jews felt themselves to be profoundly German, and indeed why 'the "fourth Reich" that established itself in Hampstead and Washington Heights, in Hollywood and Nahariya, with battered tomes of Lessing, Kant and Goethe and scratched records of Furtwängler and the Threepenny Opera, bore witness to the tenacity of roots in the German Kulturnation'. In short, why emancipated nineteenth-century Jews wanted passionately 'to proclaim that they had left the ghetto, that they had entered civilization', which now offered to admit them.

For 'the German-Jewish community enjoyed a leading, even dominant, intellectual position among other Jewries', if only because emancipated Jewry contained more German speakers than any others, even if we count only those in what was to become the German Reich in 1871. Moreover, as Ruth Gay's illuminating and copiously illustrated *The Jews of Germany* makes clear, even as it also overlooks Marx and Lassalle, German Jewry was overwhelmingly indigenous, even after the mass migration from the East began and, with school education, abandoned Yiddish for German speech.

However, the German Kulturnation was far larger than this. The very fact, observed (but not stressed) by Pulzer, that so many of the leading intellectual figures of German Social Democracy – including all but one of its prominent Marxists – had transferred their field of activity to Germany from the Habsburg Empire (Kautsky, Hilferding) or tsarist Russia (Luxemburg, Parvus, even Marchlewski and Radek), demonstrates that German was the language of culture from the Greater Russian marches to the French borders. The major difference between the Jews of Germany and emancipated Jews from the rest of the German culture zone was that the former were *only* German, whereas a substantial number of the latter were pluricultural, if not plurilingual. These, and probably these alone, constituted the idealised Mitteleuropa of which dissident Czechs and Hungarians dreamed in the 1980s, linking otherwise non-communicating cultures and peoples in the multinational empires.

Moreover, it was they who carried, perhaps even built, the German language in the remoter outposts of the Habsburg Empire, since, as the largest constituents of the educated middle class in those parts, they were the people who actually used standard literary German instead of the dialects spoken by the emigrant German diasporas of the East – Swabian, Saxon and (as German philologists confirmed, sometimes not without regret) Yiddish. German was the name of freedom and progress. Yeshiva students from Poland, like Jakob Fromer, as recorded by Ruth Gay, secretly studied German among the Talmudic commentaries by means of two dictionaries: Russian–Hebrew and German–Russian. Schiller brought emancipation from what another Polish seeker for liberation called

'the fetters of superstition and prejudice'. It is easier to senti-
mentalise the *shtetl*, now that it no longer exists, than it was
when young men and women had to live in it.

The German Jews wished passionately to be German,
though, as Pulzer observes acutely, they wanted to assimilate
'not to the German nation but to the German middle class'. Yet
the commonest of the accusations against assimilation, the great
dream of nineteenth-century social mobility, plainly did not
apply to them. It did not mean a denial of their Jewish identity,
not even in the very unusual case of conversion. As Pulzer
shows, in spite of massive secularisation and their overwhelming
commitment to being German, the German Jews survived as a
group conscious of their Judaism until extirpated by Hitler. Nor
was this due only to anti-Semitism, which, as he reminds us, was
in any case relatively mild by the standards of other countries.
As the refugee physicist Sir Rudolf Peierls puts it, 'In pre-Hitler
Germany being Jewish was a bearable handicap.' It was not
German or the much more palpable Viennese anti-Semitism
that converted Herzl to Zionism, but the Dreyfus case in France.

However, one wishes Pulzer had not chosen the term 'ethnicity' to describe what bound Jews together, since the bond was
felt to be not biological, but historical. They did not see themselves as a community of blood or even ancestral religion, but,
in Otto Bauer's words, a 'community of fate'. Still, whatever we
call it, emancipated Jews as a group did not behave quite like
non-Jews. (Eastern ones, of course, behaved very differently
indeed.) Most of Pulzer's book is devoted to demonstrating the
specificity of their political behaviour. Not surprisingly, as a
community they stood on the moderate Liberal left of the
German political spectrum, but by no means on the far left.
Even the collapse of Liberalism in the years of Hitler's rise
pushed them towards the Social Democrats, rather than the
communists. Unlike the Jews of the Habsburg and tsarist
regions of Europe, their politics were not messianic. Relatively
few, it is argued, joined or voted for the Communist Party, and

before 1933 German Zionists, also a smallish minority, saw Zionism as a personal rebirth but not as a programme of emigration. Unlike Eastern Jews, they did not see themselves as strangers in (to quote one of them) 'the land of Walther and Wolfram, Goethe, Kant and Fichte'.

In short, German Jews were at ease in Germany. Hence theirs was a double tragedy. Not only were they to be destroyed, but they had not foreseen their fate. Pulzer does his best to rationalise the failure, indeed the refusal, of Liberal German Jewry to recognise what Hitler meant, even after 1933. It is, of course, true that nobody, not even the Eastern Jews who lived among those who had massacred their relatives by the thousands in 1918–20, could expect, or even envisage, what eventually took place at Maidanek and Treblinka. Nobody could imagine it. Few could even bring themselves to believe it when the first credible reports of the genocide filtered through to the West in 1942. There was no precedent in human history for it. Nevertheless, the present reviewer, who experienced 30 January 1933 as a schoolboy in Berlin, can testify that even then a fairly apocalyptic view of Hitler's regime was taken by some. And indeed, with all their reluctance to give up Germany, many Jews prepared for the worst, even though they underestimated it. After all, almost two-thirds of the Jewish population of Germany in 1933 emigrated in the following six years and therefore, unlike their unhappy Polish brethren, survived. And yet, they did not leave even Nazi Germany willingly. Some, like a descendant of the founder of the Deutsche Bank, sent his wife and children to safety, but committed suicide after the Kristallnacht of 1938 rather than give up Germany.

All the same, even the survivors' tragedy was real. Only those who have experienced the force, the grandeur and the beauty of that culture, which made the Bulgarian Jew Elias Canetti write in the middle of the Second World War that 'the language of my intellect will remain German', can fully realise what its loss meant. Only those whose very surnames still record the

Hessian, Swabian and Franconian villages and market towns of their ancestors, know the pain of torn roots. Their loss was irreparable, because the Jewish communities of central Europe can never be reconstituted, and, even if they could be, the German culture to which they belonged is no longer a world culture but has been reduced to a regional – one is almost tempted to say a large provincial – culture.

And what did Germany lose? Paradoxically, probably less than the countries of the old Habsburg Empire, because Germany's Jews had fitted themselves into an existing middle-class culture, whereas the emancipated Jews of the Habsburg Empire created new ones, often, as in the case of Vienna's, very different from that of the Reich. Culturally, the expulsion or destruction of the Jews left Germany much as before, though more provincial and peripheral than it had been prior to 1933. And yet this is to underestimate Germany's loss. German is no longer the language of modernity for aspiring Europeans from the backwoods. It is no longer the language of the scholarly publications that every academic from Tokyo to Cambridge must be able to read. No doubt that is not only due to the exodus or the death of the Jews. However, in one respect their disappearance clearly had a dramatic effect. From 1900 to 1933 almost 40 per cent of all Nobel prizes in physics and chemistry went to Germany; since 1933 this has become only about one in ten. History records, with tragic irony or black humour, that one of the refugee Nobel laureates insisted on revisiting Germany after 1945, because of his 'inextinguishable homesickness for the German language and landscape'.

8

Mitteleuropean Destinies

It is always dangerous when geographical terms are used in historical discourse. Great caution is needed, for cartography lends an air of spurious objectivity to terms that often, perhaps usually, belong to politics, to the realm of programmes rather than reality. Historians and diplomats know how often ideology and policy masquerade as fact. Rivers, because they make clear lines on maps, are turned not only into state frontiers, but into 'natural' frontiers. Language boundaries justify state frontiers. The very choice of names on maps often faces cartographers with the need to make political decisions. What are they to call places or geographical features with several names, or those that have officially changed names? If alternative names are listed, then which are indicated as the main ones? If names have changed, how long should the former name be recalled?

My Austrian school atlas of the 1920s still reminds readers that the Norwegian capital Oslo was once Christiania, gives Helsinki only in brackets as the alternative name for Helsingfors and (prophetically in this instance) St Petersburg as the main name for Leningrad. In the standard British atlas of 1970[1] now before me, Lviv is still described (in brackets) as Lemberg, but Volgograd has lost the name Stalingrad, by which it has entered history. Dubrovnik and Ljubljana still have their subtitles (Ragusa and Laibach), but whereas Cluj in Romania still carries a reference to its Hungarian name (Koloszvar), there is no trace of its German (Klausenburg) or of any other German names in that country.

Nowhere is geography more indivisible from ideology and politics than in central Europe, if only because, unlike the western peninsula of Eurasia known as the continent of Europe, the region has no accepted borders or definition, even though there are places that will hardly be included in any version of 'central Europe', however broad, for example Oslo and Lisbon, Moscow and Palermo. Since some such term as 'central Europe or middle Europe (Mitteleuropa)' is convenient and constantly used, this leads to considerable ambiguity. Indeed, there is not even agreement about its use in cartography or discourse, whether current or historical. For the French *Guide Bleu* between the wars, 'L'Europe Centrale' comprised Bavaria, Austria, Czechoslovakia, Hungary and Yugoslavia. On the older German maps it is likely to include most of Denmark in the north and the Po valley in the south, and from somewhere near Warsaw in the east to the coasts of Flanders and Holland. I have even seen maps that extend it well to the west of Lyon and into the Danube delta.

Perhaps not uncharacteristically, on German maps central Europe usually covered Germany, or rather the area of the old Holy Roman Empire 'of the German nation'. For the primary political concept of central Europe (Mitteleuropa) is linked to the history of German national unification and imperial expansion in the nineteenth and twentieth centuries. Its first and original sense dates back to Friedrich List. List's Mitteleuropa was a mega-German economic region that included Belgium,

Holland, Denmark and Switzerland, and reached deep into the Balkans. After 1848, when Habsburg hegemony seemed possible for a moment, it was fleetingly adopted in Vienna. Bismarck, who had no interest in a Greater Germany, had none in Mitteleuropa either. However, in the age of empire the term became popular again, especially during the First World War, when a book under that title by Friedrich Naumann suggested a post-war economic and, eventually, political unity of the German Reich with Austria-Hungary. He had in mind not only the lands between the Vistula and the Vosges mountains, but also an economic and political hegemony reaching through the Balkans into the Middle East. His Mitteleuropa lay on the road from Berlin to Baghdad. Though Naumann was a Liberal and an eventual supporter of the Weimar Republic, in effect something like his concept was to be briefly achieved under Hitler, although by that time German ambitions had been enlarged to envisage a German hegemony over all (continental) Europe.

There is, however, a second, historically more recent version of Mitteleuropa. Geographically it is more restricted in the west, though more open in the south and east. This is the 'east central Europe', which has been defined as 'the eastern region of the European continent from roughly the river Elbe to the Russian plains, and from the Baltic Sea to the Black Sea and the Adriatic'.[2] This makes sense from the point of view of both economic and social history. Historically this region more or less coincides with a part of Europe socially and economically divergent from the western region, which retained systems of agrarian serfdom or peasant dependency until the nineteenth century. In effect, this central Europe coincides with the old Habsburg Empire, whose capital and the core of whose territories were, after all, situated in a region that could not be described as other than central on the map of the European continent.

Politically there is a concept of this 'central Europe' that expresses nostalgia for the Habsburg Empire. The territory of this vast agglomeration of regions and nationalities, reaching from Lake Constance in the west to the borders of Moldova in the east, was divided between seven old or new states in 1918, and is at present occupied by twelve different states.[3] History since 1918 has made those who once lived in what its national-ists called 'the prison of nations' (*Völkerkerker*) think less unkindly of the realms of the emperor Franz Joseph (1848–1916). Indeed, it is probably the only empire that is recalled with nos-talgia in all its former territories. This would have surprised its contemporaries. While it has been the only European state whose death, long expected, stimulated great literature – one thinks of Karl Kraus, Robert Musil, Jaroslav Hašek or Miroslav Krleža – with hardly an exception its literary gravediggers did not mourn for it after it had been laid to rest. The exception, as we shall see, proves the rule, for even the wonderful novel *Radetzkymarsch* by Joseph Roth looked back on the monarchy from its far eastern borders with a certain alcoholic irony.

Nostalgia about what Robert Musil called Kakania (after the initials of the double monarchy k.k. [*kaiserlich und königlich*, 'impe-rial and royal'][4]) does not mean that it could ever be revived. Nevertheless, its existence was so central to the power-system of nineteenth-century Europe that attempts were constantly made to find some equivalent central European entity between Germany and Russia.

After Versailles the French concept of a 'little entente' – with Czechoslovakia, Yugoslavia and Romania, all largely or entirely composed of former parts of the Habsburg Empire – was per-haps the first. It failed. The little entente, and its separate members, aimed to create an independent Danubian bloc. They failed. The supremacy of Hitler's Germany made these projects academic, but in its post-war plans the British govern-ment envisaged some kind of Danubian federation. The plan never got anywhere. Immediately after the war, ideas for a revival of the Little Entente once again circulated in Czechoslovakia, to be countered by equally vague plans for a

Danube federation from Hungary. Both schemes were swept away by the supremacy of Moscow, which also eliminated the much more serious plan of a Balkan federation, which had long been communist policy and had the serious backing of Tito and Dimitrov. In the twilight years of the Soviet empire, Mitteleuropa, or rather an ideal of central European identity, re-emerged among the writers of the region – Kundera, Havel, Konrád, Kiš, Vajda, Miłosz and others. It has been described correctly by Timothy Garton Ash as historically looking back towards Austria-Hungary and forward 'beyond Yalta'. Indeed, after the revolutions of 1989 a brief bid to recreate a central bloc was made in the so-called Vyšehrad Group of Poland, Hungary and Czechoslovakia, but it was essentially an attempt to separate the more 'advanced' from the more 'backward' former socialist states in order to convince the European Union to integrate them more rapidly. In fact the end of the Soviet era in this region has produced not a return to a greater central European unity, but a further disintegration of what was once the Habsburg Empire, by the fragmentation of Czechoslovakia and Yugoslavia. In short, the dream of filling the gap left by its disappearance is over. In any case, we no longer live in the era of European history when there was significant demand for a middle bloc as a bulwark between German and Russian power.

However, there is a third variant of the concept of central Europe or Mitteleuropa that is more dangerous than the nostalgia for the Habsburg Empire or some other middle bloc between Russia and Germany. It is the one that distinguishes between a superior 'us' and the inferior or even barbarous 'them' to the east and the south. This sense of superiority is by no means confined to those who live in the centre of Europe. Indeed, in both world wars and during the Cold War, it was chiefly used by the self-described 'West' to distinguish itself from the 'East' and, after 1945, specifically from countries under socialist regimes. However, it was particularly relevant to central Europe in general and especially to the Habsburg Empire, since

the border between what was variously described as 'advanced'
and 'backward', 'modern' and 'traditional', 'civilised' and 'barbarian', ran through it. To quote its celebrated statesman,
Prince Metternich: 'Asia begins on the Landstrasse' (the high-
way leading eastwards out of Vienna). And the word 'Asia'
(which was regarded as implying inferiority) recurs in the discourse of one part of central Europe about the others, as in the
works of the nineteenth-century writer K. E. Franzos
(1848–1904) – born in the Bukowina, that curious corner where
Ukrainians, Poles, Rumanians, Germans and Jews coexisted –
who wrote 'Sketches from Demi-Asia' ('a demi-Asian cultural
desert').[5] Gregor von Rezzori, another writer born in the
Bukowina, gave it an exotic African tinge as 'Maghrebinia'.[6]
This is a region in which everyone was on the frontiers of some
'Asia'. For German Carinthians it separated them from
Slovenes, for Slovenes from Croats, for Croats from Serbs, for
Serbs from Albanians, for Hungarians from Rumanians. And,
indeed, in every town the frontier ran between the educated and
the uneducated, the traditional and the modern, and sometimes (but not always) it coincided with ethnic/linguistic
boundaries. When Mitteleuropeans saw themselves as the
agents of civilisation against barbarism, the term came danger-
ously close to the racism of racial superiority and ethnic
exclusion.

As a political term 'middle Europe' is therefore unacceptable. What of it as a cultural concept? Is there a high culture, in
the arts and sciences, that has discernible regional borders?

Once there was such a 'middle European' culture: that of
the emancipated and, in many parts of central Europe, largely
Jewish middle class in the wide zone of Europe that once lived
under the hegemony of German *Bildung*. It no longer exists,
though it survived Hitler in ageing migrant colonies in London,
New York and Los Angeles. It was middle European for three
reasons. First, because only in the central belt of Europe was
German the primary international language of culture, though,

in the days when all educated Europeans knew French, not the only one. The zone of German linguistic-cultural hegemony stretched from the Rhine to the eastern borders of the Habsburg Empire and from Scandinavia deep into the Balkans. Vienna was the cultural capital for most of that peninsula. Elias Canetti, from Ruse on the lower Danube in Bulgaria, was and remained a cultural Viennese, who spoke and wrote in German to the end of his peripatetic life. Within this zone German was not only the primary international language, but the language through which those from the more backward regions and peoples acquired access to modernity. K. E. Franzos gave a characteristic expression to this ideal of German culture as a universal medium of emancipation in his short story 'Schiller in Barnow', which traces the fortunes of a volume of Schiller's poems as it passes through the hands of various inhabitants of a remote Galician village – a Polish monk, a Jew, a Ruthenian (Ukrainian) peasant, for all of whom it represents an emergence from past into future.

Hence, outside the heartlands whose population spoke only German (or rather the combination of the German literary language with a spoken dialect), typically this middle European culture belonged to a group whose members also spoke other languages and it could therefore form a bridge between peoples. One might say that the true middle European stood at some crossroads of language and culture, like Ettore Schmitz of Trieste, better known by his literary pseudonym Italo Svevo ('the German Italian'). It is no accident that the most eminent memorialiser of this Mitteleuropa and the Danube, which is its axis, is another Triestine, Claudio Magris, native of that remarkable corner of the Adriatic where Italian, German, Hungarian and various Slav cultures meet, to combine with the peasant dialects of the countryside and the multicultural music of a great maritime port.

Second, solely in one part of Europe, in practice only in the Habsburg monarchy, did the educated public consist principally

of Jews, who until the Second World War made up 10 per cent
of the population of Vienna and an even higher percentage of
that of Budapest. Before 1848 they had been largely excluded
from the capital cities of the Habsburg Empire. Overwhelmingly,
they had come into them in the second half of the nineteenth
century, from the small towns of Moravia, Slovakia and
Hungary, and eventually also from the remoter regions of what
is now the Ukraine. It was as culturally German 'middle
Europeans' that these emancipated Jews saw themselves, as they
tried to distance themselves from the traditionalist, Yiddish-
speaking Ostjuden who wandered westwards in the twentieth
century, until both groups ended their lives in the same gas ovens
of Hitler's Germany. Indeed, in 1880 the most Jewish of all
shtetls in Galicia, the city of Brody (*c.* twenty thousand inhabitants, 76.3 per cent Jewish), insisted that its children should have
their primary education exclusively in German-language schools,
and brought a special case to the Imperial Court of Justice in
Vienna to protest against the authorities' refusal to permit this.[7]

(The conceptual distinction between Ostjuden (eastern Jews),
i.e. the Jews living in the former kingdom of Poland, partitioned
between Russia, Prussia and Austria in the eighteenth century,
and the Westjuden (western Jews), i.e. specifically the Jews of the
hereditary territories (Erblande) of the Habsburg monarchy,
appears to have emerged in the Bukowina, where the clash
between an emancipated and assimilated Jewish elite and the
Yiddish-speaking majority became particularly acute in the late
nineteenth century, after the foundation of the (German-speaking) University of Czernowitz in 1875.)

Finally, the people of this culture must be called 'middle
Europeans' because the twentieth century made them home-
less. They could be identified solely in terms of geography,
since their states and regimes came and went. During the twentieth century the inhabitants of a city once linked by an electric
tram to Vienna, a few kilometres distant, as well as to Pressburg,
which was also known as Pozsony and Bratislava (all central-

European cities have several names), have been citizens of the Hungarian part of Austria-Hungary, of Czechoslovakia, of the German satellite Slovakia, of communist and, briefly, post-communist Czechoslovakia and, once again, of a Slovak state. If they were Jews who lacked enthusiasm for their own blood-and-soil national state in Palestine, the only fatherland they could look back on, like Joseph Roth (of Brody), was the old monarchy of Franz Joseph, which treated all its nations with the same gentle scepticism. And that, as everyone knew, had gone for good.

But so has that culture itself. Its physical monuments, notably the great theatres and operas – the cathedrals of the age, catering to the bourgeoisie's spiritual, but no longer necessarily religious, aspirations – are still the focus of the cities of central Europe. The buildings that dominate the circular boulevard, which was built round the old city centre when Vienna was modernised after 1860, are not, as originally intended after the defeat of the 1848 revolution, 'palaces, garrisons and churches, but centres of constitutional government and higher culture':[8] among the latter are the university, the Burgtheater, the two gigantic museums representing art and natural science, the Opera. And yet this high culture of Mitteleuropa belonged to a relatively, and often absolutely, small educated elite, though the institutions of education aimed to bring it to the mass of the population. What we treasure in it today was, in any case, of very little interest to most of the Habsburg monarchy's fifty-odd million inhabitants. How many of them could have been seated in all the opera houses of the monarchy put together? In 1913 the city of Vienna itself provided its two million inhabitants with a concert hall capacity of approximately six thousand seats in which to listen to the glories of Viennese symphonic and chamber music.

Nevertheless, even within these limits, the culture of Mitteleuropa, being essentially linked to one language, was being undermined and split by the rise of nationalism, even in the nineteenth century. Despite the work of gifted translators, the literatures in the national tongues remained little known outside their countries of origin. How much did the central European readers outside the Czech lands know or care about Neruda and Vrchlický, outside Hungary about Vörösmarty and Jókai? Indeed, divergences within central Europe are evident even in such relatively transnational fields as music and politics. Hungarian socialists were not Austro-Marxists, if only because they did not accept intellectual leadership from Vienna. Bartók and Janáček are not cousins to Bruckner and Mahler. The resentment in the Alpine provinces of Austria towards the Viennese and the Jews, the cultural as well as the musical tension between Catholic Austria and the *fin-de-siècle* Habsburg culture, now so much admired, was palpable. It was not their culture. Paradoxically, a common central European element survived best in the middle-class field of light entertainment, the dances of Slav and Hungarian origin, common to the entire region, the musical substratum of gypsy fiddlers, the Hungarian and Balkan-oriented operettas of Strauss, Lehar and Kalman. They are certainly very noticeable in the multicultural (Magyar, Czech, Italian, Yiddish) vocabulary of the Viennese dialect and in something like a general central European gastronomy, mixing the dishes and drinks of the Viennese, the German Austrians, the Czechs, the Poles, the Magyars and the southern Slavs.

Since the Second World War, and even more so since the end of the European socialist regimes, the old culture of central Europe has been pulverised by three major developments: mass ethnic expulsion or massacre; and the linked triumphs of commercialised worldwide mass culture and the English language as the unquestioned idiom of global communication. The triumph of a North American version of commercialised mass culture is not peculiar to central Europe, and little need be said about it here. The two other developments are crucial to central Europe. The mass migration or killing of national and cultural minorities, notably the Jews and the Germans, replaced essentially plurinational countries like Poland, Czechoslovakia, Yugoslavia and Romania with mononational ones, and simplified the cultural complexities of their cities. The older families in the city of Bratislava (Pressburg, Pozsony), who remember it as a meeting place of peoples and cultures, still distinguish themselves as 'Pressburaks' from the 'Bratislavaks' who, coming from the rural hinterlands of Slovakia, now determine the character of their country's capital. And, as anyone who visits them today will confirm, this is equally true of cities like Czernowitz (Chernovtsi) and Lemberg (Lwów, Lviv). Mitteleuropa has lost one of its essential characteristics.

Equally, and perhaps even more significant, is the end of German linguistic hegemony. German is no longer the lingua franca of the educated from the Baltic to Albania. It is not merely that a young Czech meeting a young Hungarian or a Slovene will most probably use English to communicate with him or her, but that none of them can any longer expect the other to know German. It is that nobody who is not a native German speaker is now likely to use Goethe and Lessing, Hölderlin and Heine as the foundation of educated culture, let alone as the way from backwardness into modernity.

Since Weimar, German culture no longer sets the tone in middle Europe. It is just one national culture among others. The old culture of Mitteleuropa may be unforgotten. It is more translated and written about than ever before. But, like the repertoire of classical symphonic and chamber concerts, which is so largely based on composers who lived and worked in an area of a few hundred square kilometres whose centre was Vienna, it no longer lives.

Politically and culturally 'middle Europe' belongs to a past that is not likely to return. Only one thing that belonged to it remains. The border that separates the rich and successful economies of the western parts of Europe from the eastern regions of the continent, which once ran through the middle of the Habsburg Empire, is still there. Only now it runs through the middle of what will be the expanded European Union.

9

Culture and Gender in European Bourgeois Society 1870–1914

Regular compendia about people in public life, or otherwise in the public domain, began to be published in Britain in the middle of the nineteenth century. The best-known of them, and the direct ancestor of the present *Who's Who*, which is in turn the ancestor of most other such biographical reference books, was *Men of the Time*. I begin this survey of the problem of public and private relations between the sexes in bourgeois culture between 1870 and 1914 with this small but not insignificant editorial change.[1]

The editorial change mentioned above was significant not because a reference book hitherto confined to males decided to include females. In fact, *Men of the Time* had long contained a small proportion of women, and the percentage regularly listed in such compendia, including, from 1897, *Who's Who*, did not rise significantly. Attempts to increase it were to be made, but the percentage remained of the order of 3–5 per cent. Not until the second great feminist wave of the 1960s and 1970s did a much larger percentage of women break into gender-neutral reference books: the *Dictionary of National Biography Supplement* for 1970–1980 contains 15 per cent of female entries. The novelty lay in the formal recognition that women as a sex had a place in the public sphere, from which they had previously been excluded except, as it were, as individual anomalies. That Great Britain, the most bourgeois of countries, had actually been ruled by a woman for over fifty years before her sex became entitled to an official place among the recognised body of public personages emphasises the significance of the change.

Let me give a second example of this recognition of women as having a public dimension. The Anglo-French Exposition of 1908 in London was, like all earlier international exhibitions of the nineteenth century, a collection of symbols including current attitudes. This one was significant for being the first time such an occasion was combined with the Olympic Games, held in a stadium specially built for the purpose, and also for including a special Palace of Women's Work. We need not trouble ourselves with the content of this building, though it is worth noting two facts. First, that according to contemporary reports, the women artists preferred to send their work to the general and non-gendered Palace of the Arts, rather than showing it under the heading of women's work; second, that the Women's Industrial Council protested that the females actually employed and working at the exhibition were being grossly overworked and underpaid.[2] The point is that the Palace of Women's Work celebrated women not as beings but as doers, not as functional cogs in the machinery of family and society but as individual achievers.

This change is also evident if we compare the criteria for including women in earlier reference books with those published in the new era. A very high proportion of those listed in a typical work of the early part of the century (*Men of the Reign*, published to celebrate fifty years of Queen Victoria's reign) are there not in their own right but through family connections (that is, as sisters, daughters, wives, widows, mistresses, or other connections of celebrated men) or (what amounts to the same thing) as members of royal or aristocratic kinship networks. The later reference books were by no means sure how such cases should be treated; they were typically represented by royal and noble ladies, but, in general, publications were increasingly inclined to omit them.

A third piece of evidence for this new public recognition of women is the evident effort that was made to find women who could reasonably be displayed in the showcase reserved for women's achievement in the public sphere. The early volumes of *Men and Women of the Time* included young ladies whose only distinction was to have passed university examinations with high marks, and the volumes also padded out the numbers temporarily with a few more noble ladies. Both practices were later dropped.[3] More striking, perhaps, is the rather prominent representation of women in the first years of the new Nobel prizes. Between 1901, when the prizes were first awarded, and 1914, they were given to women four times (to Selma Lagerlöf for literature, to Bertha von Suttner for peace, and to Marie Curie twice for science). I doubt whether any subsequent period of equal length has seen a comparable number of Nobel awards to females.

In short, towards the end of the nineteenth century we find a distinct tendency in Europe and North America to treat women as persons in the same sense of bourgeois society, analogous to males, and therefore analogous also as potential achievers. This applied very much to such a significantly symbolic field as sport, which was just then developing. In tennis, the ladies' singles championship was instituted within a few years of the men's singles in Britain, France and the United States. It may not seem revolutionary to us to permit women, even married women, to compete as individuals in a championship, but I suggest that in the 1880s and 1890s it was a more radical change than we are inclined to concede today. Of course, in one sense the growing recognition of the second sex as a body of potential individual achievers runs parallel with the growing pressure to recognise women as possessing the classical rights of the bourgeois individual. Formally or institutionally, the recognition of women as citizens was delayed in most countries until after 1917, but the strength of the tendency is indicated by the rapidity of progress during and after the First World War. In 1914 hardly any governments had given votes to women, but ten years later the right of women to vote was part of the constitution in most states of Europe and North America. More directly relevant to the question of women in the public sphere, in 1917 the British monarchy for the first time instituted a system of honours for merit open to men and women equally, namely the Order of the British Empire.

Although this infiltration of women into the public sphere was not, in theory, confined to any particular class, in practice we are naturally concerned overwhelmingly with women of the upper and middle classes, the one significant exception being, as always, in the field of entertainment. Virtually all other forms of activity, professional or not, that were likely to make women publicly known depended on leisure, material resources, and schooling, alone or in combination. These advantages were simply not available to most women of the labouring classes. And even the mere fact of acquiring a paid occupation or entering the labour market had a public significance for middle- and upper-class women that it did not have for women of the labouring classes, all of whom worked by definition, and most of whom, at some stage of their lives, were obliged, if only by financial necessity, to undertake paid occupations. On the other hand, work, and especially paid work, was believed to be incompatible with the status of a lady to which females from the bourgeois strata aspired. Hence, a middle-class woman earning money was *ipso facto* anomalous, either as an unfortunate victim or as a rebel. In both cases she raised public problems of social identity. Moreover, the educational institutions and the organised professions into which middle-class women wished to penetrate – they were beyond the reach or the horizon of the other classes – resisted their penetration. Hence, the very fact that women had succeeded was of public interest. Nobody in 1891 would have dreamed of including young men in a *Who's Who* simply because they had got a first-class university degree, but young women might be included on this ground alone. In practice this chapter is therefore concerned almost exclusively with females belonging to the bourgeoisie or those who aspired to belong to it, as well as, of course, women of higher social status.

For our present purposes I need not enquire too deeply into the reasons for the developments noted above. Evidently there was considerable pressure from middle-class women wanting to enter the public sphere. It is beyond doubt that they entered it to an extent that would have previously been unthinkable (except by a few revolutionaries). It is also beyond doubt that they could not have done so unless important sectors of males had supported them in this endeavour: namely, in the first instance, the males in a position of family authority over their women; and in the second instance, and much more reluctantly and slowly, the males who ran the institutions that the women wished to enter. To this extent the private and public spheres of the sexes are inseparable.

For obvious reasons we usually tend to stress the opposition to women's emancipation, which was indeed so stubborn, irrational and even hysterical that it is the first thing to strike any unprejudiced modern observer of the nineteenth-century scene. Thus, the Vienna Psychoanalytical Society in 1907 debated an article on women medical students, which argued that these girls only wanted to study because they were too ugly to get husbands, and that they demoralised the male students by their loose sexual behaviour, not to mention the fact that studying was not fit for women. The psychoanalysts who politely discussed this hysterical farrago were surely among the less traditionalist or reactionary male members of the Viennese bourgeoisie. However, while such men did not approve of the shrillness of the authors' denunciation, Freud's (1976) own opinion was that 'it is true that woman gains nothing by studying and that on the whole woman's lot will not improve thereby. Moreover, women cannot equal man's achievement in the sublimation of sexuality.'

On the other hand, we must never forget that behind every bourgeois girl who was given her chance there stood, at the very least, a father who gave her permission and, almost certainly, who paid the costs, because it is clear that no young woman whose appearance or visible status claimed her to be a young 'lady' would have found it easy to take a paid job without the approval of her parents or other family authority figures. But in fact there was a great deal of such parental support. One has merely to consider the extraordinary growth in the academic secondary education for girls in the last forty years before the First World War. Whereas the number of boys' *lycées* in France remained stable at about 330–40, the number of girls' establishments of the same kind rose from zero in 1880 to 138 in 1913, educating one girl for every three boys. In Britain the number of girls' secondary schools in 1913–14 was comparable to that of boys' schools: 350 as against 400. Thirty, or even ten years earlier, this would not have been the case.

The inequalities in this process are equally interesting: I cannot pretend to explain them. Thus, while girls' secondary education was utterly negligible in Italy with 7500 pupils, and growth was feeble enough in the Low Countries and Switzerland, by 1900 there were a quarter of a million girls in Russian secondary schools. Russia also led the field in university education for women, if we leave aside the college population of the United States as not comparable. The nine thousand women students there in 1910 were about double the numbers in Germany, France and Italy and about four times those in Austria.[4] It is hardly necessary to recall that the first universities that provided room for women on any significant scale were those of Switzerland in the 1880s, and what they provided for was primarily a supply of potential women students from eastern Europe.

There may or may not be a material reason for this growth of women's education, but it can hardly be doubted that there was also a positive correlation between the ideology of parents and the prospects of emancipation for their daughters. In many parts of Europe – perhaps least of all in the Roman Catholic countries – what we clearly find is a body of bourgeois fathers, one would guess mostly of a liberal and progressive persuasion, who inspired both progressive views and emancipatory intentions in their daughters and, at some time in the late nineteenth century or the early twentieth century, accepted that they ought to get a higher education – even play a part in professional and public life.

This does not mean that such fathers treated their daughters just like their sons. Probably the fact that women found it easier to break open the gates of medicine than the other professions is not unrelated to the fact that healing fitted into the conventional picture of women as particularly suited to caring activities. Even in the 1930s the father of the crystallographer Rosalind Franklin, part of a typical bourgeois kinship network of prosperous liberal Jews accustomed to more radical or even socialist children, advised her against the choice of natural science as a profession. He would have preferred to see her in some kind of social work.[5] Nevertheless, I suggest that members of such progressive bourgeois groups at some time before 1914 came to accept the new and wider social role for their daughters, perhaps even for their wives. The change seems to have come rather rapidly. In Russia the number of women students grew from fewer than two thousand in 1905 to 9300 in 1911. In 1897 there were only about eight hundred women university students in the United Kingdom.[6] By 1921 there were about eleven thousand full-time university women students, or rather less than one third of the total number. What is more, the number of women students and their percentage of the relevant age group remained virtually unchanged until the Second World War, and the percentage of women in the total of university students fell quite markedly.[7] We can only infer that the reservoir of the kind of parents who encouraged their daughters to study was already fully tapped by the end of the First World War. In Britain no additional social or cultural source of women university students was to be tapped until the university expansion of the 1950s and 1960s. And I note, incidentally, that even in 1951 women students came from upper- and middle-class backgrounds to a significantly greater extent than did male students.

We can do no more than speculate about the speed of this change. In Britain it seems to be connected with the rise of the feminist movement, which, rallying round the call 'votes for women', became a mass force in the early 1900s. (I refrain from venturing into guesses about other countries.) Certainly the suffragism of the 1900s represented an entirely acceptable option for quite conventional women of the middle and upper classes. Indeed, in 1905 a quarter of all the duchesses in Britain were listed in the directory appended to the feminist *Englishwoman's Yearbook* (1905), and three of them, together with three marchionesses and sixteen countesses, were actually vice-presidents of the Conservative and Unionist Suffrage Association. The *Suffrage Annual and Women's Who's Who of 1913*, a compendium of almost seven hundred active militants of the movement for votes, shows that they belonged overwhelmingly not just to the middle classes but to the established upper-middle strata of British society.[8] Of the identifiable fathers of these women, more than 70 per cent were officers in the armed forces, clergymen, doctors, lawyers, engineers, architects or artists, professors and public-school headmasters, higher civil servants and politicians; 13 per cent were aristocrats or landowners not otherwise described; and 12 per cent were businessmen. Officers and clergy were particularly over-represented, as were fathers with colonial experience. Among the identifiable husbands of these activists – and 44 per cent of them were married – the traditional professions were less prominent businessmen, while such new professions as journalism were considerably more numerous, but manifestly the majority of the activists belonged to the upper and upper-middle classes. It is to be noted that almost one third of the entrants in the *Woman's Who's Who* had telephones, a rather exceptional piece of domestic equipment in 1913. To complete the picture we need only add that no less than 20 per cent of these suffrage activists had a university degree.

Their relation to culture may be briefly indicated by the professions, insofar as they are listed: 28 per cent were teachers, 345 were writers and journalists, 9 per cent described themselves as artists, and 4 per cent were actresses or musicians. Thus 75 per cent of the 229 persons reporting were employed in activities directly relevant to the creation or dissemination of reproduction culture.

We may therefore accept that sometime in the last twenty or thirty years before the First World War the role and behaviour of women, as conceived in nineteenth-century bourgeois society, changed rapidly and substantially in several countries. I am not arguing that the new emancipated middle-class woman formed more than a modest minority even among her age group but, as suggested at the outset of this chapter, the speed with which she was publicly recognised suggests that, from the outset, this minority was seen as the avant-garde of a much larger army that was about to follow.

Not that the emergence of the emancipated woman was particularly welcome to bourgeois men. It is during the 1890s and 1900s that one encounters misogynist – or at any rate ultra-sexist – reactions among intellectuals and, not least, emancipated intellectuals of liberal origins, which seem to express uneasiness and fear. The most typical reaction, which one finds in various versions and varying degrees of hysteria in Otto Weininger, Karl Kraus, Möbius, Lombroso, Strindberg and the then current reading of Nietzsche, stressed that the eternal and essential feminine excluded the intellect, so that it followed that women's competition in fields hitherto regarded as essentially male was at best pointless and at worst a disaster for both sexes. The 1907 debate among the Viennese psycho-analysts, quoted earlier, is a typical example. Perhaps the intensified and consciously homosexual culture of British male intellectual youth such as the Cambridge 'Apostles' reflects a similar uneasiness.[9]

However, what needs to be stressed here is not the continued, if concealed, opposition of men to feminism but the recognition of how far the role of the bourgeois women had already changed, as indeed the quotation from Freud indicates. For one element in the *fin-de-siècle* sex war, as seen by the male belliger-ents, was the acknowledgement of the bourgeois woman's independent sexuality. The essence of woman – of any woman, including the bourgeois one, which in itself was new – was no longer decorousness, modesty and morality, but sensuality, not *Sittlichkeit* but *Sinnlichkeit*. Karl Kraus wrote numerous variations on this theme, and indeed Austrian literature from Schnitzler to Musil is full of it. And who will say, in the era of the Richthofen sisters, that this was unrealistic? Quite naturally sexual liberation was part of female emancipation, at all events in theory. Especially, of course, for the unmarried bourgeois girl who had by convention to remain *virgo intacta*. Research, as always, finds it hard to break down bedroom doors and even harder to quan-tify what goes on behind them. But I see no reason to doubt that by 1914 it had become a great deal easier in the Protestant and Jewish milieu of Europe to sleep with middle-class girls than it had been twenty years earlier, especially in politically and cul-turally emancipated circles. The sexual career of H. G. Wells illustrates this. What happened in the unknown territory of adultery is much harder to discover, and I refrain from speculation about it.

What, then, was the role of gender in this period of bourgeois culture, and how was it situated between the public and the private spheres? It has been argued that the model of female sex roles in classical, nineteenth-century, bourgeois society made the woman into the primary bearer of culture, or rather of the spiritual and moral or 'higher' values in life as distinct from the material and even animal 'lower' values represented by males. This is the image of the prosperous businessman visibly bored at the symphony concert to which his wife has dragged him against his will. There is something in this stereotype, even if we assume that the wife's interest in attending cultural functions reflected the desire to share the high social status of those who went to concerts rather than a passion for music per se. Nevertheless, it is essential to bear in mind a crucial limitation on the bourgeois woman's cultural role. In practice it was inhibited both by the man's claim to a monopoly of intellect in the public sphere (to which culture undoubtedly belonged) and by the denial to women of the sort of education (*Bildung*) without which culture was inconceivable. Of course, bourgeois women read, but largely what other women wrote for a specifically feminine market, namely, novels, fashion, news, social gossip and letters. The great novels written from within this woman's world, such as those of Jane Austen, are about intelligent and lively young women isolated not only among men, who do not expect more from their brides than that caricature of culture called 'accomplishment' – a little piano, a little sketching or watercolour and so on – but also isolated among women whose minds are given entirely to the strategy and tactics of marriage, and who are idiots in every other respect, sometimes lacking even the domestic skills of management, like Mrs Bennet in *Pride and Prejudice*. For, since the essence of a good marriage was a husband with a good income, an ability to manage was not essential.

Paradoxically, it was at the lower end of the slopes of upward social mobility that the role of women as the bearers of culture (including *kultura* in the Soviet sense, i.e., personal cleanliness and the like) was most obvious. For it was among the labouring classes that women represented the only alternative values to those of physical prowess and barbarism that ruled among men. In the bourgeois world, the male distinguished himself from the dark masses below, and incidentally from the barbarian minority of nobles above, by building success on mental rather than physical qualifications and effort. In the biographies and autobiographies of the lower orders, it is more often mothers than fathers who encourage the intellectual or cultural ambitions of sons: D. H. Lawrence is a good case in point. It is from the civilising influence of frontier women that Huckleberry Finn has to escape, like so many ideal-typical macho males. And as soon as mass primary education was instituted, it was women who became the schoolteachers par excellence in the Anglo-Saxon countries as well as in several others. Even in France as early as 1891 more women than men joined the teaching profession.[10]

I would suggest that it was only towards the end of the century that the bourgeois woman was, for the first time, in a position to become a bearer of culture in the literal sense. Incidentally, it is at this period that we find women emerging as independent patrons of culture: Isabella Stewart Gardner as an art collector, and Miss Horniman, Emma Cons, Lilian Baylis and Lady Gregory as founders, backers or managers of theatres. And, of course, we find them as active participants in commercial culture through arts and crafts businesses and the (largely feminine) new profession of the interior decorator (Elsie de Wolfe, Syrie Maugham, etc.). 'Interior decorating and furnishing is a trade in which women have been very successful of late years'.[11] Manifestly, this could not have happened without a wide extension of women's secondary and higher education, including the multiplication of art schools in post-William-Morris Britain and, in central Europe, of courses in art history. Both were probably attended by a majority of female students. However, I suggest that it was a change in the structure of the bourgeoisie itself that made culture a more central defining characteristic of this class and emphasised the role of women in it.

Three changes coincided. First, the problem of the established bourgeoisie – the families who no longer needed to rise because they had already arrived or, more generally, were the second- or later-generation bourgeoisie – was no longer how to accumulate but how to spend. And, as any family history demonstrates, this bourgeoisie generated a leisure sector, including notably the unmarried or widowed female relatives who lived on unearned incomes. Cultural activities were and are an excellent way to spend an unearned income respectably, not only because they are attractive to the educated but also because they cost less than the conspicuous consumption of a properly Veblenian leisure class. These activities could, of course, cost quite as much if need be, as Frick, Morgan, Mellon and others showed.

Second, during the same period, formal schooling increasingly became, as it has since remained, the badge of membership of those who belonged to the established bourgeoisie, as well as the best way to transform the children of the *nouveaux riches* into established bourgeois and, indeed, to join the bourgeoisie, as witness the case of the progress of the Keynes family in three generations from a provincial Baptist gardener to the economist John Maynard Keynes.[12] But *Bildung* and *Bildungbürgertum* inevitably had a strong cultural dimension. In short, while in mid-Victorian Britain Matthew Arnold could discern only barbarian aristocrats and philistine middle classes, a significant stratum of cultivated bourgeois had begun to emerge even in that philistine environment.

Third, we also see simultaneously a marked tendency to privatise and to civilise bourgeois lifestyles, once again pioneered in Britain, which created the first domestic style of bourgeois living that was actually comfortable – the suburban or rural villa or cottage, built in the vernacular style and furnished along arts and crafts lines. While this is not the place to discuss the reasons for this development, the point to note is, first that the new style was imbued with aesthetic and artistic values – think only of Morris wallpaper – and second, that women, as the mistresses of the domestic sphere by bourgeois definition, therefore became centrally concerned with culture. Even Beatrice Webb had to take time off from social and political activity to look for William Morris furnishings.[13] And indeed in Britain at least three commercial firms were then founded, and are still in existence, building their fortunes on fabrics, furniture and interior decorations in the aesthetics and arts and crafts manner, namely Heal's (furniture); Sanderson, which still sells the wallpaper and curtains designed by Morris himself; and Liberty, which was to provide the Italians with a name for *Jugendstil*. And *Jugendstil* or art nouveau in all its regional variations is, more than anything else, the avant-garde style based on arts applied to domestic living.

In fact, all three developments were bound to bring women into the centre of cultural life. After all, they formed the majority of the leisured bourgeois stratum living on unearned income or an income earned by someone else. As we have seen, in several countries they were rapidly catching up with men in secondary education. What is more, in Britain and the United States they now tended to stay at school longer than the boys, though fewer of them went to universities. In the domestic division of bourgeois labour, they were unquestionably the spenders of income. But even utilitarian spending on what was now often called the house beautiful had a distinct and conscious cultural dimension. Producers of culture were aware of it, even when, like William Morris himself, they were not happy to be taken up by leisured ladies with money to spend.

All this would have increased the cultural role of bourgeois women even without their autonomous drive for emancipation, which was inevitably also a drive to achieve equality in education and culture. Nor should we forget the specific links between the avant-garde of the arts and the avant-garde of the social – including feminine emancipation – which was particularly strong in the 1880s and 1890s. And we should not overlook the fact that it became conventional among bourgeois menfolk to prefer that 'in the room the women come and go / Talking of Michaelangelo' (T. S. Eliot) to seeing them engaged in more controversial activities.

There can be no doubt that educated women in this period therefore became more cultured, felt obliged to undertake cultural activities and took on a greater importance for the maintenance of cultural production, especially in the performing arts. The typical audience envisaged by writers of nineteenth-century boulevard plays was hardly one composed of females, but between the wars, as the British commercial playwright Terence Rattigan put it, they wrote for an ideal 'Aunt Edna' coming to the London West End for the matinée. In contrast, the original public for the American cinema was almost certainly poor, rough and 75 per cent male. America imported, and eventually produced, screen classics (i.e., prestige movies with a cultural reference) largely to mobilise the interest and money of the new middle-class woman and her children. I should be surprised if the Medici Society, which from 1908 produced reproductions of Italian old masters, or the publishers of the Insel Bücherei, had not had a public of young women firmly in their sights.

Nevertheless, it is impossible to argue that during this period the striking transformation of bourgeois culture was essentially carried out by women or, indeed, that culture showed any specific skewing towards one gender. Even in a branch of literature as traditionally and markedly feminine as the writing of novels was (and still is) in the Anglo-Saxon world, one has the impression that 'serious' women novelists temporarily became somewhat less prominent than they had been in the days of Jane Austen and George Eliot, or were again to be between the wars.[14] And, of course, 'writers', who had previously formed the great bulk of women featured in the biographical compendia (together with performing artists), in this period formed a rapidly diminishing proportion of the female entries. What seems to have happened is that culture became more central to the bourgeoisie as a whole.

I would suggest that it did so largely through the emergence, in the period after 1870, of a stratum of youth as a distinct and recognised entity in bourgeois public life. Although this youth now undoubtedly included young women on far more equal terms than before, it also, naturally, comprised young men. The links between *Jugend* and culture, or more specifically between it and *die Moderne*, are too obvious to require comment. The very terminology of the period (*Jugendstil, Die Jungen, Jung-Wien*, etc.) demonstrates it. Youth, or rather the period of secondary and higher education, was evidently the time when most bourgeois acquired cultural knowledge and tastes, and they did so increasingly from or through their peer group. The vogue for Nietzsche and Wagner, for instance, seems clearly to have been generational.

However, given that the number and proportion of bourgeois men who acquired secondary and higher education was so very much larger than that of young bourgeois women, we would therefore expect the community of those seriously interested in culture to have been primarily masculine on purely statistical grounds.

What is at least equally to the point, a much larger number of sons of the bourgeoisie than before now chose (and were in a position to do so) to spend their lives in cultural pursuits; a much larger number of parents or relatives supported them in this choice; and the development of capitalist society made it increasingly possible. We can all think of figures of obvious cultural significance during this period who depended on subsidies from the family business or from relatives or other well-wishers, at any rate until they became self-sufficient: Sir Thomas Beecham, the conductor; Frederick Delius, the composer; E. M. Forster ('in came the dividends, up went the lofty thoughts,' to use this novelist's own phrase); Hugo von Hofmannsthal; Karl Kraus; Stefan George; Thomas Mann; Rainer Maria Rilke; Marcel Proust; and György Lukacs. In what might be called the cultured region of Europe, even businessmen can be found who retired from their affairs to devote themselves to culture: Reinhardt of Winterthur is an example. His case was perhaps exceptional, but not that businessmen should wish their children to win the social status and recognition that came precisely from a life identified with something that was by definition not business. What is new in this period is that this status could now be derived not only from public service or politics, or even from the aristocratic and luxurious lifestyle financed via family fortunes, but from a life devoted to the arts or, more rarely (one thinks of the British Rothschilds), the sciences. This indicates the new social acceptability of the arts, including that strand hitherto least acceptable to the puritan or pietist values of the classical bourgeoisie: the theatre. Yet in the 1890s the sons and even the daughters of the British bourgeoisie were becoming professional actors and actresses, as eminent theatrical figures were given titles of nobility.

In summary, the late nineteenth and early twentieth centuries were a period when culture became a much more important mark of class identification for those who belonged, or wished to belong, to the bourgeois strata in Europe. However, it was not a period when a clear cultural division of labour between the sexes could be said to operate, even as an ideal-typical model. In practice, of course, women's role in culture was favoured, primarily for two reasons: first, because most adult bourgeois men expected to earn their living and therefore, presumably, had less time for daytime cultural activities than bourgeois married women, most of whom were not employed; and second, as already suggested, because the bourgeois home was increasingly 'aestheticised', and the woman was (and by tradition remained) the primary homemaker and home furnisher, greatly abetted by the rapidly developing advertising industry. Nevertheless, it is evidently not possible to apply the caricature image of Hollywood films to the males of the educated bourgeoisie: the image of the roughneck millionaire, bored by his wife's social and cultural ambitions. This model may appear plausible enough for first-generation accumulators or even for some of those tired businessmen returning home after a long day at the office and dreaming of the relaxations conventionally associated with tired businessmen. But it can hardly apply to the large stratum of the middle classes, who had passed through a secondary and higher education, and who defined themselves socially by this fact and by being 'cultivated' (*gebildet*); it especially does not apply to their children. At the very least we must distinguish between the two different types of bourgeois who provided the theme for E. M. Forster's novel *Howards End* (1910): the Schlegels and the Wilcoxes, the cultivated and the uncultivated. Nor should we forget that even the roughneck millionaires of this period soon learned that collecting pictures could be as good a form of conspicuous consumption as collecting racehorses, yachts or mistresses.

This chapter therefore does not accept a cultural labour of division between men, whose involvement in the sphere of the market, exchange and communications outside the domestic domain simply gave them too little time to be culturally active, and women, who were seen essentially as the bearers of culture and spiritual values. For the reasons suggested earlier, I do not believe that this was more than occasionally true in the early part of the nineteenth century. Women's separate sphere was supposed to be neither clever nor educated nor cultured, except in the most superficial sense – and superficial was precisely what culture in the bourgeois world-view was not supposed to be.

During the early period of bourgeois women's emancipation, women did indeed capture the right to high culture as well as other rights hitherto confined *de jure* or de facto to the other sex. But they did so precisely by moving away from a specific women's sphere with specific functions. And insofar as they remained within a specific female sphere, it was one that had not much cultural content in terms of bourgeois high culture. On the contrary, the major developments within the separate women's sphere during this period were a systematic exploitation of women as a market for goods and services, both for purchases in general and for literature in particular. On the one hand, advertising addressed specifically to women emerged; on the other, women's journalism was produced in the form of special publications for women, and special women's pages in general journals and periodicals. Both of these trends quite consciously concentrated on what they felt to be the appeals that would most effectively move women to buy, and focused on the subjects they considered to be of the most general interest to women as women: family, home, children, personal beautification, love, romance and the like. High culture was not among them, except for a small minority of the extremely rich and snobbish, anxious to be socially up to date in every respect. No doubt many emancipated and cultured women also devoured fashion pages and read romance novels without thereby derogating from their status, but even today not many such women actually like to boast about their taste for romantic fiction.

None of this means that the women of 1880–1914 tried to imitate, let alone be, men. They knew quite well that men and women were not alike, even when they did the same things, recognised each other as complete equals, or played the same public roles, as a glance at Rosa Luxemburg's letters and Beatrice Webb's diaries shows. What it does mean is that by this time the insistence on women having a separate sphere, including the claim that they had a special responsibility for culture, was associated with political and social reaction. Emancipated men and women alike aspired to live in a public milieu that did not discriminate against either sex. But in this public milieu, culture in the bourgeois sense was probably more central to the definition of *Bürgerlichkeit* than before or, perhaps even, since.

10

Art Nouveau

Aesthetics do not exist in a vacuum, especially not the aesthetics of a movement – or, if you prefer, a family of movements – as profoundly committed to art as part of daily life as art nouveau, a movement almost by definition not only with a style but for a lifestyle. 'The only possible point of departure for our artistic creation,' wrote the great architect of *fin-de-siècle* Vienna, Otto Wagner, in his 1895 textbook *Modern Architecture*, 'is modern life.' What I want to talk about this afternoon is what it was that 'modern life' in the literal sense – the environment that generated art nouveau, and the social needs of the artistic movements to which it belonged – set out to serve. More specifically, the city at the end of the nineteenth century. For, as Rosemary Hill has observed in one of the most perceptive notices of the present exhibition, 'If there is one almost universal truth about Art Nouveau it is that it was urban and metropolitan.'[1]

It was urban and metropolitan in several obvious ways. It was – you have only to look round this exhibition – the architecture of subway stations: the Paris Métro, the Vienna

Stadtbahn. 'Its building types' (if I may quote Dr Hill again) 'were apartment houses, concert halls and swimming baths' (I assume she is thinking of the great bath at the Hotel Gellert in Budapest). It was an almost entirely secular style, except for the great and, by any standards, one-off Catalan architect Gaudi. And around the turn of the century it was, without any question, 'the forward-looking choice for the institutions of modern city life, for the offices of the *Glasgow Herald* and *Die Zeit*, for photographic studios in Munich and Budapest, for hotels, for the Paris Metro and for department stores [like Galéries Lafayette and Samaritaine in Paris].' Indeed, in Italy the style was actually named after a department store, namely Liberty. I am told that to this day you can see the art nouveau influence on the ironwork at Harrods, whose modern frontage dates from 1900–5. Nor should we forget another part of the modern city infrastructure produced at this time (in this instance by Philip Webb, an old collaborator of William Morris), London's New Scotland Yard of 1891.

This is hardly surprising. By the late nineteenth century the metropoles of western and central Europe – the cities of one million or more – had almost reached their twentieth-century dimensions and therefore required the service institutions we now associate with such cities, notably a rapid urban transit system. That is why, apart from some steam-powered pioneering in London, underground and overground electric railways were built at that time: in London itself, in Berlin, in Paris, in Vienna, even – the first on the continent – in Budapest. I say 'service institutions' deliberately, for what they did was more important than how imposing they looked. Unlike the great symbolic structures of nineteenth-century bourgeois modernity (railway termini, opera houses, parliaments, or even those great substitute palaces, the popular theatres), monumentality – that is to say, inspiration by some historical style accepted as high-class – was not part of their remit. This actually left rather more scope for non-traditional styles in such service-buildings as mass-transit stations, department stores and savings banks. However, there is one other important contribution of art nouveau to the urban scene: it is the poster that found the general style so congenial.

And yet, if monumentality was not what art nouveau specialised in, it undoubtedly paid a great deal of attention to its external public appearance. There is no mistaking the impact of art nouveau on the cities most closely associated with it: Helsinki, Glasgow, Barcelona, Munich, Chicago, Prague. Of course their rate of growth was such that a large and visible sector of middle-class housing was built in the period when this style was fashionable, as is obvious in Helsinki. (And remember, leaving aside the new service institutions and an occasional millionaire's town house in Brussels and Barcelona, art nouveau building was essentially the construction of middle-class living accommodation.) And yet it isn't just the rate of growth that explains why art nouveau belongs to the public face of some cities so much more than to others: to Glasgow so much more than to London, to Munich more than to Berlin, even – though this does not come out of the present exhibition – to the Midwest of Sullivan and Frank Lloyd Wright more than to New York. By and large – Vienna and the planned global show of the 1900 Exposition in Paris are the big exceptions – art nouveau is not characteristic of national metropoles, but of the self-conscious and self-confident bourgeoisies of provincial or regional ones. That is perhaps why, in spite of the obvious family connection between all its variants, there is no unique art nouveau style, just as there is no single name for it. In some ways it is like rock music. Groups belong to the same family, but every one, or at least every interesting one, strives for its own specific 'sound'. I shall return to this point later.

What was the novelty of the *fin-de-siècle* city? It was, it had to be, a city based on mass transit – that is to say a place where people no longer lived, worked and played within walking distance. Such cheap mass transit became available from the early 1880s – in New York from the end of the 1870s – and the inhabitant of the metropolis suddenly became what we would call today a user of public transport. To give you an idea of the speed of this change: in the twelve years after the Cheap Trains Act of 1883 forced railway companies to offer low-price tickets on a large scale, the number of workmen's tickets in South London increased from about twenty-six thousand per year to about seven million.[2] Before then, at least according to London trade union rules, any worker living within four miles of his place of work was supposed to walk there and back, and anyone working beyond a radius of four miles was supposed to get a lodging allowance. But this implied a considerable innovation: a systematic consideration of city ecology and social problems, or – to use the term that emerged rapidly in the first years of the new century, its first use being recorded in 1904 – 'town planning'.

Two developments made mass transit necessary, but were also accelerated by it: residential segregation or suburbanisation, and the development of highly specialised areas within the metropolis, such as special centres for shopping, for entertainment, and for various types of economic activity. Consider the emergence of what used to be called 'theatreland', as a specialised part of London's West End, and consequently, a little later, of Soho as a restaurant area. The vast majority of the West End theatres were built, or rebuilt, between the mid-1880s and the First World War. The same is true of the new all-London music halls, like the Palladium, the Holborn Empire and the Victoria Palace, which now supplemented the enormously flourishing music halls in the working-class districts. Yet even this implied a degree of city planning, that is to say, a consideration of the metropolis as a whole. No theatre existed in Shaftesbury Avenue before 1888, and none could have existed much before then, since Shaftesbury Avenue – the name itself suggests an element of social reform – was a new construction, an early example of urban planning. The term 'town planning', by the way, came into use in the early 1900s and established itself almost immediately. In short, thinking about the social problems of the metropolis as a whole could no longer be avoided.

Compare the mid-Victorian and *fin-de-siècle* transport developments. The building of the railways had almost certainly led to the most massive disruption of the urban fabric of London since the Great Fire of 1666, and both events were alike in having an impact on the city that was not deliberate: they simply destroyed large parts of it in an uncoordinated way. On the other hand the new mass-transit systems were not only planned for commuters, but were also consciously conceived as agencies of suburbanisation – that is to say, for redistributing the population across the expanding area of the metropolis, not least those individuals who could not, or no longer wanted to, live in the now specialised areas of the inner city. Remember that this was the era when the old metropolitan nucleus expanded, often systematically, into a 'Greater Berlin' or a Greater Vienna or New York, by taking over formerly independent communities like Brooklyn or Steglitz.

Only some metropoles – notably Paris – resisted this trend. And this, in turn, meant more than coordinating the government of what had previously been a congeries of communities. In 1889, London acquired an all-London council for the first time in history. It also meant providing the structures for the increasingly specialised city districts, perhaps even the housing and infrastructures for the redistributed inhabitants.

For remember also – it is rather relevant to the new urbanism – the rise of labour movements, which suggested the need to do something about the appalling state in which so much of the urban working class lived.

Take the provision of something that was once Britain's glory, and is so no longer, namely the system of free public libraries. A glance at Pevsner will show you that in various parts of London they were principally built in the 1890s, as indeed were the local swimming baths – and, not surprisingly, in the aesthetic arts and crafts style that in Britain corresponds to continental art nouveau. That is because the inspiration was both social and aesthetic. Nor is it surprising that the town planners and community builders had strong social convictions. They came from the British progressive-socialist milieu. Aesthetics and social idealism went together.

But here we come up against a peculiar contradiction at the heart of art nouveau and the *fin-de-siècle* family of avant-gardes of which it is a part. I am suggesting that it was very much the style of a certain moment in the evolution of the European middle classes. But it was not designed for them. On the contrary, it belonged to an avant-garde that was anti-bourgeois and even anti-capitalist in its origins, as was the sympathy of its practitioners. Indeed, if this avant-garde had any socio-political affinity, it was for the new, mainly socialist, labour movements that suddenly sprang up in the 1880s and early 1890s. The finest Dutch architect of the new style, Berlage, built the headquarters of the most powerful Amsterdam Union, the Diamond Workers. Horta himself designed the Belgian Workers' Party headquarters in Brussels, the Maison du Peuple, which was destroyed in the 1960s, that most disastrous of all decades in the history of modern urbanisation. And he designed it specifically – and I quote him – as a building with 'the luxury of air and light so long absent from the slum houses of the workers'.[3] Indeed, Belgian socialist leaders were passionate supporters of the artistic avant-garde of the time, which meant symbolism in poetry and painting, social realism or 'naturalism' in sculpture, and art nouveau in architecture. That is why its style (the preference for flowing organic forms, which we still admire in William Morris's designs), its social critique and its ideal of art as an integral part of a living and communal environment for the people (that is to say, for ordinary people) were all so deeply inspired by the British arts and crafts movement.

For Britain was the first European country to be transformed by industrial capitalism and it therefore produced, with Ruskin and Morris, the most powerful home-grown denunciation of its social and cultural consequences, not least its effect on the production of the arts and the human environment, and on the search for a social-aesthetic alternative. Morris, in particular, was received on the continent as the propounder of a socially and therefore aesthetically revolutionary gospel, especially in two other industrialised countries: Belgium, where the term art nouveau was actually coined, and Germany.

Interestingly enough, art nouveau made its impact not so much through politics, even via the socialist movement, but rather directly through socially conscious practitioners of the arts, designers, town planners and, not least, the organisers of museums and art schools. That is why the aesthetic ideology of the tiny and insignificant British socialist movement of the 1880s became a major European presence. The socialist iconography of Walter Crane became the model for the much larger continental socialist movements.

That is also why Nikolaus Pevsner's *Pioneers of Modern Design* was right in seeing Morris and arts and crafts as the direct ancestor of the modern movement in architecture: that most lasting dream of twentieth-century modernism, architecture as the construction of social utopia. To this end, Ashbee's 'Guild of Handicraft' was set up in London's East End in 1888. Ebenezer Howard, inspired by a reading of the American socialist Edward Bellamy's utopian *Looking Backward*, a very influential text in the 1880s and 1890s, set out to build the classless urban/rural utopias of his 'garden cities', or rather green city-communities of human size. Dame Henrietta Barnett, widow of the founder of Toynbee Hall in the East End, passionately wanted her new Hampstead Garden Suburb to be a community where the middle classes and the poor lived together in beauty and comfort – though apparently without pubs. She did not see it as the one-class settlement for prosperous professionals that it has turned out to be. And the planners and architects of these communities – Patrick Geddes; Raymond Unwin who built Letchworth Garden City and much of the Suburb; William Lethaby who organised the London County Council's new Central School of Arts and Crafts, both the latter being Fabians – came from the milieu of those who had worked with William Morris.

And yet, arts and crafts was not merely a design for utopia, but the production of elaborate and necessarily expensive pieces of domestic equipment and decoration. It was a way of furnishing and decorating the space for a new kind of middle-class living – and, so far as the women were concerned, the persons inhabiting it. In fact one of the British innovations that captured the imagination on the continent was that essential part of the Ruskin–Morris tradition, namely building for beautiful *comfort* rather than building well as prestige display. Continental ideologists like Muthesius and van de Velde soon made themselves the spokesmen of this model, though in very different ways. Indeed, in countries with a strong and living tradition of luxury crafts, like France and Austria, the British arts and crafts were received minus their politics, as in Vienna[4] or even with very different politics, as in France.[5] And there is an obvious gap, if not a contradiction, between the Morris who dreamed of an art by and for the people, and the firm that produced high-price products for the minority who could afford them.

This brings me to the second of my two main themes: the transformation of the middle class in the decades on either side of 1900. I have discussed this at some length in the third volume of my history of the nineteenth century, *The Age of Empire*, and in a previous chapter, but let me try, briefly, to summarise an argument that still convinces me. I begin with a curious paradox.

In the century of the conquering bourgeoisie (I borrow this title from a French historian) members of the successful middle classes were sure of their civilisation, generally confident and not usually in financial difficulties, but only very late in the century were they physically *comfortable* ... the paradox of the most bourgeois of centuries was that its life-style became 'bourgeois' only late ... and that, as a specifically class way and style of living, it only triumphed momentarily.[6]

And the moment this change became obvious was also the moment of art nouveau, the first all-conquering and consciously, programmatically, 'modern' style. Not for nothing does a recent book speak of 'the unashamedly bourgeois comfort of art nouveau'.[7]

There were four reasons for this change in the way the middle classes lived. The first was that the democratisation of politics undercut the public and political influence of all but the very grandest and most formidable individuals. From leading lives where 'private life and the public presentation of status and social claims could not be distinct', they moved into a less formal, more genuinely private and privatised lifestyle. Victor Horta, the great Belgian architect of art nouveau, describes his clients, drawn largely from the comfortable professionals of the Freemasons' lodge 'Les amis philanthropes', as 'people whose profession prevented them from taking public action and taking any interest in political matters and whose direct character led them more towards privacy and beauty than towards the masses and general vulgarity'.[8] Not that this stopped them from being anticlerical and politically progressive.

The second was a certain loosening of the links between the triumphant bourgeoisie and the puritan values that had been so useful for accumulating capital in the past. The money had already been made, or it no longer required abstention. In short, spending became as important as earning, and even those who couldn't compete with the ultra-rich learned how to spend for comfort and enjoyment. And this inevitably meant giving a higher priority to aesthetic considerations, especially spending by women. Was it not, as the *Revue des Arts Decoratifs* wrote, woman's role and mission in society to embody 'nature's freshness' in her seasonally changing physical adornments and interior surroundings?[9] Is it surprising that the Exposition of 1900 took 'The Parisian Woman' as its monumental symbol?

The third was the loosening of the structures of the patriarchal family. On the one hand there was a substantial degree of emancipation for bourgeois women; on the other, the emergence of those between adolescence and marriage as an independent category of 'youth'. Remember that the German word for art nouveau is *Jugendstil*, that is, 'the style of youth'. If I may repeat myself: 'The words "youth" and "modernity" sometimes became almost interchangeable, and if "modernity" meant anything, it meant a change of taste, decor and style ... [This] not only affected the form of leisure ... but greatly increased the role of the home as the setting for [and the creation of] its women.'[10] In a way this new lifestyle became as obligatory as the old one had been. Let me remind you of that otherwise extremely anomalous bourgeois household set up in the 1890s – that of the great Fabian couple Beatrice and Sidney Webb. Their home (depending on £1000 a year in unearned income, a pretty ample sum in those days) was intended essentially as a space for political networking and a campaigning headquarters for social reform. Aesthetics, domestic relaxation – indeed, family and home-making – were the last of Beatrice Webb's concerns, and the Webbs' parties were spectacularly unconcerned with comfort, food and drink. And yet, even Beatrice – as she records in her diary – took time off from the important things in life to go to Heal's to buy William Morris wallpaper and curtains.

But there was a fourth reason. This was the substantial growth of those who belonged, or claimed to belong, or aspired passionately to belong, to the 'middle class' as a whole. One of the things that bound all its members together, without any question, was shopping. 'They plunge into it as one plunges into a career;' wrote H. G. Wells in that quintessentially Edwardian masterpiece *Tono-Bungay*; 'as a class they talk, think and dream possessions.' The possessions displayed in this exhibition are at the millionaire end of the market, but we must never forget that art nouveau artefacts or things bearing the trademarks of the movement – organic, plant-like curves and tendrils, feminine bodies trailing hair and drapery – were available in all price ranges, or were, indeed, universally available. When next you go to France, look at the one-franc piece. It was designed in 1895 specifically to strike the note of modernity, both aesthetic and moral. It has not been redesigned since. And, while I wrote about art nouveau in my *Age of Empire* in the late 1980s, I found myself stirring my tea with a cheap spoon, made in Korea, whose decorative motifs visibly still derived from art nouveau.

But another, and even more important, element of middle-class consciousness – for the finances of so many aspirers to middle-class status were too restricted for leisure shopping – was a comfortable domestic lifestyle with special provision for relaxed indoor leisure in the characteristically named 'lounge'. Such a life would preferably be lived far from the lower orders, among families 'like ourselves' – that is to say, in middle-class districts and suburbs – who shopped in the new department stores, so many of which were being erected at that very time by the new architects. It was for the lower end of these social groups that something like factory production cheapened the products of art nouveau. The suburb was an essential part of the new metropolis. Of course, outside the Anglo-Saxon world it had yet to reach the lower levels of the middle class. Living in a central European 'villa' or 'cottage' indicated a considerably higher income and social status than living in Upper Tooting, of whose imitation 'Liberty' interiors *Punch* made fun in 1894.[11]

What made it even more of a 'bourgeois' art was that, in one way or another (mostly as an expression of regional pride or national self-assertion), it was taken up by the bourgeois elites who actually ran the cities and organised their modernisation at this time. Here the possibility of crossing modernism with a suitable national style, real or invented, was tempting – Asiatic in Budapest, Nordic in Helsinki, Slav in Bohemia. Barcelona is a marvellous example where town planning coincided with the 'modernist' style in which the local Catalan bourgeoisie gloried in its own rise and wealth, and marked itself off from its fuddy-duddy rulers in Madrid. Electrification and the local art nouveau, characteristically known as 'modernisme' went together, trying to turn a provincial capital into a world city, to create what its ideologist called 'that imperial Barcelona which propels the wealth and culture of all Catalonia, indeed of all the hispanic people of the triumphant Iberia of tomorrow'.[12] And, incidentally, it was the style in which the young bourgeois couples chose to furnish their new apartments in the new bourgeois quarters.[13]

Let's put it another way: around 1900 some version of art nouveau was the idiom in which second and third cities tried to establish their superior modernity to imperial capitals, urban Pepsi-Colas against the dominant Coca-Colas, though most of them were not quite as imperial in their ambitions as Barcelona. Not that this applied to the state-sponsored art nouveau of Vienna and Paris, but the special political circumstances of the French and Habsburg governments do not concern us here. In any case art nouveau was not the only style for the *fin-de-siècle* bourgeoisie; nor was it the only style in which urban equipment was renewed around 1900. To take an obvious example, it barely affected the London Tube.

And yet this leaves us with a question that all visitors to this exhibition must have asked themselves: why did it last such a short time, unless we include the impact of the British arts and crafts movement, which cannot quite be fitted into art nouveau, whose role in the genesis of the modern style was convincingly argued by Nikolaus Pevsner?

And, indeed, in the long run the art nouveau family of styles did not actually prove very suitable for the solution of these problems of urban growth and organisation, whether practical or symbolic. In the careers of the best architects, art nouveau and the styles corresponding to it (for example, arts and crafts in Britain) are a stage on the road to modernism. The dominant style of the new century's architecture was to be stripped, recti-linear, would-be functionalist. It shared the passionate modernity of art nouveau, its rejection of classical and other historical models. It shared the functionalist aspirations of architects like Otto Wagner in Vienna, but it rejected two things deeply embed-ded in art nouveau: the idealisation of pre- or non-industrial craftsmanship; and, above all, the desire to express modernity symbolically through elaborate ornamentation inspired by living shapes. Both aspects handicapped art nouveau. Obviously, any style suited to the new century's society of mass consumption – even mass middle-class consumption – had to reject anti-indus-trialism, since it had to be suitable for mass production and made compatible with the machine.

Curiously this proved to be easier for the William Morris kind of arts and crafts, in spite of its idealisation of the Gothic past, because its passionate social commitment to a better, a more beautiful, a more comfortable living environment for the common people implied production for everyday *use* for all. That is why, as Pevsner recognised, there is a straight road from William Morris to the Bauhaus. There was no equivalent tech-nical compulsion to reject ornament, curved or otherwise, in the name of pure functionalism. However, one must admit that the tendency to a certain baroque lushness, particularly of the showpiece art nouveau sponsored by the French government in the 1900 Exposition, really could get in the way of making products fit for their purpose. For instance, the readability of print on art nouveau posters.

In any case there were some things for which art nouveau was simply not suited. When the *Jugendstil* architects of the German *Werkbund*, like Peter Behrens, worked for the big industrial cor-porations, such as AEG, which was also affiliated to it, they inevitably found themselves designing in a very different manner from the way they built a private house. Nor did large social projects like municipal housing estates lend themselves much to art nouveau. So it is not surprising that, in its extreme form, art nouveau lasted only a few years. But there may be another reason for its short life. The silver age or 'belle époque' of the European bourgeoisie before 1914, to which its heirs continued to look back nostalgically, came to an end. In most of Europe the self-confident, moneyed, city-building, servant-keeping families did not survive the First World War. Still, the art form did survive on the other side of the Atlantic, via a direct, though less curvaceous, descendant of French art nouveau, namely art deco. It survived as the public face of American metropolitan prosperity in the 1920s. The cityscape of New York is, to this day, dominated by two architectural monuments in that style, namely the Rockefeller Center and the Chrysler Building, completed just in time for the great Wall Street Crash of 1929. However, even in the USA the belle époque ended with the Great Depression of the 1930s.

11

The Last Days of Mankind

The work of Karl Kraus cannot be separated from his life, because he himself, in the words of Bertolt Brecht, 'made his own person into a yardstick of the worthlessness of his age'. And yet there is not much to be said about the outward appearances of his life. He was born in 1874 in a small town in Bohemia, the younger son of a rich Jewish paper manufacturer. His family's wealth later gave him the economic independence on which his role in cultural and public life, and his lifestyle, that of a consciously idiosyncratic loner, were both based. In 1877 the family moved to Vienna, where Kraus spent practically all his life, apart from the long journeys, making trips to the countryside and to Germany, that were customary at the time among the well-to-do middle classes. It was in Germany that he later found, probably not many more admirers, but fewer enemies, among writers and performing artists. He died in Vienna aged sixty-two, on 12 June 1936.

He chose to play the role of an outsider on principle. Like Groucho Marx, he refused to join any club that would accept someone like him as a member. He belonged to no school, even if he can be categorised as part of the second Viennese avant-garde, which distanced itself from the 'modernism' of the 1880s, from Hermann Bahr and Hugo von Hofmannsthal, Gustav Klimt and the *Jugendstil*, Arthur Schnitzler and natural-ism. He had no school of his own, although he attracted and influenced other talented outsiders (in Vienna, Schoenberg, Wittgenstein, Loos, Kokoschka, the young Social Democrats and Expressionists; in Germany, later, Benjamin and Brecht), and stood up for underestimated writers. He contributed to no newspaper or journal. In the end it was a logical step for him to publish a magazine of his own, as and when he pleased, and eventually write all of it himself. Anyone who wanted to hear his views had to make a conscious choice, either to seek out his writ-ten words or to seek him in person, through the spoken and sung word on his famous performance evenings, where he also appeared entirely on his own.

His public life consisted of this lifelong monologue addressed to the world. Privately he led a life in seclusion, so to speak, from the great public, which he rejected as such, walking alone through the streets of Vienna, 'a small, slightly built man, clean-shaven, short-sighted, with noble, sharply marked features', recognised and greeted by passers-by – Vienna is a large provin-cial town – but systematically rebuffing the greetings of those not personally known to him. He belonged to no circle. He worked long and intensively, was an enthusiastic swimmer and relentlessly pursued his enemies with the satisfaction of the righteous warrior, to whom the unrighteous supplied the oppor-tunity to prove his own superiority. He remained unmarried, although during the First World War he proposed marriage to Baroness Sidonie Nádherný von Borutin, whose love made the time of *The Last Days of Mankind* less intolerable for him. (Kraus liked to frequent the circles of the bohemian nobility, and also, according to his friend Princess Lichnowsky, had 'a secret which enabled him quietly and informally to captivate the better members of society'.) The marriage did not take place, since the poet Rainer Maria Rilke is said to have pointed out to the baroness the disadvantages of a union with a middle-class Jew, however brilliant and agreeable.

He was hated. He was revered. Most certainly, he was taken seriously. The Viennese press on the whole ignored his existence. For his admirers he was the yardstick of a corrupt era. Whether literary figures 'are genuine and true, or superficial and dishonest, can be recognized by their attitude to Karl Kraus', wrote Friedrich Austerlitz in the *Arbeiter-Zeitung*, although Kraus had not spared this newspaper either. Only National Socialism was able to silence him. He no longer understood the times after the Nazis rose to power, and died in solitude.

The young Kraus's extraordinary talent – for the stage, which remained denied him for physical reasons, perhaps even more than for literature – became evident early in his life. At the age of eighteen he wrote for periodicals and held his first public lecture. In the course of the 1890s he made a name for himself as a journalist, critic and literary-political polemicist – against Hermann Bahr and the modernists of the 1880s, against the modern Zionism of Theodor Herzl. The *Neue Freie Presse*, the most important newspaper of the liberal Habsburg middle classes, was sufficiently impressed to offer the twenty-five-year-old a post as the successor to the brilliant Daniel Spitzer ('the good Austrian is above all the cautious Austrian') as editor of the satirical *Feuilleton* or arts section.

Kraus turned down the offer and, in the same year in which he renounced the Jewish community, founded his own periodical, *Die Fackel* (*The Torch*). The small, bright red, sporadically published magazines whose contributors gradually dropped away, to be replaced by deadly commentaries on quoted foolishness or malice, were the microphone through which he directed his words towards, or rather against, the world. Through them he became 'Fackelkraus', adapting the role of the biblical prophet to the late Habsburg era and the newly developing media culture – with the same passion, but in a more stylised prose and with much more wit. Polemics were for him as much a moral as an aesthetic necessity. Thanks to his financial independence he was able to continue them up to his death, although after 1933, when he lost his German as well as part of his Austrian readership, he seriously considered closing down the magazine. Death saved him from this decision in favour of intellectual suicide. Like everything else written by Kraus, *Die letzten Tage der Menschheit* (*The Last Days of Mankind*) was first published in *Die Fackel*.

Biblical prophets, moralists and even moral satirists have little interest in political agendas. Kraus himself wrote of the 'apolitical tendency' of *Die Fackel*, of his 'view undimmed by any party-political spectacles'. But we cannot by any means call him unpolitical, even if questions such as monarchy or republic, the right to national self-determination and universal suffrage left him cold. He consciously kept outside party politics, to the chagrin of the socialists, who would have liked to claim the great opponent of the system as one of their own, and whom he attacked less systematically and perhaps with more regret than the other parties and politicians. For a moment, after the First World War, it even seemed as though their common opposition to the war created a closer relationship. This was an illusion. Kraus did not fit into any political pigeon-hole and remained outside party politics, even when he spoke out on the questions of the day. Political issues were of secondary importance to him, because he was convinced that 'it was not in the representative bodies, not in the parliaments, but in the editorial offices that the effective powers were at work'.

Kraus heard, or rather read, the signals that summoned him to the last battle, in the newspapers. He recognised in the bourgeois journalism of the pre-war years, and above all in the *Neue Freie Presse*, the germ – no, somehow already the reality of our own era of the media, built upon the emptiness of the word and the image. He knew 'where the spirit perishes and where its carcass, the phrase, tastes best to the hyenas'. The press not only expressed the corruption of the time, but was itself its great corrupter, simply through 'the commandeering of values through words'. The saying by Confucius, which he discovered late but with satisfaction, seemed to be spoken out of his own mouth:

> If language is not correct, then what is said is not what is meant; if what is said is not what is meant, then what must be done remains undone; if this remains undone, morals and art will deteriorate; if justice goes astray, the people will stand about in helpless confusion. Hence there must be no arbitrariness in what is said. This matters above everything.

Karl Kraus dedicated his life to the ordering of the world through words. The corruption of values through words – spoken, heard, above all read – gives *The Last Days of Mankind* its form and structure. It is not by accident that each act of the tragedy begins with the shouts of news vendors and headlines.

The Last Days of Mankind became one of the great masterpieces of literature of the twentieth century, because the age ('these great times which I knew when they were such little times') at last deserved the volleys of ordnance that Kraus had launched at smaller targets up to 1914. His field had always been world history, which as we know is the world's Supreme Court of Appeal, but he wrote it as a local reporter from Vienna, whose ideal-typical location, marking the beginning of each act of *The Last Days*, is represented by the Sirk-Ecke, the corner of the Ringstrasse and the Kärntnerstrasse, where all of fashionable Vienna met for the daily promenade. His cosmos was the microcosm. It was only with the assassination of Archduke Franz Ferdinand in Sarajevo – still an ominous name today – that the microcosm automatically extended into a macrocosm, and the local chronicle became recognisable as a commentary on the end of a whole world, as the 'tragedy of mankind'.

The Last Days of Mankind was written during the First World War, which Kraus had opposed from the start and publicly condemned in his lectures. He wrote the first drafts of most of the scenes in the summers from 1915 to 1917, and reworked them in 1919 for publication in book form. In the same year it was published in three special editions of *Die Fackel*, and in 1922, in somewhat more extensive form, by his own publishing firm, in the *editio princeps* of 792 pages. In its original version, this drama, 'whose dimensions would according to earthly measurements of time fill about ten evenings ... was intended for a theatre on Mars', so not for any terrestrial performance. It was not until 1928 that in principle – and contrary to the justified protests of his admirers – he gave permission to the Social Democratic Arts Centre in Vienna for the performance of an abridged and, to be frank, inevitably inadequate stage version. Kraus himself gave readings of variants of the stage version in the spring of 1930, in Vienna, Berlin, Prague and Moravská Ostrava, but never again after that. It was not published until 1992.

The present version of *The Last Days of Mankind* is thus merely a small, and incidentally – with regard to the rise of nationalism – politically somewhat adapted selection from the great Martian drama. It can and should therefore not replace a reading of the actual work. But this edition contains something not to be found in the larger work, though also essential for its readers: the drawings of Georg Eisler. The original edition of *The Last Days* included only two illustrations: the notorious title page of the 'Austrian countenance' of the jovial hangman, enthroned above a corpse, surrounded by other Austrians in and out of uniform, who also want to get into the picture; and the final image of a crucifix destroyed by artillery fire on the open field. (One was the reproduction of a picture postcard that was hawked around the monarchy after the execution of Cesare Battisti, an Italian socialist; the other had been sent to

Kraus by the young Kurt Tucholsky.) An illustrated edition of a world tragedy, which, like genocide, must elude all direct representation, seems at first glance presumptuous. But what Georg Eisler is commenting on and explaining in his drawings is not the topic, but the author. As a Viennese, Eisler, as it were, absorbed Kraus with his mother's milk. The son of a pupil of Schoenberg and himself a pupil of Kokoschka, who had the strongest connections with Kraus of all visual artists, Eisler also grew up with Kraus as an artist. No one is in a better position to create a bridge from the text of *The Last Days* to the modern reader.

For this text is today accessible only with difficulty. For Viennese of my generation and Eisler's, *The Last Days* is simply part of our lives. The copy of the first edition, which I continually reread, bears on its title page the name of my mother, one of Kraus's many admirers from a middle-class Viennese background. The 'Austrian countenance' accompanied my childhood. Too young to have experienced the First World War and the death of the monarchy, I came to know both through this book. I discovered the murder of Archduke Franz Ferdinand on Karl Kraus's Ringstrasse, in the prelude to the play, which was unfortunately not included in the stage version. ('A newsvendor: Extra edition! Murder of the heir to the throne! The culprit arrested! A passer-by (to his wife): Thank God, not a Jew.') I first learned world history in the accents of the lieutenants Pokorny, Nowotny and Powolny, of the subscriber and the patriot, of old Biach and the boys Gasselseder and Merores, to whom Georg Eisler has now given faces and shapes. Even the Viennese dialect is still that of my childhood. For Viennese of my age, *The Last Days*, despite all allusions to forgotten figures and forgotten events of the day, is comprehensible, even taken for granted. But this is hardly the case for others, particularly for non-Austrian readers, who stumble directly on this colossal, unfathomable, documentary-visionary work.

But does this work need any commentary? Is it today – and

136

was it not always – a matter of indifference to us, who and what the scenes of *The Last Days* are about? Who provoked the anger and contempt of Kraus? These scenes and figures, such as the forgotten war correspondent Alice Schalek and the quotations from yellowed leading articles, exist for us, and for the future, only through Kraus. Is it not enough to know that 'the most unlikely conversations conducted here have been spoken verbatim; the most glaring inventions are quotations'?

Yes and no. Certainly it is immaterial that, for example, Hans Müller, who speaks a few idiotic lines in the first scene of the first act, was a justifiably forgotten, but at the time successful and well-known, dramatist. A tiny footnote is enough to rescue the point of the fourth scene of the first act, the conversation of the four (actual) military leaders through the generations; 'Der Riedl', to whom the Habsburg general writes a banal postcard 'from the distant encampment', was the owner of a favourite Viennese coffee house.

On the other hand it is part of the age whose rotting limbs Kraus observed up to the point of amputation: that it consists *only* of what is specifically read and seen, what is overheard verbatim. It is not a question of understanding 'the slackly dissolving dialect of the last Viennese, who is a jumble of a Viennese and a Jew', which is less problematic for today's German reader than Shakespeare's text is for the modern English secondary-school pupil, but of catching the characteristic tone of voice of the time. This is especially vital for a writer like Kraus, because his idea of the word was actually an auditory one. Written and performed text, both substitutes for the career as an actor that had been denied him, belong together. His wonderful but often contrived prose, which in the printed text demands continuous and intense attention, clearly came to life when read aloud. 'I am perhaps the first case of a writer who experiences his writing at the same time in theatrical terms,' he commented. 'What I write is written acting.'

It is probably no accident that Kraus at more or less the same time (1910–11) decided to run *Die Fackel* as a pure monologue and returned to the public reading evenings that he had given up since the early 1890s.

'I have rescued the essence [of the time],' he wrote in one of the monologues of *Die Nörgler* (The Grumbler) in the complete edition of *The Last Days*, 'and my ear has discovered the sound of actions, my eye the gesture of speech, and my voice, when only repeating, has quoted in such a way that the fundamental tone has remained fixed for all time.' It is precisely this 'gesture of speech', the actions and attitudes, the body language, which is part of the inflection of the time, that are reflected in Eisler's drawings. They are an important contribution to the understanding of the text.

But this is also important for another reason. *The Last Days of Mankind* was not only an outcry against the First World War and the corruption of the tragedy of mankind by journalism. ('Let them see how they're praying.') The book was also a passionate plea against Habsburg Austria, which Kraus, not without justification, considered responsible for the outbreak of hostilities; against that 'Austrian visage', which drifts in endless diversity, but always the same superficiality, through the scenes of his drama. 'Is it not that face, not Austria, not the war,' he wrote in his *Nachruf* (obituary) on the monarchy, soon after the war, 'is it not that avid and bloodthirsty phantom, demanding in need and in death, in dance and party fun, and hate and sport, which has haunted us from its grave in the night of the centuries? ... For this one, that one, one and many, they were murderers not only because it was the time for murder but for lack of imagination.' It is the face of the officers on the Sirk-Ecke ('the Ringstrasse front of that fortress of sin'), of the generals who were interested in the map of the theatre of war only when in front of the photographer (the word 'photo-opportunity' had not yet been discovered), the reporters and the literary figures who were eager for conflict, but were otherwise engaged in Vienna. For Kraus the old monarchy was not only doomed to die – as every Viennese government official knew – but it also deserved the death sentence.

Never, probably, has an empire been carried to its grave with more mockery than that of the Habsburgs. And yet we face the paradox that the death of no other empire of our century, rich in empires as it has been, has produced so much important literature. Think of Musil, of Joseph Roth, and not least of Jaroslav Hašek's *Good Soldier Schwejk* and *The Last Days of Mankind* itself – all works that specifically deal with the downfall of the old monarchy.

What links all these contributions to the genre of 'funeral eulogies of Austria' is a sense of the absurdity of this regime, the comedy of its tragedy, which cannot quite be avoided even by the most merciless denunciations. Even the (few) sentimental retrospective looks at the time of Franz Joseph have an ironic smile.

Nothing, for example, is more inhuman than the topic of the scene in the military hospital (Act 4, Scene 6, of *Last Days*), which can incidentally be compared to the wonderful eighth chapter of *The Good Soldier Schwejk* ('Schwejk as Malingerer'). And yet the mouth of the appalled reader cannot help contorting into a laugh. But who can laugh about Dachau and Mauthausen? We do not even laugh at the officers, soldiers and cripples in the pictures of George Grosz, which correspond exactly to the contemporary Ringstrasse scenes in the final acts of Kraus's drama. The officers Nowotny, Pokorny and Powolny are horrific because they are also comic; no less horrific, but decidedly more comic than the German figures in *The Last Days*. And this is not because Kraus had a sharper ear for Viennese speech than for German ways of speaking, but because one could maintain of the situation of Austria in the war that it was desperate, but not serious.

The German Empire was absurd only to foreigners, never to its own citizens. This specific climate of the Habsburg monarchy, so favourable to literature, can also be brought closer to us by Eisler's drawings.

This climate also explains why the war represented more for Kraus than the irruption of cruelty and mass murder into ordered society. He recognised it immediately as the collapse of a whole world, that is, the bourgeois-liberal civilisation of the nineteenth century, to which he himself belonged, even though reluctantly. For in many respects the Vienna of the later years of Franz Joseph was the meeting of the enlightened Josephinist bureaucrats with the enlightened Jewish bourgeoisie, both committed to the great cycle of public architecture along the Ring, ideological manifestos of the bourgeois liberalism of its century and its classic expression. Both were beleaguered: a thin stratum of the 'cultured' German-speaking readers of the *Neue Freie Presse*, hovering over the masses of the Slavic rural population, and beleaguered as supporters of a state that had no future. What is certain is that, from the end of the century, the Viennese were already much more sharply aware of the crisis of this civilisation than elsewhere in Europe. Kraus, who desired the downfall of the liberal world, was prepared for it. But since it was Vienna he was attacking, or at least the readers of the *Neue Freie Presse*, not only as 'Kakanians' (to use Robert Musil's term) but as a paradigm of the total development of the bourgeois-liberal, technological-capitalist society, the war became for him the last days not only of Austria, but of mankind. For after this collapse there could be no going back. There was only a forward step into an unimaginably apocalyptic future.

But the dying monarchy gave Kraus something more. It allowed him to write a work even *during* the war, which in another place could have been written only after it had ended as a way of dealing with a traumatic but personal past, as for example with the war literature that began to appear in Germany ten years after the collapse. Where else in the Habsburg monarchy would an open opponent of the conflict have been allowed to protest against it, publicly, in speech and writing? Where else could such a lecture 'be shaped in front of an audience consisting partly of officers and other military personnel, into an aggressively pacifist declaration which' – this is the spring of 1918 – 'unleashed almost unanimously enthusiastic agreement in the audience', or at any rate was denounced as such by the centre for resistance to enemy propaganda of the imperial and royal Ministry of War? And where else could a police superintendent for the district in question, 'who had attended this lecture as a government representative', inform his department that Kraus had actually given a talk against poison gas, 'which made an extremely unpleasant, even distressing impression' on the superintendent, 'but he had found no reason to intervene'.

The Viennese police had come to an agreement with the writer that work already published in *Die Fackel* could be read in public without further ado, but he was requested to submit as yet unpublished pieces for censorship. Kraus on the other hand, summoned by the police after a denunciation, reacted with a formal complaint of libel by an unknown person who had falsely reported the content of his anti-war speech. And where else but in Habsburg Austria could absolutely nothing further have happened, until world history closed the file on Habsburg Austria itself, shortly before the surviving relic of its Ministry of War closed the file on the Kraus case?

The historical range of events and experiences appropriate for Kraus was comparatively narrow. There are things in our century that wipe away even the most poisonous smile from the face of the most passionate satirist. Karl Kraus himself said of National Socialism: 'On the subject of Hitler, nothing occurs to me,' and when in the end something did occur to him, his language was no longer adequate. 'The word fell asleep when that world awoke.' In the history of the Soviet Union there was a place for the satirist in the time of the New Economic Policy and in the Brezhnev era, which incidentally is sometimes reminiscent of the last years of the Habsburgs; but not in the grim times of Josef Stalin, which to this day no one makes fun of, even in retrospect.

Kraus had the good fortune to live almost to the end of his

days in a world and in an era in which he could write freely, and in which inhumanity was not yet so great that it forced words and, even more, satire into silence. He was still able to find the words for the first great act of tragedy of the twentieth century, the world war of 1914. He found them in the leading articles, the announcements, the overheard conversations, the newspaper reports of a time in which he recognised that a tragedy was being played out here in which not King Lear, but the Fool, not Hamlet but Rosencrantz and Guildenstern, were the central characters. He found words for the unsayable at a time when it had not quite yet become unsayable.

Bertolt Brecht wrote the best and most lapidary obituary of him: 'When the age laid a violent hand on itself, he was that hand.'

12

Heritage

What is left, what is remembered and what is still fit for use in the heritage of classical bourgeois culture?

'High' culture is both a mechanism for generating permanent products in the form of preservable objects – buildings, paintings, books, etc. – and a set of variable flows of actions we may call 'performance' – singing, acting, dancing, etc. – which are impermanent by nature, although, thanks to twentieth-century technology, they may leave permanent records – records, films, hard or soft disks. More to the point, some performances take place in special buildings that can form part of what is considered the preservable cultural heritage, though not all do. Indeed, since the rise of the domestic implements for presenting culture – radio in the 1930s, television and eventually the increasingly adaptable portable devices of the early twenty-first century – the scope for the formal locations of public performance has become very much more restricted but national pride, if not megalomania, have nevertheless continued to multiply these locations and networks. They have been notably stimulated by increasing numbers of global performance events such as the Olympic Games.

This essay is not specifically concerned with culture in the broader anthropological sense, although in fact its procedures and the objects it generates are today increasingly also seen as part of the national heritage to be preserved in specialised museums and cultural sites. But, as we shall see, it cannot avoid the tricky problems of 'cultural identity', about which more will be said below.

Until the rise of a mass-market-led culture in the nineteenth century, patronage commissioned and collected most of the objects of high culture, except those generated by that first child of technological revolution, the printing press. Hence the persistence, which still dominates collectors of unique, unrepeatable and consequently expensive 'works', of what is still called 'the art market'. In Europe the producers of non-reproducible art depended largely on the courts of monarchs, princes and nobles, city patriciates and millionaires and, of course, on the Church. Grand architecture still depends essentially on this form of primarily prestige-seeking patronage and may be flourishing better than the rest of the visual arts for this reason.

Patronage always played less of a role in the performance arts, which were firmly rooted in the practices and entertainments of the common people, but certain specific elaborations of these were taken up by Church and court culture, and therefore also became largely dependent on such patronage. Some still are, notably opera and ballet. The role of patron has been taken over, usually, by the state or other public entities and more rarely (as in the USA) by the *campanilismo* of a local billionaire patriciate. I note in passing that, unlike football teams, major performance centres have not so far been taken over as luxuries by single super-billionaires. The typical nineteenth-century bourgeois solution – of collectives of more or less wealthy art lovers, subscribing regularly or buying permanent seats or boxes in theatres – has faded away.

Cultural production, including performance, for profits in a mass market, relying as it does on Benjamin's 'era of technical reproducibility', is essentially a twentieth-century product, except for the output of the printing press. In theory their fortunes depend on sales, and therefore call for no institutional support, subsidy or conservation. There is no reason why Agatha Christie's *The Mousetrap* should not continue for another half-century under its own steam. Conversely with the decline in cinema-going the great bulk of British cinemas, ranging from intimate spaces to the auditoriums of the Kilburn State seating five thousand, have disappeared from sight and from the map with less protest than a single arch outside Euston Station. They lived and died by the box office. However, it does sometimes occur that performance productions geared to the market fail to find a sufficiently large permanent public. They may therefore need subsidy or assistance because their practitioners and products, such as jazz and some avant-garde films, are regarded as valuable culturally or for other non-economic reasons, but cannot earn an adequate commercial return. They may therefore find themselves integrated into the infrastructure of cultural protection such as the enclave of classical music (for example, the Lincoln Center in New York) and, increasingly, the institutions of higher education.

At this point a distinction must be made between 'national culture', usually defined in terms of an existing or anticipated ethnic-linguistic unit, and the body of high-prestige products and activities established (mostly in nineteenth-century Europe) as a corpus of universal 'high culture' or 'classic' culture and adopted as such by the elites of enthusiastically modernising – that is to say, Westernising – non-European societies. Thanks to this corpus's high prestige and potential for ostentatious expenditure by successive generations of the newly rich and powerful, this remains the case to this day, especially in the visual arts and music, shaping the content of museums and galleries, the repertoire of concerts and operas, the recruitment of musicians and singers, in Tokyo, Beijing and Seoul as in Stockholm and Los Angeles, largely as a historic succession of 'great works' by 'great artists'.

The divergence between national and universal culture is well illustrated by the difference between the first and second museums of Oskar Reinhardt of Winterthur, one of the great Swiss-German collectors. His first museum specialised in eighteenth- to nineteenth-century German, Austrian and Swiss painting, much of it attractive but not, as it were, on the cultural tourist circuit. On the other hand, in his private villa Reinhardt established a second gallery of universally accepted 'great art', which remains one of the great private twentieth-century art collections. The contents of such museums are not national, though located in particular places, and do not belong to a single national heritage, whatever their original mode of accumulation (through theft, conquest, the monarchy, money or patronage). Whether some such collections become the foundation of officially designated national museums or not, their intended scope is supranational. However, a new problem has arisen in the world of decolonisation and modern globalised tourism, namely the concentration of the corpus of universally accepted 'high art', mainly in the museums and collections of former Western (that is, until the twentieth century largely European) imperial powers and the accumulations of their rulers and the rich. This has led to demands to repatriate such works to their territories of origin by states now occupying these, as in Greece, Turkey and West Africa.

While this still leads to much controversy it is rather unlikely that the geographical distribution of universal high art will change fundamentally, since no major museum in the emerging world, however rich, can any longer compete with the overwhelming concentration of globally accepted 'high art' in Europe and the USA, and the Western collections, thanks to conquest, theft and fraud, are by no means devoid of the treasures of the other great cultures. However, this distribution will be affected by another development of the last half-century: the rise of the museum that forms the major cultural attraction irrespective of its content. These impressive and usually adventurous buildings have been constructed by architects of universal esteem and are intended to provide major global poles of attraction in otherwise peripheral or provincial centres. What goes on inside them is irrelevant or secondary, as in the pioneer case of the Eiffel Tower, which exists simply to be admired for itself. Daniel Libeskind's famous Berlin Jewish Museum actually loses much of its symbolic power from the attempt to fill it with suitable exhibits. The Sydney Opera House of the early 1970s is a familiar example, but in the 1990s the otherwise relatively unimpressive city of Bilbao turned itself into a global tourist centre on the strength of Frank Gehry's Guggenheim Museum. Nevertheless collections of worldwide significance in Spain, like the Prado and the Thyssen-Bornemisza, still have no need to rely on settings of architectural acrobatics. On the other hand contemporary visual art since the breakdown of modernity in the 1950s has tended to find such self-dramatising and functionally unfixed spaces congenial for performance and display. In so doing it may genuinely undermine the difference between 'global' and 'local' art, taking over part of the old appeal, as seems to have been happening between Tate Britain and Tate Modern in London.

The problem lies not with the heritage of products of purely national or provincial scope, which usually enjoy the protection of patriotic authorities and collectors, and, indeed, often of the fact that there is little interest in them outside their 'nation'. It lies with the products, national in origin or not, which are regarded as part of the international canon of 'the arts', whether by conquerors or, as is today more likely, by the market. These are the artworks worth bidding for, stealing, smuggling and faking.

This raises the problem of fitting the arts into cultural identity. What is 'cultural identity'? There is nothing new about the concept of a collective sense of belonging to some group of 'us', defined negatively by not belonging to other groups of 'them'. In fact all of us are simultaneously members of several such collectivities, although nation states and, since the 1960s, the ideologists of 'identity politics' have insisted that one such role should claim primary or exclusive attachment from its members. The old English socialist militant who claimed on his deathbed that he believed in Jesus Christ, Keir Hardie and Huddersfield United would not have passed this test unless he had declared his first loyalty to the Union flag. However, a sense of collective identity in itself has no special cultural dimension, though it may use or construct some cultural signs as markers of difference, though certainly not language, which was so often identified with the basic values of a people by the intellectuals who set about constructing it for this purpose. And indeed it was not and could not be rooted in the lives of peoples who could not have understood any national language until taught it by a state education system or conscripted into a state's military forces.

Hence in the context of 'heritage', 'national culture' has a meaning and it is political. Insofar as most political units in the world today are or aspire to be 'nation states', 'national culture' overwhelmingly has the state as its framework. Since the construction and reconstruction of a suitable 'heritage' for the 'nation' is the primary spiritual function of any new territorial nation state, it has a built-in incentive for preservation, all the more so as this is readily combined with mythopoeia. This is so even in regions where numerous states share the same language or religion – for example, in the vast zones where English or Arabic is the accepted general language, or where Roman Catholicism or Islam the universal religion. While culture and education remained confined to elite minorities, this was to some extent offset by the cosmopolitanism of such elites, as it is today for the small minorities of businessmen, technicians and intellectuals who live in various global villages. At the other end of the social scale it was also offset by the localism of people who did not speak the national language and whose basic cultural unit was much smaller than the nation. In Italy the gradual nationalisation of the Italian language, which was spoken by only a tiny percentage of Italians at the time of unification, has taken place through the media's need for a spoken idiom comprehensible to all speakers of Italian dialects. Dialects, lacking the power of states, are clearly retreating before linguistic homogenisation except possibly as regional or even local accents, even if most everyday communication in regions like Sicily still continues to be in Sicilian.

However, the general transformation of peasants into Frenchmen or Italians or Ruritanians by administration and education nationalised the masses, as the rise of large middle and lower-middle classes both expanded and nationalised the elites. For instance, they created bodies of men and women to whom the classics of world literature were accessible only if translated into their national languages or turned into Italian and French opera librettos. And, by the same mechanism, they could separate what had somehow become recognised as part of 'world literature' from that which is in practice confined to the national market (at least until the era of television) like *zarzuelas* in Spain, Gilbert and Sullivan in Britain, and so many historical novels in nineteenth-century Germany, a country that took to them with special enthusiasm. Probably democratisation further tied national language and culture to the state.

Education formed and still forms the major link between the two. It was taken over and run under the auspices of states or other public authorities and this is still the case except in a few theocratic areas. It is difficult to see how this could be otherwise in the absence of effective supranational political units or authorities. This situation certainly introduces distortions and opens the way to a lot of political brainwashing. Clearly 'history' cannot be treated only in terms of the past of a particular current political unit, even supposing it has a long continuous past, unlike the great majority of the world's nation states. Yet, given the role of the past in the formation of single and collective identities, it is unreasonable not to expect the past history of a particular *Heimat*, small, large or even national, to be a central part of what citizens of an educational system learn. Whatever our reservations, it is hard to deny that education (that is, in modern times state-wide public education) functions as an engine of national socialisation and identity formation.

This gives the state considerable power – and not only the dictatorial state. Obviously, the kind of state that used to be called *totalitarian*, concentrating all power and communication in its own hands and attempting to impose a homogeneous set of beliefs on the citizens, is undesirable, but in Europe we no longer have such states, not even in Russia.

The main danger from the state in liberal societies is not the imposition of an official culture or the monopoly of cultural funding. The state no longer has that monopoly. It is trying to interfere with the pursuit of historical truth by power or law. There are plenty of examples of this, especially in the past thirty years when history, in the form of publicly funded ceremonies and commemorations, museums, heritage sites, theme constructions, etc. has multiplied. Regime changes and new nationalisms have created a uniquely large number of states whose politicians require a suitably new and patriotically useful history or public historical tradition. This is most obvious in newly independent states, some of which have actually been established and led by professional historians or rather preachers of a national myth, for example, Croatia and Georgia. Add to this the politicians' wish to make concessions to democratic pressure groups or potentially desirable voters, which insist on their own historical truth or political correctness. Recent examples from France, the USA and Scotland come to mind. Establishing historical truth by decree or Act of Parliament has tempted politicians, but has no legitimate place in constitutional states. States should remember what Ernest Renan said: 'Forgetting history or even getting it wrong is one of the major elements in building a nation; which is why the progress of historical studies is frequently a danger to nationalism.' I regard it as the primary duty of modern historians to be such a danger.

Nonetheless, the state is not the only major danger to culture in liberal-democratic capitalist societies today. It coexists in uncomfortable instability with the independent force of an increasingly globalised and rapidly growing capitalist economy, which, in the era of consumer society including the mass media, may be a more powerful engine of politico-ideological socialisation and *Gleichschaltung* or homogenisation. Moreover, as witness the beaches of the Mediterranean, only public authority and (sometimes) laws limit the state's usually disastrous impact on the country's physical and historic heritage. Indeed, insofar as the state is uncontrolled, it constantly undermines and destroys the contemporary concept of 'heritage', whose essence is to protect an endangered past against further erosion by neglect, by the market, by revolutionary conviction that 'the past must be swept away' ('du passé faisons table rase') or by fundamentalist theological conviction.

Public authority is the only way of ensuring this protection, unless, as sometimes happens, it also doubles as a destroyer of the past, or of unsuitable parts of it.

And yet even the most devoted champions of heritage must recognise that in the last half-century the very concept of cultural heritage has become problematic – perhaps even the apparently unambiguous concept of physical or material heritage. It probably reached its peak after the Second World War, when city ruins were fairly universally replaced by literal reconstructions of the symbolic public buildings and sites that had been destroyed. Conserving what actually remained became a major issue later, particularly after the 1960s, the nadir of city building. Yet in both cases 'heritage' was an artifice, however necessary. The impact of the contemporary tsunami of visitors on fragile sites that need to be preserved, whether in city (one thinks of Venice) or countryside (even to forest trails and mountain tops) puts them at unprecedented risk or destroys their character. In extreme cases it imposes rationing or even exclusion.

But what is chiefly at issue is the very concept and shape of high culture as the spiritual core of nineteenth-century bourgeois society, as expressed in the institutions and buildings that transformed contemporary city centres. Even today it remains at the heart of high culture and its conservation. It belonged to the small minority of the educated, some parts of whom defined their social status by it, as in the German *Bildungsbürgertum*, but in a society open to merit and aspiration there was no upper limit to *Bildung*. After all, did not illiterate Brazilians name their offspring Milton and Mozart? And indeed, secondary and tertiary education, as well as the rise of massive educated middle strata, have vastly increased the demand for this type of culture. It consisted essentially of a generally accepted canon of individual 'works' created by unique artists of great skill and, ideally, genius, or alternatively unique contributions to the performance of such works by individual singers, instrumentalists and conductors/directors. And this corpus of the high arts was to be not simply enjoyed but absorbed with both aesthetic and spiritual emotion by the individual citizen or, as is more likely today, by tourist-pilgrims to its holy places.

It has long been evident that this model of culture had survived but it no longer dominated the twentieth century, for reasons discussed elsewhere in this book, in particular because it was largely abandoned after the Second World War by the creators themselves. What did the traditional model of the high arts mean to the lives of populations indifferent to Rembrandt or Bruckner, in times increasingly drenched, night and day, by images, shapes and sounds not produced or distributed for any purpose other than inflating sales in a mass-consumer society? What did personal skill and emotional investment of 'the artist' contribute in an era when these were no longer central to the production of 'a work', not only because of technological obsolescence, but when it was no longer clear what constituted 'a work'? What was the difference between the picture on the gallery wall and the unending flows of often undemanding daily shapes, with or without usually undemanding texts, produced as advertisements, strip cartoons or for one-line laughs?

In a sense, works produced in such a context as 'art' were jokes at the expense of those who would treat a Lichtenstein blow-up of a cartoon-strip image as an analogy to the *Mona Lisa*. The art of Andy Warhol was deliberately designed as anti-art or non-art; without emotion or affect or, indeed, the pretence of more than minimal craft skill, an endless series of silk-screen images of the ephemeral, mass-produced in his 'factory', and of objects, challenging the very principle of telling art from non-art by looking. 'Conceptual art', an invitation to charlatans with the instincts of the great American showman P. T. Barnum, abolished the work itself, which could be constructed by anyone following instructions, if it needed to exist at all outside the creator's mind. Damien Hirst demonstrated how rapidly displaying split sharks in formaldehyde could be turned into the biggest fortune in British art. Indeed, as Robert Hughes put it, the 'brand name had completely replaced both sacredness and solidity'.

Half a century earlier the original missile strike against the arts by Dada and others had sought to destroy art and the society it expressed by provocation and ridicule. Duchamp's moustache on the *Mona Lisa* and his urinal were primarily declarations of war, though student japes as well. The 'conceptual art' inspired by them in the second half of the twentieth century had no such revolutionary purpose. It wanted – or perhaps more precisely it took for granted – integration into the capitalist system, but for the products of 'creative activity' no longer identifiable by the traditional criteria of 'works of art' such as skill and permanence. Often technically deficient new practitioners like rock groups advertised their rejection of the craft standards of the old studio, and of the music professionals who made them recordable, by deliberately unprofessional behaviour. Or, indeed, the moral obligations and work discipline, which drove the traditional performer of evanescent events in theatre, ballet, opera, concert hall or circus, let alone the designer of never-repeated public rituals, to maintain professional standards of high quality, would be shed.

The more logical of the post-artists recognised from the start that the product was a commodity for sale like everything else. What is more, they realised what the film industry had long known: that in a society of mass culture it was personality and public impact that sold their commodity rather than merit. Face and sensation sold, while professionalism, essential as ever, moved into the shadows; talent, though not in short supply, was optional. The joke is that the salesmen in the ever-swelling market for traditional 'high art' continued to insist that they successfully sold the new serial productions as unrepeatable one-off creations, on the strength of their certified uniqueness.

The extreme example of this is Andy Warhol, whose products in 2010 accounted for 17 per cent of all contemporary auction sales, not without some powerful assistance from the artist's estate. Nevertheless, his work is a tribute to the sheer physical impact of these oversized but deliberately throwaway batteries of icons, and perhaps a recognition of Warhol's apparently casual intuition for recognising what fills the subconscious mind of the USA. He expresses it as a disconnected but not incoherent set of images of hope, greed, fears, dreams, longings, admiration and the basic settings of material life, whose totality may well constitute the closest visual equivalent of the 'great American novel' of which the writers of the USA once dreamed.

Some of the new post-art has thus been fitted into the old cultural framework. Much of it cannot, or can be fitted in only by the unplanned changes quietly undergone by the structures of heritage, such as have kept public sculpture alive by new concepts of landscape and townscape and new exhibition spaces vast enough to have room for the gigantism which, as architects have long realised, guarantees attention and effect. How much of the great simultaneous circus show of sound, shape, image, colour, celebrity and spectacle that constitutes the contemporary cultural experience will even survive as a preservable heritage, as distinct from changing sets of generational memories occasionally revived as retro fashions? How much of it will be remembered at all? As the cultural tsunamis of the twentieth century prepare for those of the twenty-first, who can tell?

Part III

UNCERTAINTIES,
SCIENCE, RELIGION

13

Worrying About the Future

There is a major difference between the traditional scholar's questions about the past 'What happened in history, when and why?' and the question that has, in the last forty years or so, come to inspire a growing body of historical research, namely 'How do or did people feel about it?' The first oral history societies were founded in the late 1960s. Since then the number of institutions and works devoted to 'heritage' and historical memory – very notably about the great twentieth-century wars – has grown explosively. Studies of historical memory are essentially not about the past, but about the retrospect to it of some subsequent present. Richard Overy's *The Morbid Age* belongs to another, and less indirect, approach to the emotional texture of the past: the difficult excavation of *contemporary* popular reactions to what was happening in and around people's lives – one might call it the mood music of history.

Though the field of this type of· research is fascinating,

especially when done with Richard Overy's inquisitiveness and surprised erudition, it faces the historian with considerable problems. What does it mean to describe an emotion as characteristic of a country or an era, and what is the significance of a socially widespread emotion, even one plainly related to dramatic historical events? How and how far do we measure its prevalence? Polling, the current mechanism for such measurement, was not available before *c.*1938. In any case such emotions – the extremely widespread dislike of Jews in the West, for instance – were obviously not felt or acted on in the same way by, say, Adolf Hitler and Virginia Woolf. Emotions in history are neither chronologically stable nor socially homogeneous, even in the moments when they are universally experienced alike, as in London under the German air raids, and their intellectual representations even less so. How can they be compared or contrasted? In short, what are historians to make of the new field?

The specific mood Overy enquires into is the sense of crisis and fear, 'a presentiment of impending disaster', the prospect of the end of civilisation that, in his view, characterised Britain between the wars. There is nothing specifically British or twentieth-century about such a mood. Indeed, in the last millennium it would be hard to point to a time, at least in the Christian world, when it found no significant expression, often still in the apocalyptic idiom constructed for the purpose and explored in Norman Cohn's works. (Aldous Huxley, in Overy's quotation, sees 'Belial's guiding hand' in modern history.) There are good reasons in European history why the sense that 'we' – however defined – feel under threat from external enemies or inner demons is not exceptional.

The pioneer work in this genre, Jean Delumeau's history of fear in western Europe from the fourteenth to the early eighteenth century (*La peur en Occident*, 1978), describes and analyses a civilisation 'ill-at-ease' within 'a landscape of fear' peopled by 'morbid fantasies', dangers and eschatological fears. Overy's problem is that, unlike Delumeau, he does not see these fears as reactions to real experiences and real dangers, at least in Great Britain, where, by general consent, neither politics nor society had collapsed and civilisation was not in crisis between the wars. Why, therefore, is it 'a period famous for its population of Cassandras and Jeremiahs who helped to construct the popular image of the inter-war years as an age of anxiety, doubt or fear'?

With learning, lucidity and wit, notably in its brilliant choice of quotes, *The Morbid Age* disentangles the various strands of catastrophic expectation – the death of capitalism, the fears of demographic decline and corruption, 'psychoanalysis and social dismay', the fear of war – mainly through the writings, public and private, of what Delumeau, who did the same for his period, called 'those who had the word and the power': in his day the Catholic clerics; in Overy's, a selection of bourgeois intellectuals and reflective persons in the political class. The attempts to escape from the anticipated disasters by pacifism and what the author calls 'utopian politics' are seen largely as yet another set of symptoms of the pessimist epidemic.

Let us grant, for the moment, that he is correct about the gloominess of 'those who had the word and the power', in spite of some obvious exceptions: the researchers who knew, with Rutherford, that they were living in the glory days of the natural sciences; the engineers who saw no limits to the future progress of old and new technologies; the officials and businessmen of an empire that reached its maximum extent between the wars and still seemed well under control (except for the Irish Free State); the writers and readers of that quintessential inter-war genre, the detective novel, which celebrated a world of moral and social certainty, of stability restored after temporary interruption. The obvious question is, how far did the views of Overy's articulate minority represent or influence the thirty million or so electors who constituted the king's subjects in 1931?

In Delumeau's late medieval and early modern Europe, it may be answered with some confidence. In the Christian West of his period there were organic links between what priests and preachers thought and what the faithful practised, though even then we cannot regard them as congruent. The Roman Catholic clergy had both intellectual and practical authority. But what influence or practical effects between the wars had the words – to take only the case of the writers who rate more than two lines in Overy's index – of the Eugenics Society's Charles Blacker, of Vera Brittain, Cyril Burt, G. D. H. Cole, Leonard Darwin, G. Lowes Dickinson, E. M. Forster, Edward Glover, J. A. Hobson, Aldous and Julian Huxley, Storm Jameson, Ernest Jones, Sir Arthur Keith, John Maynard Keynes, Archbishop Cosmo Lang, Basil Liddell Hart, Bronisław Malinowski, Gilbert Murray, Philip Noel-Baker, George Orwell, Lord Arthur Ponsonby, Bertrand Russell, Bernard Shaw, Arnold Toynbee, the Webbs, H. G. Wells or Leonard and Virginia Woolf?

Unless clearly backed by an important publishing house or journal, as with Victor Gollancz and Kingsley Martin's *New Statesman*, or an actual mass organisation like Lord Robert Cecil's League of Nations Union or Canon Sheppard's pacifist Peace Pledge Union, they had the word, but little else. As in the nineteenth century they had a good chance of being talked about, and of influencing politics and administration within the enclosure of the established elite, if they belonged to it by origin or had been recognised by it, especially if they belonged to the networks of Noel Annan's 'intellectual aristocracy', as did several of the announcers of doom. But how far did their ideas shape the 'public opinion' that lay outside the range of the writers and readers of letters to *The Times* and the *New Statesman*?

There is actually little evidence in the culture and way of life of the inter-war working and lower-middle classes, which this book does not investigate, that it did. Gracie Fields, George Formby and Bud Flanagan did not live in the expectation of social collapse, nor did the West End theatre. Far from morbidity, the working class of Richard Hoggart's (and my) youth consisted largely of people who 'feel they cannot do much about the main elements in their situation, feel it not necessarily with despair or disappointment or resentment but simply as a fact of life'. True, as Overy shows, the dramatic rise of the mass media allowed the 'core ideas' of his morbid thinkers to be widely disseminated. However, spreading intellectual gloom was not the object of the omnipresent movies or even the mass newspapers, reaching circulations of two million and more in the early 1930s, though BBC radio, almost universally available by the mid-1930s, gave their spokesman a tiny fraction – one would have wished Overy to make an estimate – of its vast output. It is not irrelevant that *The Listener*, which reprinted radio talks and debates, had a circulation of fifty-two thousand in 1935, as against the 2.4 million of the *Radio Times*.[1]

The book, revolutionised in the 1930s by Penguin and Gollancz, was almost certainly the most effective form of intellectual diffusion: not to the mass of the manual working class for whom the word 'book' still meant 'magazine', but to the old educated and the rapidly growing body of the aspiring and politically conscious self-educated. Even among these, Overy's footnotes show, circulations of over fifty thousand – the order of magnitude of the Left Book Club and above the contemporary level of a best-seller – were unusual, except in the tense pre-war months of 1938–9. Overy's admirable inquiries into publishers' records show that Walter Greenwood's depression novel *Love on the Dole* ('few other cultural products of the slump reached so wide an audience') sold 46,290 copies between 1933 and 1940. The potential book readership in 1931 (adding together the census categories of 'professional and semi-professionals' to that of 'clerical and kindred workers') was about two and a half million out of the almost thirty million of the British electorate.

Admittedly, 'the theses of some defunct (or living) thinker' (to adapt Keynes's phrase) do not spread by such conventional means, but by a sort of osmosis whereby a few radically reduced and simplified concepts – 'the survival of the fittest', 'capitalism', 'the inferiority complex' and 'the unconscious' – somehow enter the public or private discourse as recognised brand names. Even by such relaxed criteria, several of Overy's doom-laden forecasts hardly reached outside the corral of the intellectuals, activists and national decision makers, notably the demographers' fear of population collapse (which proved mistaken) and what we now see as the sinister plans of the eugenists for eliminating those defined as genetically inferior. Marie Stopes made her impact on Britain not as an advocate of sterilising the subnormal, but as the pioneer of birth control, which in this period came to be recognised among the British masses as a useful addition to the traditional practice of coitus interruptus.

Only where public opinion spontaneously shared the fears and reactions of elite intellectuals can their writings serve as expressions of a general British mood. Almost certainly they coincided on the central problem of the age, the fear of war; probably also in some ways on the crisis of the (British) economy. In these respects the British did not, as Overy suggests, experience the European predicament between the wars at second hand. Like the French they lived with the dark memory of the mass killings of the 'Great War' and (which was perhaps even more effective) the living evidence on the street of the crippled and disfigured survivors. Britons were realistic in their fears of another war. Especially from 1933 on, war loomed over all lives, those of women, about whose take on inter-war Britain this book is silent, perhaps more even than men.

In the impressive second half of this book, Overy, who made his deserved reputation as a historian of the Second World War, brilliantly describes the sense of an inevitably approaching catastrophe in the 1930s, which was to overpower the appeal of absolute pacifism. But it did so precisely because it was not a mood of hopelessness, comparable to that voiced in the spectacular understatement of the secret government report on nuclear war of 1955, quoted by Peter Hennessy ('Whether this country could withstand an all-out attack and still be in a state to carry on hostilities must be very doubtful'). To expect to die in the next war, as my contemporaries not unreasonably did in 1939 – Overy quotes my own memories to this effect – did not stop us from thinking that the war would have to be fought, would be won and could lead to a better society.

British reactions to the crisis of the inter-war British economy were more complex, but here the argument that British capitalism had less cause for alarm is surely wrong. In the 1920s Britons seemed to have more obvious causes to worry about the future of their economy than other nations. Almost alone in the world, Britain's manufacturing production – even at the peak of the 1920s, when world output was over 50 per cent above the pre-war figure – stayed below the 1913 level, and its rate of unemployment, very much higher than Germany's and the USA's, never fell below 10 per cent. Not surprisingly the Great Slump hit other countries much harder than the already faltering Britain, but it is worth remembering that the impact of 1929 was so dramatic as to make Britain abandon in 1931 the two theological foundations of its nineteenth-century economic identity: free trade and the Gold Standard. Most of Overy's quotes of economic doom come from before 1934.

Certainly the crisis produced agreement among the articulate classes that the system could not go on as before, either because of the basic flaws of capitalism or because of 'The End of Laissez-Faire' announced by Keynes in 1926, but discussions on the future shape of the economy, whether socialist or shaped by a reformed, more interventionist and 'planned' capitalism, were strictly confined to minorities: the first of up to half a million in and around the labour movement; the second probably of a few hundred of what Gramsci would have called the 'organic intellectuals' of the British ruling class. However, memory suggests that Overy is right in thinking that the most widespread reaction to the troubles of the economy among the king's non-writing subjects, outside the new wastelands of the old industrial regions, was not so much the feeling 'that capitalism did not work, but that it should not work the way it did'.[2] And insofar as 'socialism' reached beyond the activists into the 29 per cent of the British electorate who voted for the Labour Party at the peak of its inter-war success, it represented a moral perspective in which capitalism would be transformed by the magic of nationalisation.

Yet neither the belief in socialism nor in a planned capitalism implied morbidity, despair or a sense of apocalypse. Both viewpoints, in different ways, assumed that the crisis could and should be overcome, encouraged by what seemed to be the extraordinary immunity to the Great Slump of the Soviet Five-Year Plans, which in the 1930s, as Overy rightly notes, made the words 'plan' and 'planning' into a political 'open sesame' even for thinking non-socialists. But both standpoints also looked forward to a better or at least a more viable future. Only the forlorn rearguard of unreconstructed pre-1914 liberal individualists saw no hope. For the great guru of the London School of Economics, Friedrich von Hayek, who does not appear in this book, both socialist and Keynesian prescriptions for the future were predictable stumbles on *The Road to Serfdom* (1944).

This should not surprise us. A great many Europeans had the experience of Armageddon in the Great War. The fear of another and very likely more terrible war was all the more real because the Great War had given Europe a set of unprecedented and fear-inducing symbols: the aerial bomb, the tank, the gas mask. Where past or present provided no adequate comparison, most people were inclined to forget or underestimate the hazards of the future, however minatory the rhetoric surrounding them. That many Jews who stayed in Germany after 1933 took the precaution of sending their children abroad shows that they were not blind to the perils of living under Hitler, but what actually awaited them was literally inconceivable in the early twentieth century, even by a ghetto defeatist.

No doubt there were prophets in Pompeii who warned of the dangers of living under volcanoes, but it is doubtful whether even the pessimists among them actually foresaw the total and definitive obliteration of the city. Certainly its inhabitants were not expecting to live their last days.

There is no single label for how social collectives or even individuals envisage or feel about the future. In any case 'apocalypse', 'chaos' or 'the end of civilisation', being beyond everyday experience in most of Europe between the wars, were not what most people really anticipated, even when they lived, uncertain about the future, in the ruins of an irrecoverable old social order, as many did after 1917. These things are more easily recognised in retrospect, for during genuinely apocalyptic episodes of history – say, central Europe in 1945–6 – most non-uniformed men and women are too busy trying to keep going to classify their predicament. That is why, contrary to the champions of air-power, civilian populations in great cities did not wilt under the bombs and firestorms of the Second World War. Whatever their motivations, they 'carried on' and their cities, ruined and burning, continued to function because life does not stop till death. Let us not judge the intimations of disaster between the wars, even when they proved correct, by the unimagined standards of subsequent havoc and desolation.

Overy's book, however acute in observation, however innovative and monumental in its exploration of archives, demonstrates the necessary oversimplifications of a history built round feelings. Looking for a central 'mood' as the keynote of an era does not get us closer to reconstructing the past than 'national character' or 'Christian/Islamic/Confucian values'. They tell us too little too vaguely. Historians should take such concepts seriously, but not as a basis for analysis or the structure of narrative. To be fair to the author, he does neither. His purpose has clearly been to compose an original set of variations to compete with the other riffs by professional historians on what is assumed to be a universally familiar theme: the history of

Britain between the wars. But it is no longer familiar except to the old. The Overy Variations in the key of C (for crisis) are an impressive achievement, though one misses any serious comparison with the situation in other European countries. Since he writes well, his book also becomes what it was not intended to be, a tourist guide to *terra incognita* for readers to whom the Britain of George V is as remote and unknown as that of George II. It should be read with intellectual pleasure and profit for its perceptiveness and its discoveries of much that was unexplored in some parts of British intellectual life, but not as an introduction to inter-war Britain for the inexperienced time-traveller.

14

Science: Social Function and World Change

Let me begin this review with a motor trip in 1944 by two scientists down the valley from Lord Mountbatten's headquarters in Kandy (in Sri Lanka) to the jungle. The younger recalls the conversation of the older. He was 'interested and expert in everything around him – the war, Buddhist religion and art, the geological specimens he would retrieve from every ditch, the properties of mud, luminous insects, the ancestry of cycads, but his recurrent theme was the fundamentals of biology and of the enormous development just becoming possible through the advances in the physical and chemical techniques of the 1930s'.

The young scientist was John Kendrew, one of the many inspired by such conversations to win the highest scientific award, which escaped his travel companion. But it might have been anyone, male or female, who ever came within earshot of that stumpy bohemian visionary genius with the uncontrollable head of hair and reedy voice. John Desmond Bernal (1901–71) has evidently amazed and dazzled his biographer as much as everyone else who ever came into contact with this 'polyvalent' and 'extraordinarily attractive person' (in the words of Joseph Needham), considered by competent judges 'one of the greatest intellectuals of the twentieth century' (Linus Pauling).

There are two reasons for reading the biography of this brilliant and tragic figure: sheer human curiosity about an individual recognisable even at first sight as singular and fascinating; and, since he stood at their conjunction, the need to understand the interconnections between the scientific, sociopolitical and cultural revolutions of the twentieth century and their interlocking hopes and dreams about the future. Between the wars nobody was a more visible icon of the scientists' commitment to the future than Bernal, who, in the shape of 'John Cabal' (Raymond Massey in Bernal-like make-up), actually appeared as the protagonist in Korda's 1936 film of H. G. Wells's *The Shape of Things to Come*. And, though he was a living proof that there is no basic division between art and science, nobody in the suspect culture of science was a more obvious target for the sour provincialism of F. R. Leavis.

Andrew Brown's *J. D. Bernal: The Sage of Science*[1] is better at satisfying the biographical than the historical questions about him. It is not the first book based on the Bernal Archive, now in the Cambridge University Library, but its 538 fairly dense pages certainly tell us more of the facts than all its predecessors, even without those contained in the six boxes of love letters, which, when opened in 2021, will supplement our knowledge of the Sage's legendary polygyny. One concludes it, fascinated but insufficiently satisfied.

In his autobiographical mode, Bernal himself thought his life should be written in three colours: red for politics, blue for science and purple for sex. The book is strongest on Bernal's

Irish dimension, important for both his ideological and perhaps even his scientific development. Had the later Stalinist left behind all the 'militaristic view of social change' that went with his youthful nationalist commitment as a Sinn Fein revolutionary? On the red side of his life it is distinctly less perceptive than the essay on 'Political Formation'[2] presumably because the author is too anxious to balance his enormous admiration for the man and the scientist by insisting on his rejection of the Stalinist. The present reviewer is not competent to assess Brown's evidently well-qualified discussion of Bernal's science, but his analysis of Bernal's crucial failure to play as central a part in the molecular biology revolution as might have been expected seems inferior to Robert Olby's entry for Bernal in the new *Oxford Dictionary of National Biography*. Also, he shows insufficient interest in the nature of the thinking that turned so many eminent figures in the evolutionary life sciences to Marxism or, rather more surprisingly, to the writings of Engels and, incidentally, towards the USSR[3] – J. B. S. Haldane, Joseph Needham, Lancelot Hogben, C. H. Waddington and Bernal himself. There was more to the unusual and short-lived phase of 'red science' than politics.

As to the sex, Brown rightly brings out the crucial importance of Freudianism – the idea rather than the theory – in the early generation of red intellectuals and as a force for Bernal's personal emancipation, though he omits his repudiation of it in the 1930s, which had no effect on his behaviour. Indeed, the strength of Bernal's libido and the charm that so few resisted are equally impressive, but are we any closer at the end of this book to understanding the astonishing and evidently lifelong loyalty of his wives and lovers, or for that matter anything about his emotions, except that he evidently attracted and respected intelligent women, whether or not he bedded them, that he was – surprisingly – deaf to music, was totally disorganised in life and lab, and never did any shopping for himself?

'A shilling life will give you all the facts,' wrote Auden. Thanks to Brown we now have a lot of them. How far do they help us understand Bernal and his times? He was the son of a prosperous Catholic farming couple in County Tipperary with distinctly wider horizons than was usual in this milieu, whose gift for mathematics and science – indeed, whose all-embracing curiosity – were evident almost from infancy. Unlike other authors, Brown does not stress the family's Sephardic side, no doubt because in the Bernal household intellectual stimulation evidently came from his well-travelled and studious mother, the child of New England Presbyterian clerics, and not from his rustic father. (Indeed, by the Israeli criterion of maternal descent, the son and grandson of unquestionably non-Jewish women could not be considered a Jew.)

Sent to Bedford, a minor public school with good scientific credentials in England, in the usual manner – fortunately, he would not accept his father's first choice, Stonyhurst – he won a scholarship to Cambridge, read and thought omnivorously, established an undergraduate reputation as 'Sage', an all-purpose genius. He shifted from Catholic piety to atheism; from active support for the IRA's war against Britain to socialism and the wider anti-imperialism of the October Revolution; and to Freudianism, which liberated him from sexual inhibition as well as from 'the phantasies of religion and rationalism'. He lost his virginity as an undergraduate – late by current, but not by the middle-class student standards of the time, but early enough to become a married undergraduate with a child and a partner, Eileen Sprague, who stubbornly maintained her status as his only legal wife for the remainder of his life. He was to establish a second household with children in the 1930s with Margaret Gardiner and a third with Margot Heinemann in the 1950s, both of whom also survived him.

Though the brilliance and originality of his mind were

extraordinary and evident, his progress as a scientist was curiously uneven. He was forced to shift from mathematics to physics, and his failure to get a first-class physics degree closed the Cavendish Laboratory to him for a while – not that the great Rutherford liked Bernal's personal and scientific style, let alone his communism. His way into science was to be through crystallography, which 'appealed to him as naturalist, a mathematician, a physicist and a chemist'[4] and suited his combination of experiment, model and theory. For some wonderfully enjoyable and bohemian years Bernal joined the Nobel-winning Bragg family in London, before returning to Cambridge in 1927. The next twelve years would be the most rewarding, in scientific terms as well as in his impact on politics. During this period he came to prominence as a communist intellectual, became the founder of modern molecular biology (in Francis Crick's words, Bernal was his and Watson's 'scientific grandfather') and, through his enormously influential *The Social Function of Science*,[5] the foremost theorist of science planning and science policy. Cambridge was his base until he took over P. M. S. Blackett's chair of Physics at Birkbeck College, not then one of the major hubs of scientific research, in 1938, where he remained for the rest of his life, building up a distinguished crystallography department after the war. His reputation attracted young researchers of the highest ability – Francis Crick (before he went to Cambridge), Rosalind Franklin, Aaron Klug – but Bernal remained on the margins of the revolution in the life sciences he had done so much to inspire. He was to recognise the DNA model immediately as 'the greatest single discovery in biology', but his name is not attached to it.

In fact, from early 1939 to 1946 he was effectively outside the academy as part of the extraordinarily successful mobilisation of British scientists in the Second World War. Although one of the main inspirers and creators of 'operational research', he seems to have had no connection with the atom bomb project. For a few years, science and politics, theory and practice were one. Even laymen can appreciate his most dramatic achievements, like correctly predicting the effect of the 1940 German bombing of Coventry and his spectacular research on the invasion beaches of Normandy as well as his nonchalant bravery. Not surprisingly, the chapters on this period are the most readable for non-scientists. In 1945–6 the wartime insider once again became the communist outsider and potential traitor, though the Establishment had more trouble getting used to the political transition than George Orwell, who lost no time in denouncing Bernal's Stalinism and 'slovenly style'. It is notable that he was still asked in 1945–6 to calculate the relative military effort needed to knock out the USSR, the USA and Britain in a future nuclear war, a task he carried out with his usual icy intelligence and verve. It was to be his last official duty. There has never, incidentally, been any evidence or serious suggestion of relations with the Soviet intelligence services.

Was it only the Cold War that ended what looked like the triumphant post-war career of a major scientist at the peak of his creative capacities? The *Oxford Dictionary of National Biography* plausibly suggests that his political activism after 1945 made it difficult for him to re-establish his pre-war standing. Certainly his total public identification with Stalinism did him serious harm. Bernal's peer-group reputation among scientists never quite recovered from his attempt to justify the charlatan Lysenko whose views became the official orthodoxy of Soviet biology in 1948. Nevertheless, it does not explain his failure to make more than a peripheral personal contribution to the great molecular biology revolution, or his shift from research to encyclopaedic and historic writing. As Brown records, the preparation of the titanic *Science in History*[6] 'at times threatened to overwhelm' him.

Bernal continued to exercise his prodigious gift of 'shooting an arrow of original thought into any target present to him' to good effect, but his own scientific reputation does not rest on his post-war research, except perhaps for his work on the structure of liquids, which Brown discusses excellently. There were many reasons for this. As Rosalind Franklin has recalled, Birkbeck physics laboured under conditions primitive even by the standards of post-war bombed London. These difficulties were not made any easier by jealousies and hostilities within the college and, when the international situation reached crisis point, Bernal was subjected to political and ideological attacks from without. He worked with unremitting and growing intensity, but the scientific results he achieved were less impressive than might have been predicted in 1939.

By 1951 his powerful physique began to crack under the pressures of a superhuman schedule that combined full-time scientific work and academic duties with constant global campaigning on behalf of the Soviet-sponsored peace movement, on top of a programme of writing, lecturing and conferencing that was little short of the obsessional. He began to have trouble climbing mountains, and his gait became more unbalanced – he himself compared it to that of Lear's Pobble. Thus in one academic year, 1961–2, in addition to his travels on behalf of the peace movement, he lectured in Chile and Brazil, in Berlin, Munich, Yale (a series of postgraduate lectures on 'Molecular Structure, Biochemical Function and Evolution'), at the Ghana Academy of Science, at a research conference on physical metallurgy in New Hampshire, at the Physical Society of France, the British Association, and institutions or associations in Glasgow, Manchester and Newcastle, not to mention the Bakerian Lecture at the Royal Society as well as talks to various scientific and student societies. Since he had also published five books in the 1950s, this left little room for more than intermittent research.

Eventually, the overload caught up with him. Starting in 1963, a series of strokes laid him low although he did not retire from the chair of crystallography he had finally extorted from Birkbeck until 1968. His last years, with his time divided between Margot Heinemann and his daughter Jane and the two other wives who reasserted their claims on him, were tragic. Gradually his extraordinary brain lost the physical capacity to communicate with the outside world. In the end even those closest to him, having a lifetime familiarity with his voice and handwriting, could no longer decipher his sounds and signs. He passed his last two years transported from one house to another, in silent solitary confinement in the prison of a decaying body, and died on 15 September 1971, aged seventy.

Even the life of the most singular individual makes no sense except in the setting of his or her time and place. Bernal's hopeful dream of humanity's progress and liberation through a combination of political, scientific and personal revolution – via Lenin, Freud and the revelations hidden in the beauty of crystals – was his own, and so was his tragedy, but both could only belong to someone who reached adulthood in the first half of the twentieth century. As a man, he belonged to the era of capitalist and imperial crisis, as an Irish and subsequently a communist revolutionary. As a scientist he was acutely conscious of living in what a then influential book by the French sociologist, Georges Friedmann, called 'the crisis of progress'.[7]

For 150 years before the outbreak of the First World War there had been little doubt in educated secular Western minds that civilisation, through a single pattern of global advance, was inevitably moving forward to a better future, faster or slower, whether continuously or discontinuously. Its reality could not be denied even by those who worried about its problematic consequences. But where was humanity going after 1914, in what seemed to be the irreparable ruins of the nineteenth-century world, amid wars, revolutions and economic collapse? Only three pillars, reinforcing one another, still held up the temple of progress: the forward march of science; a confident, rationalised American capitalism; and, for ravaged

Europe and what later came to be called the 'Third World', the hope of what the Russian Revolution might bring: Einstein, Lenin and Henry Ford. The advance of science was safe enough, but social crisis, intellectual danger and even its own progress increasingly pressed its practitioners into looking outside the laboratories to society.

In the 1920s even the young USSR looked to Henry Ford, and in his youth Bernal, though communist, accepted that human needs could be satisfied through either 'a rationalised capitalism or Soviet state planning'. The American model crashed in the world economic crisis, the central cataclysm of the era, taking with it the local versions of liberal corporate capitalisms in Germany and Japan. A crude industrialisation on the Soviet model seemed to be roaring ahead. For believers in progress the only way to the future looked like a new planned socialist society, created by history and transformed by a triumphant science. The peculiarity of Bernal's career is that he never lost the belief, acquired in the 1930s, that this could only be achieved by a society like the USSR, even in its Stalinist form.

The move of science into the public arena seemed both logical and necessary to a dynamic core of young natural scientists of that era. On the one hand, the small band of pioneer explorers, making discoveries around every corner ('in this glorious new world of science', as the young Bernal put it), knew that they lived in triumphant times. Revolutions in their field since 1895 had opened up an era of spectacular, limitless and world-transforming progress in the understanding and control of nature. The scientists alone knew how it was done. Only they really knew its potential. Bernal was not alone in making daring speculations about 'the shape of things to come'. His specific, and perhaps most lasting, contribution to the assertion of the power of science was to analyse how it actually operated as a social and intellectual agent, and how it should be organised for effective development.

Equally obvious was the ignorance of those who ran the Western world. It was as spectacular as their military and economic failures since 1914. They were helpless in an era of revolutionary upheaval and, as the worldwide capitalist economic cataclysm made clear, of poverty in the midst of plenty. ('Social need' and 'national well-being' entered the public vocabulary of British science in the early 1930s.) Society needed scientists. Though research and theory had been traditionally averse from controversial politics, like it or not, science, previously an outsider, had to enter the field of public activity, as a body of propagandists for science itself, as prophets and active pioneers. And, from the hour that Hitler took power in a Germany that burned its books and decimated its researchers, scientists became the glory of Europe, as defenders of the future of civilisation. At this crucial moment, the apparent immunity of the USSR to the Great Slump discredited market economics and made 'planning' look like an instant social miracle drug. Soviet Russia became something of a model even for the non-Bolsheviks. Across frontiers of states and ideologies, 'planning' appealed to socialists who believed in it on the grounds of ideology, to scientists and technocrats who practised it anyway, and to politicians who began to realise that slump and war made it necessary.

With bitter irony, history decided that victory by total war effort and not the good society was to be the greatest achievement of planned progress through the combined mobilisation of people, politics, science and social hope. The Second World War fused political and scientific decisions and turned science fiction into reality, sometimes nightmare reality. The atom bomb was the social application of a political judgment against Hitler made in 1939 by the purest nuclear theorists and experimenters. The conflict not only justified Bernal's predictions of the need of a planned 'big science' that would allow it to break out into new realms of understanding and social usefulness, but it also had to realise them. There was no other way to build a nuclear weapon. War and only war was to give science and technology – nuclear, spatial, computer-generated – the resources and the support structure that propelled both disciplines into the second half of the century. And because it put new and limitless powers into human hands, war escaped from control and reversed the relation between sorcerer and apprentice. The sorcerers, who had created these powers, conscious of their danger, found themselves helpless when faced with the apprentices who justified, and gloried in, their use. The bomb-makers became anti-nuclear campaigners and, in the Cold War, objects of suspicion and contempt to the bomb-users.

Robert Oppenheimer and Desmond Bernal (who probably spent more time after 1945 campaigning against nuclear war than on any other of his many activities) were among the many victims of this reversal, though in different ways. In one respect Oppenheimer, the chief architect of the atom bomb, was the more tragic case. Hounded out of public life by enemies and witch-hunters on the excuse of pre-war communist associations, his fall was greater, and the case against him was transparently spurious. Given his political allegiance, Bernal could not have been surprised to be treated as a 'security risk' after 1945. Yet in another way his case was equally tragic, since he was brought low by those whose politico-scientific vision of the future he shared, but who chose to splinter it dramatically during the first war, risking the superpower confrontation of the Cold War.

During the tense months of the 1948 Berlin Airlift, Stalin decided to raise the fortifications of the USSR against ideological infiltrations and other dangers from the West by an *ex cathedra* decision that henceforth there would be two mutually hostile sciences. Only one of these was right and obligatory for all communists, because authorised by the Party. In Maoist terms, being 'red' was more important than being 'expert'.

That, rather than an argument about the nature of the reproduction of organisms, was the issue in the Lysenko affair, directly 'authorised and in effect dictated by Stalin',[8] as recent research shows, which, not surprisingly, put an end to the era of 'red science'. Bernal discredited himself by giving the obligations of being 'red' priority over those of being the 'expert'.

Unconscious of historical irony, Stalin had singled out as orthodoxy's chosen scapegoat precisely the field of life-science research that had most attracted Western scientists to Soviet thinking and which had produced the most eminent Marxists and Marxisants of the era of 'red science'. They were vulnerable in Russia because, unlike physicists and mathematicians, who had to be allowed to go about their business whatever their ideological sins, geneticists produced neither arms nor, apparently, enough short-term improvements in agriculture. The problematic agrobiological theories of T. D. Lysenko were officially declared correct, materialist, progressive and patriotic against reactionary, scholastic, foreign and unpatriotic bourgeois genetics. (As a result, some three thousand biologists promptly lost their jobs, and some their liberty.) Soviet doctrine and Soviet practice in the Lysenko affair were equally indefensible.

Why Bernal, almost alone among Western scientists, chose to make an aggressive public defence of both and reinforce it, some years later, by an implausible obituary of 'Stalin as a Scientist' is still not clear. It is not enough to say that he put party duty before scientific conscience, though his attempts to make an intellectual case for Lysenko could hardly have convinced himself. Technically, he was not even a Communist Party member. However, he was by then an important public figure in the international sphere of the USSR. Possibly he was moved by concerns about world peace and the hope of influencing developments within the Soviet Union. As Brown shows, he did eventually become a friend and confidant of

Khrushchev. Whatever his motives, his stance served neither his cause, himself, nor his reputation.

Bernal clearly failed in his political aims and, though he never expressed any criticism of the Soviet Union, he must have been disappointed in his political hopes. He was far more influential as a prophet of the post-1945 organisation, structure and public funding of science. From projects like CERN to the 'citations index', we still live with his heritage. But what did he achieve as a scientist?

Very few scientists have had a more impressive peer assessment. 'The scope of Bernal's brain was legendary,' wrote Jim Watson, not a man given to feelings of inferiority. 'I regarded Bernal as a genius,' wrote Francis Crick, who shared the Nobel Prize with Watson. Linus Pauling thought Bernal the most brilliant scientist he had ever met. His biographer has traced statements by at least a dozen Nobel laureates, older and younger than Bernal, expressing 'admiration or even awe'. Yet the very universality of his interests, the very speed of his responses and his consequent impatience all tempted him away from the concentration essential to measurable achievement. Probably the most balanced assessment was written in 1964 by C. P. Snow:

In natural gifts he stands very high, he is the most learned scientist of his time, perhaps the last of whom it will be said, with meaning, that he knew science ... And yet his achievement, though massive, will not dominate the record as it might have done. The number of scientific papers, all over the world, produced under other names, which owe their origins to Bernal, is very large. But he has suffered from a certain lack of the obsessiveness which most scientists possess and which makes them carry out a piece of creative work to the end. If Bernal had possessed this kind of obsessiveness he would have polished off a great deal of modern molecular biology and won Nobel prizes several times over.[9]

Should we therefore think less of his achievement? It is the paradox of scientific knowledge that, being cumulative (unlike some of the creative arts), its practitioners are remembered for personal prominence in a sphere where progress is collective and independent of single individuals. The greatest geniuses in the sciences are historically replaceable, because their innovations would have been made by others, sooner or later, and are inevitably part of a continuing collective endeavour, unlike the works of a Shakespeare or a Mozart, which are uniquely theirs. We rightly honour Mendeleyev but the chemical elements would have found their periodic table without him. The names Crick, Watson and Wilkins on the 1962 Nobel Prize stand for a regiment of researchers who made their breakthrough possible and who continued to develop their ideas. On the other hand, the mechanism of reward and name-recognition is inadequate to record the contribution of men like Bernal, though at least four of his pupils and disciples won Nobel prizes in the three years from 1962 to 1964, without counting Crick, who had wanted to work for him, and Rosalind Franklin from Bernal's own laboratory, who, but for her death, would have been in the running. His work is not a solid but an impulse, an atmosphere.

Everybody knows what Roentgen achieved in science, even though we may know or need to know nothing else about him: he discovered X-rays in 1895. Until 2012, few knew who Higgs was or is, but he gave his name to the mysterious Higgs boson, about which physicists had argued for years. Nothing in science permanently carries Bernal's name. Most of those who knew him and felt the impact of this extraordinary figure are dead. Once the generations who responded directly to the stimulus of such a man of preliminary or unspecifiable contributions die, his reputation is in the hands of the historians alone. They will need to be not only experts in the history of science, but men and women who can reconstruct the mood and temper of his age – of global catastrophe and global hope – when no one is left who can remember it. Henceforth Andrew Brown's book will be their necessary point of departure.

15

Mandarin in a Phrygian Cap:
Joseph Needham

Except in Stefan Collini's edition of the famous 1959 Rede Lecture, the great battle about 'The Two Cultures' which divided the arts and sciences in Cambridge, and the intellectual pages of Britain at the time, is hardly remembered. It laid claim to the centrality of science and launched an attack on 'literary intellectuals' by the now almost forgotten C. P. Snow (1905–80); unjustly so, because his ponderous novels about hope, power and prestige tell us much about the public and academic life of his period. In a sense it was a polemic about the 1930s, the age of glory of the scientists and the low, dishonest or otherwise depreciable decade of the disappointed poets. In a narrower sense it was a Cambridge rearguard engagement between the arts and the self-confident natural sciences, well on the way to their eighty-two Nobel prizes, who knew that the future greatness (and funding) of the university would essentially be in their hands. Probably nothing irritated arts dons more than the scientists' certainty that the future was theirs. In a wider sense, the debate was about the relation between reason and imagination. In Snow's view the scientists had both, while the literary intellectuals were fatally hobbled by their ignorance and suspicion of science and the future. Only one of the two cultures really counted.

Snow overplayed his hand, though not as absurdly as his chief antagonist, F. R. Leavis, but fundamentally he was right. In the first half of the twentieth century, the canyon between the two cultures was probably wider than it had ever been, at least in Britain, where secondary schools already divided 'arts' from 'science' in the mid-teens.

In fact, arts intellectuals were closed off from the sciences, but not scientists from the arts, since the basic education for the upper social strata had always been one of letters, and the then small community of scientists came chiefly from this milieu.

Nevertheless, the contrast is striking between the range of knowledge and interests of a group of inter-war scientists – mostly, but not exclusively with biological interests – and the limitations of those in the arts. The leading group of 1930s poets, other than perhaps Empson, admired technology (as witness all those pylons in their poems), but, unlike the romantic poets of the early nineteenth century, seem to have had no sense of living in an era of scientific wonders. Shelley and Keats, J. B. S. Haldane observed, were the last poets to be abreast of developments in chemistry. Conversely, scientists could lecture on Iranian art (Bernal), write books about William Blake (Bronowski), acquire honorary degrees in music (C. H. Waddington), investigate comparative religion like J. B. S. Haldane and, above all, write and have a sense of history.

They also tended to combine the imaginations of art and science with endless energy, free love, eccentricity and revolutionary politics. It is a combination highly characteristic of the era between the world wars, or more specifically of the 1930s. No man belonged more obviously to it than Joseph Needham (Li Yuese in Mandarin), who was perhaps the most interesting mind among the constellation of brilliant 'red' scientists of that decade. He was also perhaps the most unusual in his ability to combine revolutionary behaviour and convictions with acceptance by the established world of *Who's Who*, eventually as Master of his Cambridge college and a Companion of Honour. Not everyone in the years of the Cold War was sufficiently disarming for his career to survive having – wrongly – accused the USA of using bacteriological weapons in the Korean War.

Certainly his achievement is impressive. Needham's great work, *Science and Civilisation in China*, transformed knowledge of the subject both in the West and, to a considerable extent, in China itself. That titanic project naturally dominates the lively new biography by Simon Winchester, a writer who has specialised in books tying individuals to great achievements. Its original American title was *The Man Who Loved China*. Needham's life, before his energies and emotions were turned to China, is dealt with in twenty-three fairly cursory pages. It is not unfair to a very readable and rightly successful book to say that it cannot claim to be a balanced assessment of its remarkable and neglected subject.[1]

The first volume of *Science and Civilisation in China* was described – by a critic who had no sympathy for Needham's politics or personal behaviour – as 'perhaps the greatest single act of historical synthesis and intercultural communication ever attempted by one man'. The sheer scale and twenty-first-century relevance of this achievement makes it certain that this is what he will be remembered for. Though Needham was elected to the Royal Society at the age of forty-one after the publication of a large volume, *Biochemistry and Morphogenesis*, his own scientific work would probably never have been in the Nobel range, nor does he seem to have inspired those who achieved new breakthroughs, as did J. D. Bernal and J. B. S. Haldane. On the other hand, he had already demonstrated his ambitions as a historian of science (introducing it as a subject to Cambridge some years later) in the three volumes of *Chemical Embryology*.[2] This not only summarised the state of the field in terms of biochemistry, but provided an impressive history and prehistory of the subject, subsequently published as such. Even after he had plunged into Chinese matters, he provided an irresistible sketch of 'the pre-natal history of chemistry' in the introduction to *The Chemistry of Life*,[3] in which he described the ancient beliefs in the 'breath of life' as 'pneumatic protophysiology', and in which he considered the links between alchemy and the invention of Bénédictine and other monastic liqueurs. More unexpectedly, he also published a small popular book on the Levellers in the English Revolution under the pen-name Henry Holorenshaw.

History and public activism were at the core of the 'red science' of the 1930s. One marvels at the sheer range and intensity of these scientists' academic and extra-curricular activities. In Needham's case they included putting the 'S' into UNESCO as founder and first director of that organisation's Section of Natural Sciences (1946–8). But even here he did not neglect history, though the project concerning the scientific and cultural history of mankind, in which he took an interest, is best forgotten.

History was central to the red scientists not merely because they knew themselves to be living in times of extraordinary change. The sense of development and transformation over time – if only through the great question of the origin of life – provided a bond between the sciences and the most exciting problems for biologists. All of them were absorbed by the changing relations, both past and present, between science and society. All memoirs of the period agree on the dramatic impact of the Soviet papers presented at the 1931 London International Congress on the History of Science, to which the USSR sent an unusually distinguished delegation. Its Marxist slant deeply impressed the British (including Needham who attended it), not so much by the quality of the papers as by the new perspectives that they opened up on the relations between science and society. The 1931 Congress and his discovery of China in 1937 have been suggested as the two primary events that shaped Needham's life.

So far as we know, Needham, a Marxist, never joined or was particularly close to the Communist Party, though his characteristic 'millenarian fervour'[4] made him, if anything more instinctively radical than more hard-headed left-wingers. He urged J. B. S. Haldane to choose the socialist Materialism of the future – Haldane joined the Communist Party soon after – and he reviewed the Webbs' *Soviet Communism* in 1936 with what has been described as 'enthusiasm bordering on rapture'.[5] However, his widely advertised enjoyment of nudism and morris dancing, while giving him an aura of English eccentricity to which the otherwise conservative Fellows of Gonville and Caius College assimilated his political heterodoxy, did not help his standing in the politics of the left. Admittedly, the long-lasting *ménage à trois* of Joseph and Dorothy Needham with Lu Gweijen (to whom Winchester ascribes his passion for China) was not yet established before the war, but the flaunted sexual emancipation of their admired seniors was tolerated rather than imitated by the communist generation of the 1930s.

As was the most surprising characteristic of Needham, which distinguished him from the other prominent red scientists: his lifelong attachment to religion and its ceremonials. His High Anglicanism certainly did not get in the way of his political convictions in the 1930s. He worshipped in the wonderful church in Thaxted, which, since the living was in her gift, had been supplied with a revolutionary socialist priest, Conrad Noel, by a strongly socialist landowner who also doubled for a while as King Edward VII's mistress. In the course of time Needham modulated from the Anglicanism that he knew to be a local phenomenon ('because I happened to be born in the European West and Anglican Christianity was the typical form religion took for my time and race')[6] to a sort of Daoism, which he saw as both democratic and at the roots of science and technology in China. In any case he came to think that his views of religion had been 'certainly too neo-platonic, idealistic, pietistic and other-worldly'.[7] Nevertheless, though also an Honorary Associate of the Rationalist Press Association (the present Humanists) he never ceased to believe in religion as 'the distinctive sense of the holy, the appreciation of the category of the numinous [which] does not imply a creator God' and in 'its embodiment in corporate observance and rite'.[8] And he certainly did not believe it was in conflict with science, although he approved of Confucius's view that the existence of gods and spirits must be accepted, but kept at a distance. Nor was his form of religion distinct from politics. Communism, he thought in 1935, provided the moral theology appropriate to our time, but was opposed to scientism.

Stalin's communism definitely was not, but Needham never wavered in his rejection of scientism or reductionism in any form, including the Marxist. This was not only because it left out so much that was important in reality, but also because it also undermined science as he understood it. A passage from his 1932 review of Aldous Huxley's famous dystopia *Brave New World* in (of all places) F. R. Leavis's *Scrutiny* is worth quoting. He saw current intellectual tendencies (in his view Wittgenstein, the Vienna Circle and the – leftist – Lancelot Hogben) leading 'by reasonable extrapolation' towards the Huxleyan *Brave New World*, because they

urged that the concept of reality must be replaced by the concept of communicability. Now it is only in Science that perfect communicability is attainable. And, in other words, all that we can profitably say is, in the last resort, scientific propositions clarified by mathematical logic ... We are left with Science as the only substratum for Reason, but what is worse, Philosophy or Metaphysics too are relegated to the realm of the unspeakable, so that Science, which begins as a special form of philosophy, and which retains its intellectually beneficial status if it retains its status as a Philosophy, becomes nothing more than the Mythology accompanying a Technique.[9]

Needham's ambition as a researcher had long been to create a biochemical embryology that would meld the reductionism of the chemists with the inevitable concern of biologists for organisms and processes as a whole. An anti-mechanistic (he preferred the term 'organic') view of science had an obvious appeal for developmental biologists, such as the group brought together in the Theoretical Biology Club of the 1930s by the then influential but now largely forgotten J. H. Woodger, which included both the Needhams and C. H. Waddington (who was to be the specific target of von Hayek's attack on the Marxists in *The Road to Serfdom*). It pioneered the concept of living things organised in hierarchical levels, classically presented in Needham's *Order and Life* (1936). He posited that whole organisms could not be fully grasped at any one of the lower levels of increasing size and complexity – the molecular, macro-molecular, cell, tissue, etc. – and new modes of behaviour would emerge at each level, which could not be interpreted adequately either in terms of those below or even at all, except in their relations. As Needham wrote in his 1961 introduction to *The Chemistry of Life*: 'The hierarchy of relations from the molecular structure of carbon to the equilibrium of the species and the ecological whole, will perhaps be the leading idea of the future.' Process, hierarchy and interaction were the key to a reality that could be understood only as a complex whole.

And – though one would not discover this from the pages of

Simon Winchester – Needham's ideas drew him towards the country and the civilisation to which he devoted the rest of his life. China was, he wrote, the dialectical home of Yin and Yang, of an 'extreme disinclination to separate spirit and matter', of a philosophy that, it has been well said, saw the cosmos as a vast symphony that composed itself and within which other lesser symphonies took shape. He knew too much about Chinese reality to see it, in George Steiner's phrase, as a place where 'utopia was concrete', and still less to see himself, in the fashion of a twentieth-century Marco Polo, as a mere bringer of amazing news from foreign parts to a West that had allowed much of the eighteenth-century thinkers' intellectual respect for China to evaporate in the century of European world triumph.

Needham loved and admired China and the Chinese, but paradoxically his heart went out to the imperial past rather than to the revolutionary present, to which he was committed and which he defended, though he seems to have become a critic of Mao's policies in the 1970s, even before the death of the Great Helmsman. He felt at home not only with the Chinese view of nature, so lovingly reconstructed in *Science and Civilisation in China* but with a civilisation based on morality without supernaturalism, a great culture not based on the doctrine of original sin, a country where no priesthood ever dominated. It was admirable even in 'the ancient right of rebellion, so characteristic a doctrine of the Confucian scholars', enunciated by the scholars of the Chou dynasty. He saw in China not an 'Asiatic despotism' – a phrase that he thought had been invented by eighteenth-century French thinkers who compared it to European absolutism – but in terms of 'that democratic duality of life in traditional China which has been experienced by all those who have known Chinese society at first hand'.

Above all, he cherished the tradition of the old scholar-gentry, recruited by examination to form the cadres of government in medieval China, but which also collectively formed 'a public opinion' of Confucian scholars who 'never lost their independent ideological authority' and a capacity to resist imperial attacks on traditionally accepted values. What Western system could have found a place in its government for the equivalent of a William Blake, a Giordano Bruno, a Faraday? Characteristically this defence of the Chinese tradition – few are more heartfelt – appeared in an American Marxist journal in a lengthy critique of an ex-communist tome, *Asiatic Despotism*, which Needham correctly dismissed as a jumbo-sized Cold War pamphlet and 'the greatest disservice that has yet been done to the objective study of the history of China'.[10]

Wearing his newly acquired traditional scholar's gown in blue silk on his arduous travels through wartime China, Joseph Needham was obviously conscious of his affinity with its contemporary mandarins. And yet the crux of his world-view was precisely the irreversible historical break with the past that ended China's long era of technological superiority, which *Science and Civilisation in China* tried to explain, though not to everyone's satisfaction.

What happened after the rise of modern natural science *c*. AD 1600 could not resemble what had come before, with the result that 'both capitalist and socialist societies today are qualitatively different from all preceding societies'. There was no way back to the past, but there was a way forward. Needham never abandoned his belief in potential progress. Science and technology did not create the good society, but they could create the tools to bring it about, not least in China. 'This is perhaps the promised peace on earth, and whoever puts first the real needs of real people will inherit it.'[11]

All the same, Needham will not be remembered for his passionate longing for a better human future, nor even for his biology-inspired organic Marxism, but for his extraordinary achievement in exploring and re-creating a past. Nevertheless, he remains a neglected thinker, except in textbooks of developmental biology. Simon Winchester's *Bomb, Book and Compass* does not do him justice. He still awaits a biographer with a fuller understanding of a remarkable man and the times and contexts that made him.

16

The Intellectuals: Role, Function and Paradox

Could a social function for intellectuals – that is to say, could intellectuals – have existed before the invention of writing? Hardly. There has always been a social function for shamans, priests, magi or other servants and masters of rites, and we may assume also for those whom we would today call artists. But how could intellectuals have existed before the invention of a system of writing and numbers that needed to be manipulated, understood, interpreted, learned and preserved? However, once these modern instruments of communication, calculation and, above all, memory had arrived, the exiguous minorities who were masters of these skills probably exercised more social power for a time than intellectuals have enjoyed ever since. The masters of writing could, as in the early cities of the first agrarian economies in Mesopotamia, become the first 'clergy', a class of priestly rulers. Until well into the nineteenth

and twentieth centuries, the monopoly of literacy in the let-
tered world, and the education necessary for its mastery, also
implied a monopoly of power, safeguarded against competition
by education in specialised, ritually or culturally prestigious
written languages.

On the other hand, the pen was never mightier than the
sword. The warriors could always conquer the writers, but without the latter there could be neither polities, nor larger
economies, nor, even less so, the great historical empires of the
old world. The educated provided the ideologies of imperial
cohesion and the cadres of its administration. In China they
turned the Mongolian conquerors into imperial dynasties while
the empires of Genghis Khan and Tamerlane soon broke up for
lack of them. The first masters of the educational monopoly
were to be what Antonio Gramsci has called 'the "organic intellectuals" of all major systems of political domination'.

All this belongs to the past. The emergence of a class of
laymen literate in the regional vernaculars in the late Middle
Ages created the possibility of intellectuals who were less closely
determined by their social function, and appealing, as producers and consumers of literary and other communications, to a
new though small public sphere. The rise of the modern territorial state once again required a growing body of functionaries
and other 'organic' intellectuals. These were increasingly
trained in modernised universities and by the secondary-school
teachers who had graduated from them. On the other hand, the
rise of universal primary education and, above all, after the
Second World War the huge expansion of secondary and university education, together created a vastly greater reservoir of
the literate and intellectually educated than ever before.
Meanwhile, the extraordinary expansion of the new media
industries in the twentieth century massively expanded the economic scope for intellectuals unconnected with any official
apparatus.

Until the middle of the nineteenth century we are talking

about a very small group. The body of students who played so great a role in the 1848 revolutions consisted of four thousand young men (not, as yet, any women) in Prussia and seven thousand in the entire Habsburg Empire outside Hungary. The novelty of this new stratum of 'free intellectuals' did not lie simply in the fact that they shared the education and cultural knowledge of the ruling classes, which were themselves by now expected to have the literary and cultural formation the Germans call *Bildung*, a trend increasingly shared by the business classes, but also in the fact that they enjoyed a far greater possibility of earning a living as freelance intellectuals. New technical and scientific industries, and institutions for the production of science and culture, universities, the fields of journalism, publicity and advertising, stage and entertainment, all provided new methods of earning their living. Towards the end of the nineteenth century, capitalist enterprise had produced so much wealth that a number of the children and other dependants of the business middle classes could devote themselves entirely to intellectual and cultural activities. The families Mann, Wittgenstein and Warburg are cases in point.

If we accept the marginal group of the *Bohème*, free intellectuals had no recognised social identity. They would simply be regarded as members of the educated bourgeoisie (in J. M. Keynes's words, 'my class the educated bourgeoisie') or at best as a sub-group of the bourgeoisie as *Bildungsbürger* or *Akademiker*. Not until the last third of the nineteenth century are they described as a collective of 'intellectuals' or 'the intelligentsia': from 1860 on, in a turbulent tsarist Russia, then in a France shaken by the Dreyfus affair. In both cases what seemed to make them recognisable as a group was the combination of mental activities and critical interventions in politics. Even today current language often tends to associate the words 'intellectual' and 'in opposition' – which in the days of Soviet socialism meant 'politically unreliable' – not always correctly. However, the rise of a mass reading public and therefore the propagandist potential of the new media, provided unexpected possibilities of prominence for well-known intellectuals that even governments could utilise. Even after a century it is embarrassing to recall the miserable manifesto of the ninety-three German intellectuals, as well as those of their French and British peers, designed to reinforce the spiritual case for their respective belligerent governments in the First World War. What made these individuals such valuable signatories of such manifestos was not their expertise in public affairs, but their reputation as writers, actors, musicians, natural scientists and philosophers.

The 'short twentieth century' of revolutions and wars of ideological religion was to become the characteristic era of political engagement for intellectuals. Not only were they defending their own causes in the epoch of anti-Fascism and later of state socialism, but they were recognised on both sides as acknowledged public heavyweights of the mind. Their period of glory falls between the end of the Second World War and the collapse of communism. This was the great age of counter-mobilisations: against nuclear war, against the last imperial wars of old Europe and the first of the new American world empire (Algeria, Suez, Cuba, Vietnam), against Stalinism, against the Soviet invasion of Hungary and Czechoslovakia and so on. Intellectuals were on the front line of almost all of them.

One such example, the British campaign for nuclear disarmament, was founded by a well-known writer, the editor of the period's most prestigious intellectual weekly, a physicist and two journalists; it immediately elected the philosopher Bertrand Russell as its president. The eminent names in art and literature rushed to join, from Benjamin Britten to Henry Moore and E. M. Forster, among them the historian E. P. Thompson, who was to be the most prominent face in the European nuclear disarmament movement after 1980. Everyone knew the names of the great French intellectuals – Sartre, Camus – and those of the dissident intellectuals in the USSR: Solzhenitsyn and Sakharov. Prominent intellectuals were on the masthead of the influential literature of communist disillusion ('The God that Failed'). The secret services of the USA even found it worth their while to fund and found special organisations like the Congress for Cultural Freedom to win European intellectuals away from their unfortunate lack of enthusiasm for Cold War Washington. This was also the period when, for the first time since 1848, the universities of the Western world, now dramatically expanding and multiplying, could be regarded by their governments as nurseries of political and social opposition and, indeed, sometimes of revolution.

This age of the intellectual as the chief public face of political opposition has retreated into the past. Where are the great campaigners and signatories of manifestos? With a few rare exceptions, most notably the American Noam Chomsky, they are silent or dead. Where are the celebrated *maîtres à penser* of France, the successors of Sartre, Merleau-Ponty, Camus and Raymond Aron, of Foucault, Althusser, Derrida and Bourdieu? The ideologists of the late twentieth century preferred to abandon the task of pursuing reason and social change, leaving them to the automatic operations of a world of purely rational individuals, allegedly maximising their benefits through a rationally operating market that naturally tended, when free of outside interference, towards a lasting equilibrium. In a society of unceasing mass entertainment, the activists now found intellectuals to be less useful inspirers of good causes than world-famous rock musicians or film stars. The philosophers could no longer compete with Bono or Eno unless they reclassified themselves as that new figure in the new world of the universal media show, a 'celebrity'. We are living in a new era, at least until the universal noise of Facebook self-expression and the egalitarian ideals of the internet have had their full public effect.

The decline of the great protesting intellectuals is thus due not only to the end of the Cold War, but to the depoliticisation of Western citizens in a period of economic growth and the triumph of the consumer society. The road from the democratic ideal of the Athenian agora to the irresistible temptations of the shopping centre has shrunk the space available for the great demonic force of the nineteenth and twentieth centuries: namely, the belief that political action was the way to improve the world. Indeed, the object of neoliberal globalisation was precisely to reduce the size, scope and public interventions of the state. In this it was partly successful.

However, another element determined the shape of the new era. This was the crisis of traditional values and perspectives, perhaps, above all, the shedding of the old belief in the global progress of reason, science and the possibility of improving the human condition. Ever since the American and French Revolutions, the vocabulary of the eighteenth-century Enlightenment, with its firm confidence in the future of the ideologies rooted in these great upheavals, has disseminated to the champions of political and social progress all over the globe. A coalition of these ideologies and their patron states won perhaps its last triumph in the victory over Hitler in the Second World War. But since the 1970s the values of the Enlightenment are retreating, faced with the anti-universal powers of 'blood and soil' and the radical-reactionary tendencies developing in all world religions. Even in the West we see the rise of a new irrationality hostile to science, while the belief in an irresistible progress gives way to the fear of an inevitable environmental catastrophe.

And the intellectuals in this new era? Since the 1960s the enormous growth in higher education has transformed them into an influential class of political significance. Since 1968 it has been evident that students en masse are easily mobilisable, not only nationally but even across frontiers. Since then the unprecedented revolution in personal communications has greatly reinforced their capacity for public action. The election of the university teacher Barack Obama to the presidency of the USA, the Arab Spring of 2011 and developments in Russia are among recent examples. The explosive progress of science and technology has created an 'information society' in which production and the economy are more dependent than ever before on intellectual activity, that is to say, on men and women with university degrees and on the centres of their formation, the universities. This means that even the most reactionary and authoritarian regimes have to allow a certain degree of freedom to the sciences in universities. In the former USSR, academia provided the only effective forum for dissent and social criticism. Mao's China, which virtually abolished higher education during the Cultural Revolution, has learned the same lesson since. To some extent this has also benefited China's humanist and arts faculties, though these are economically and technologically less essential.

On the other hand, the huge growth in higher education tended to transform the degree or tertiary diploma into an essential qualification for middle-class and professional jobs, therefore turning graduates into members of the 'superior classes', at least in the eyes of the less educated mass of the population. It has been easy for demagogues to present the 'intellectuals' or the so-called 'liberal establishment' as a presumptuous and morally unsatisfactory elite, enjoying economic and cultural privileges. In many parts of the West, notably the United States and Britain, the educational gap is at risk of becoming a class division between those whose university certificates became surefire entry tickets to career prestige and success, and the resentful rest.

They were not the really rich, that tiny percentage of the population who succeeded in the last thirty years of the twentieth century and the first decade of the twenty-first, in acquiring wealth beyond the dreams of avarice: men and sometimes women whose individual assets were as large as the GDP of many medium-sized countries. Overwhelmingly their fortunes came from business and political power, although some of them were no doubt intellectuals by origin whether as graduates or, as in many striking cases in the USA, college drop-outs. Paradoxically the luxury they flaunted with increasing self-confidence after the fall of communism provided a kind of link with the uneducated masses, whose only chance of emerging from their condition was to join the few hundreds in any country who reached the top without letters or business gifts – football players, stars of media culture and winners of gigantic lottery prizes. Statistically a poor person's chance of following a similar trajectory was infinitesimal, but those who managed it really did have money and success to flaunt. In some ways that made it easier to mobilise the economically exploited, the failures and losers of capitalist society, against what American reactionaries called 'the liberal establishment', with whom they seemed to have virtually nothing in common.

It was only after some years of the most severe depression in the Western economy since the 1930s that resentment of economic polarisation began to displace resentment of imputed intellectual superiority. Curiously its two most visible expressions were formulated by intellectuals. The general collapse of confidence in the ability of the free market (the 'American dream') to produce a better future for all – indeed, the growing pessimism about the future of the existing economic system – was first brought into the open by economic journalists and, with the rarest exceptions, not by the super-rich themselves. The occupation of sites close to Wall Street and other centres of international banking and finance under the slogan 'We are the 99 per cent' as against the 1 per cent of the super-rich, clearly struck a notable chord of public sympathy. Even in the USA polls showed support of 61 per cent which must clearly have included a large body of anti-liberal Republicans. Of course these demonstrators, establishing their tented camps on enemy soil, were not the 99 per cent. They were, as so often, what has been called the stage army of intellectual activism, the mobilisable detachment of students and bohemians, conducting skirmishes in the hope they would turn into battles.

Nevertheless the question arises: how can the ancient, independent critical tradition of the nineteenth- and twentieth-century intellectuals survive in the new era of political irrationality, reinforced by its own doubts about the future? It is a paradox of our time that irrationality in politics and ideology have had no difficulty in coexisting with, indeed in using, advanced technology. The United States and the militant Israeli settlements within the occupied areas of Palestine demonstrate that there is no shortage of professional IT specialists with a belief in the literal story of creation in the book of Genesis or in the Old Testament's more bloodthirsty calls for the extirpation of the unbelievers. Mankind today has characteristically got used to lives of internal contradiction, torn between a world of feeling and a technology impervious to emotion, between the realm of human-scale experience and sense-knowledge and that of meaningless magnitudes, between the 'common sense' of everyday life and the incomprehensibility, except to exiguous minorities, of the intellectual operations that create the framework in which we live. Is it possible to make this systematic non-rationalism of human lives compatible with a world that depends more than ever on Max Weber's rationality in science and society? Admittedly the globalisation of the media of information, of language and of the internet no longer make it totally possible for even the most powerful state authority to isolate a country physically and mentally from the remainder of the world. Nevertheless the question remains.

On the other hand, while high technology can be used, though not further advanced, without original thinking, science needs ideas. Hence even the most systematically counter-intellectual society today has a greater need of people who have ideas, and of environments in which they can flourish. We may safely assume that these individuals will also have critical ideas about the society and the environment in which they live. In the emerging countries of East and South-East Asia and the Muslim world, they probably still constitute a force for political reform and social change in the old manner. It is also possible that they may in our times of crisis once again constitute such a force in a beleaguered and uncertain West. Indeed, it may be argued that at present the locus of the forces of systematic social criticism is to be found in the new strata of the university-educated. But thinking intellectuals alone are in no position to change the world even though no such change is possible without their contribution. That requires a united front of ordinary people and intellectuals. With the exception of a few isolated instances, this is probably harder to achieve today than in the past. That is the dilemma of the twenty-first century.

17

The Prospect of Public Religion

What has happened to religion in the past fifty years is striking. For most of recorded history it has provided the language, often the only language, for discourse about the relations of human beings to each other, to the wider world and to our dealings with the uncontrollable forces outside our everyday lives. Certainly this has been so for the masses, as evidently it still is in India and the Islamic region. Religion continues to provide the only generally accepted model for the celebration of the great rites of human life from birth through marriage to death and, certainly in temperate zones, the rites of the eternal cycles of the year – New Year and harvest, spring (Easter) and winter (Christmas). Rarely have they been effectively replaced by secular equivalents, possibly because the rationality of secular states, not to mention their hostility or indifference to religious institutions, led them to underestimate the sheer force of ritual in private and communal life. Yet few of us can escape that force. I recall a funeral service organised by an Oxford college on behalf of a systematically unbelieving Soviet lady for her passionately atheist British husband because, as she said, it didn't seem right to see him off without some ritual. Totally irrelevant as it was, the Anglican service, in a faith she neither knew nor cared about, was the only one available to her at that moment. Indeed, the most rationalist among us may use even the most primitive spells for propitiating the directors of our unknown future, the 'touch wood' or 'fingers crossed', which are the equivalent of the Christians' DV (God Willing) or the Muslims' Inshallah.

In the contemporary world religion remains important and, in spite of the new militancy of Anglo-Saxon atheists (which bears witness to its importance), also prominent. In one respect there can be no doubt about a dramatic revival in religion since the 1960s, in that it has plainly become a major *political* force, though not an intellectual one. The great Iranian revolution was the first since the American revolution of the eighteenth century to be conducted in terms of religion, abandoning the discourse of the Enlightenment, which had inspired the movements for social change as well as its great revolutions, from the French to the Russian and the Chinese. The politics of the Middle East, among Jews and Muslims alike, became the politics of holy books and, to a surprising extent, so did the politics of the USA. It is easy to point out that, far from being an ancient tradition, this pattern is a twentieth-century innovation. Orthodox Judaism, traditionally opposed to Zionism, was Zionised by the Six-Day War of 1967 as Israel's victory seemed miraculous, justifying some rabbis in abandoning the conviction that the return of all Jews to Israel should take place only after or upon the arrival of the Messiah, who up to that moment had patently not arrived, even though an aged head of an American Chassidic sect claimed that status for himself.

Not until the early 1970s did an extremist secession from Egypt's Muslim Brotherhood revive a theological justification for the killing 'as an apostate' of anyone outside a very narrow form of orthodoxy. The fatwa authorising the killing of innocents came in 1992 from within Al Qaeda. It has been shown that the Iranian revolution of 1979 introduced not a traditional

Islamic polity, but a theocratic version of the modern territorial state. Nevertheless, politics formulated in terms of religion has made an impressive return, from Mauretania to India. Turkey visibly moved away from a militantly secularist regime under the aegis of an Islamic mass political party. The foundation of a powerful Hinduist party in 1980 (in government 1998–2004) marks a movement to reduce the multiplicity of Hinduism to a single exclusive and intolerant orthodoxy. In current global politics no one is inclined to underestimate this trend.

Whether there has been a general global rise of religious faith and practice is less clear. There have been spectacular transfers from one branch to another, notably within Christianity. A growth of religious zeal in the rapidly expanding communities of evangelical and Pentecostal/charismatic Protestantism is evident in the Americas and elsewhere. So, since the 1970s, is a notable Islamic resurgence in previously fairly placid regions such as Indonesia.[1] I shall say something about these issues later. However, with the exception of Africa, where Christianity and Islam in particular made impressive advances in the last century, it cannot be claimed that the major world religions have gained much ground since 1900. Of course the overthrow of the Soviet Union and other institutionally atheist states has allowed suppressed religions to re-emerge – in Russia to be formally re-established – though probably, Poland may be an exception, not recovering their pre-communist level. And in Africa, the monotheistic faiths have gained ground not at the expense of secularism, but at the expense of the traditional animist religious beliefs, though the latter have sometimes morphed into syncretic combinations of the new monotheism with the old cults. Only in three African countries do indigenous and syncretic beliefs still represent the majority.[2] In the secularised West, attempts to construct new or to adopt strange and generally vague spiritual cults to replace the atrophy of the old faiths have had little success.

This unquestioned rise in the public presence of religion has been seen as disproving the long-held view that modernity and secularism were destined to advance in tandem. But this is not so. It is true that ideologists and activists, and indeed many historians, grossly underestimated the extent to which the thoughts of even the most secularised were emerging from the age when religion supplied the only language of public discourse. They overestimated too the quantitative impact of secularisation in the nineteenth and twentieth centuries, or, rather, they discounted the vast swathes of humanity – primarily women and the peasantry – who successfully resisted it. Essentially, nineteenth-century secularisation, like its political flip side, anticlericalism, was a movement of educated middle- and upper-class males and plebeian political activists. But how many historians paid adequate attention to gender, or for that matter to the movement's impact in the countryside? They also tended to overlook the disproportionate role of religion in the formation of the nineteenth-century entrepreneurial classes and capitalist networks: the pietist textile masters in France and Germany; the specifically Huguenot, Jewish or Quaker banks. They paid little heed to those for whom religion in an age of social upheaval became Marx's 'heart in a heartless world'. In short, nothing is easier than to present the history of the West in the nineteenth century as a series of religious advances. While this may be the case, it does not change the fact that modernisation and secularisation plainly went together in Europe and the Americas during the past two and a half centuries and there they continue to do so. This process may even have speeded up in the past half-century.

Conversions from one faith to another cannot conceal the continued decline of the obligations and the practice of religion in the West and also, if the acceptance of inter-caste marriages is an indication, in India. In fact, this trend has accelerated since the 1960s. This is most obvious in the largest of the Christian denominations, the Roman Catholic Church, which is consequently in a historically unprecedented major crisis. Unlike in the sixteenth century, the threat to this Church lies not

only in religious dissidence but in indifference or tacit disobedi-
ence, as in the massive turn of Italian women to birth control
since the 1970s. Catholic vocations began to collapse in the
middle 1960s, and with them the personnel of religious institutions. In the USA numbers dropped from 215,000 in 1965 to
75,000 in 2010.[3] In Catholic Ireland, the diocese of Dublin
could not find a single priest to ordain in 2005. In the current
Pope's own home town, the traditionally pious Regensburg, no
more than seventy-five people could be prevailed upon to turn
up to welcome him on his visit.

The situation of other traditional Western religions is similar.
Traditionally, collective identity in Wales, at least among Welsh
speakers, was asserted through various versions of puritan and
Temperance Protestantism. Yet the contemporary rise of a
political Welsh nationalism has emptied the chapels of the
Welsh countryside while political sociability has moved to secular locations. Indeed, there are signs of a curious reversal of
force. Traditional religion, which once reinforced or even
defined a sense of national cohesion among some people –
notably the Irish and the Poles – now relies for its strength on its
association with nationalism or an alleged ethnicity. This is
clearly visible in Orthodox Christianity, whose various branches
are distinguished from each other essentially by region or ethnicity.[4] In comparison with their fellow Americans, the 5.5
million US Jews are unusually secular. About half of them
describe themselves as secular, non-religious or associated with
some other faith. In any case, most of the religious ones belong
to more or less liberalised versions of the faith (72 per cent of
synagogue members in 2000) – Reform and even to some extent
Conservative Judaism – which are firmly rejected by rabbinical
orthodoxy.[5] For such a community, largely assimilated and
increasingly intermarried, the religious practice that had traditionally defined Jews and held them together could do so no
longer. An emotional identification with a (historically novel)
political fact, Israel, tended to replace religious practice and

endogamy as a criterion of 'being a Jew'. Even within the minority drawn to ultra-orthodoxy, this identification tended to supplement the complexities of ritual practice.

There can really be no serious doubt that the world of the American, French and Liberal revolutions and their offspring, that of the communist and ex-communist regimes, is in every sense more secular than it has ever been in the past, not least in the characteristic separation of a confessionally neutral public realm from the purely private one assigned to religion. But even outside the Western world, to quote a notable expert on Islam,

> politics apart, popular mentalities and styles of life were thoroughly secularised over the course of the 19th and 20th centuries. That is not to say that people lost their faith or piety (though this was much diluted for many), but that the confines of communal and local life, governed as they were by religious authority, ritual and the calendrical punctuation of time, were broken with mobility, individualisation and the rise of spheres of culture and entertainment unrelated to religion, and subversive of its authority.[6]

Moreover, the role of the traditional Western religious bodies continues to decline. In 2010, 45 per cent of Britons said they did not belong to any particular religion.[7] Between 1980 and 2007, the number of religious weddings dropped from just over half to one third of these ceremonies.[8] In Canada the combined rate of attendance at all religious services dropped by 20 per cent in a similar period.[9] Indeed, given the high value of a reputation for church attendance in the USA, even the supposed piety of that republic is largely a construct based on the fact that those answering polling questions on the subject systematically overestimate their own religious activities. It has been estimated that the weekly attendance at religious services in the USA may be more like 25 per cent or even as low as 21 per cent.[10] Moreover, certainly for American males, always the

less religious gender, it has been said that their 'religious involvement signals social establishment and security' rather than
spiritual urges.

It would be absurd to suppose that this continued and perhaps accelerating process of secularisation will lead to the
disappearance of religious worship and the rituals associated
with it, let alone that it will lead to mass conversions to atheism.
It means, above all, that the affairs of the world are and will be
increasingly conducted as though there were no gods or super-
natural interventions, irrespective of the private beliefs of those
who conduct them. As the great astronomer Laplace told
Napoleon, who wanted to know where God came into his science: 'I have no need of this hypothesis.' Who can tell a
structural engineer, nuclear physicist, neurosurgeon, fashion
designer or computer hacker brought up as a strict Muslim or
as a Pentecostal Christian from one brought up as a Scots
Calvinist or in Mao's China? The gods are irrelevant to their
work, unless belief in some religion imposes limitations on what
they are allowed to do or insists on propositions incompatible
with their activities. In that case either orthodoxy tacitly abandons its veto, as Stalin did with the physics needed to construct
nuclear arms – as in a dramatic scene in Vassili Grossman's *Life
and Fate* – or the domination of dogmatic religion leads to intellectual stagnation, as in Islam since the fourteenth century.

For two reasons this has come to raise greater problems in the
course of the past century than was once supposed. On the one
hand, there was an increasingly wide gap between the theory
and practice of the sciences on which the running of the
modern world depends, and the narratives and moral propositions of several leading religions, notably the Christian and
Muslim, especially in any field affecting human beings and
societies. On the other hand, the modern techno-scientific
world grew increasingly incomprehensible for the great majority of those who live in and by it, while the traditional systems

regulating morals and human relations, consecrated by religion, crumbled under the explosive transformations of their lives. The 40 per cent of Americans who believe that the earth is no older than ten thousand years clearly have no clue about the nature and physical history of our planet, but most of them are no more inconvenienced by this ignorance than supermarket checkout servers are by an ignorance of topology. For most of history, human societies have functioned with populations most of whom were relatively or absolutely ignorant and a good proportion not very bright. It is only in the twenty-first century that the bulk of humanity, being so constituted, is becoming surplus to the requirements of production and technology. Meanwhile as a large body of voters in democratic countries, or under rulers committed to fundamentalist dogmas, they raise major problems for science and the public interest, not to mention truth. What is more, the increasing exclusion of the insufficiently educated from the rewards offered by a meritocratic and entrepreneurial society has embittered the losers and mobilised them as 'know-nothings' against 'the liberal establishment' (their targets including knowledge as such), rather than, more logically, as the poor against the rich.

In some ways the confrontation between a marginalised religion and a science under attack from various quarters has become more acute since the 1970s than at any time since Andrew D. White's two-volume *A History of the Warfare between Science and Theology in Christendom* (1896). For the first time in many decades there is today a militant movement propagating atheism. Its most prominent activists are natural scientists. It is true that, intellectually, theology has virtually given up challenging science on its own ground, confining its arguments to devising theories that will make the accepted results of contemporary science somehow compatible with divinity. Even the believers in the literal truth of Genesis now cover their nakedness with the figleaf of a 'creation science'. What mobilises the believers in reason is not the absurdity of their opponents' arguments, but their newly demonstrated political force.

For in the past as well as once again increasingly in the present, the secularisation of global activities has been, overwhelmingly, the work of minorities, mainly of the educated – whether the literate in a world of illiterates, the secondary-school and university graduates in the nineteenth and twentieth centuries, or the doctorals and post-doctorals of the twenty-first century who have access to the real know-how of the information society. The traditional, popular, radical and labour movements, whose activists were largely self-educated, must also be regarded as a campaigning secular minority. The only exception, a genuine grass-roots movement of modernisation, is the drive for the physical and sexual emancipation of women from their historic constraints, insofar as it has been allowed to take place; and even this owes its official institutional recognition (divorce, birth control, etc.) to the work of secular activist minorities. In the nineteenth century these secularising minorities were disproportionately effective – because educated elites provided the cadres of the modern nation states; because labour and socialist movements were remarkably powerful mobilisers and organisers; and not least because the major forces resisting secularisation – women, peasants and a large sector of the unorganised 'labouring poor' – were largely excluded from politics. Outside the developed capitalist countries, their domination lasted until the late twentieth century. In short, it belonged to the era before the democratisation of politics.

Democratised politics inevitably gave greater, and increasingly decisive, weight to the masses in whose lives religion continued to play a far larger part than among the activist elites. Intelligent secular practitioners of the new democratic politics were well aware that they had to pay attention to religious feelings even within their own constituencies. Thus in 1944, after Mussolini's fall, the Italian Communist Party, emerging from long years of illegality, recognised that it could not hope to

become a major force in its native land, unless it allowed practising Catholics to join. A decision to lift the ban was taken,
breaking with the party's tradition of insisting on atheism. The
miraculously predictable periodic liquefaction of the blood of
San Gennaro, patron saint of Naples, took place even when that
city was under communist administration. Nationalist reforming
leaders in the Islamic world knew well enough that they had to
conciliate the traditional piety of their countrymen, but they did
not share it. The founder of Pakistan, the entirely secular M. A.
Jinnah, who mobilised Indian Muslims successfully for a separate state, envisaged a clearly secular, liberal-democratic
constitution in which all religions would be the private affair of
its inhabitants, but the state would not be involved in them.
Essentially this was also the position of his opposite number,
Jawaharlal Nehru, in India, which has so far remained a secular
state, and, for that matter, of the Founding Fathers of the USA.
For the benefit of a pious people, Jinnah embellished these pro-
posals with references to Islam (its democratic traditions, its
commitment to equality and social justice, etc.) but they were so
few and so unspecific that even enthusiastic Islamists have found
it impossible to claim him with any confidence as the champion
of the Islamic state to which a military ruler was later to commit
Pakistan.

Secular reforming leaders within the Euro-North American
colonies and dependencies might finesse their own lack of religious zeal with appeals to popular xenophobia, anti-imperialism
and the Western innovation of nationalism, which was then
seen as inclusive, cross-confessional and cross-ethnic. (Indeed,
the pioneers of Arab nationalism in the Middle East were more
likely to be Christians than Muslims.) On this basis the brief
British hegemony in the Middle East ('Britain's Moment') was
supplanted after the Second World War in Egypt, Sudan, Syria,
Iraq and Iran. But even in the rare cases when modernising
rulers had the political or military power to break the institutional power of majority religions, in practice they had to make

allowances for its continued hold on the masses. Even the root-and-branch moderniser Kemal Atatürk, who abolished the Khalifate, eventually disestablished Islam and changed his people's clothes, alphabet and, with less success, their attitude to women, did not attempt to eradicate their religious practice, though seeking to replace it by an all-Turkish nationalism. Control was in the hands of a militantly secular state elite, backed by an army dedicated to the values of its founder Atatürk and ready to intervene when these seemed to be threatened. The army has taken such action on several occasions – in 1970, 1980 and 1997 – and still feels bound to do so, even if the situation no longer gives its leaders a free hand.

The democratisation of politics brought into the open the conflict between mass popular religion and the secular rulers, nowhere more clearly than in Turkey, where Islamist groups and political parties favouring the establishment of an Islamic state grew active in the 1960s and 1970s, surviving attempts to outlaw them. Turkey is today governed by an elected Islamic government and a constitution allowing the popular election of an Islamic president, though not one committed to the full programme of a state ruled by Sharia rather than secular law. Since the overthrow of a firmly secular authoritarian government in Tunisia, a mass electoral Muslim party seems to envisage a similar solution.

Conflict has been, or is likely to be, equally or even more acute in most other states populated by a majority of Muslims. In Algeria, it led to a bloodthirsty civil war in the 1990s, won by the army and the modernising elites. In Iraq, foreign invasion defeated an authoritarian modernising regime and, under foreign occupation, produced a state divided between two competing Muslim fundamentalisms, Shia and Sunni, in which the surviving secular politicians seek room for manoeuvre for a barely existing national government. In Syria, a secular regime is at this moment in a state of increasingly confessional civil war that may destroy the country and would most probably benefit

Wahhabite Sunni fundamentalists. In Egypt, where the problem first arose with the emergence of the Muslim Brotherhood in 1928, Islamist movements have sometimes been banned or permitted a marginal de facto existence, but they have always been excluded from the making of political decisions. They now form the largest body of deputies in the democratic elections that followed the overthrow of the authoritarian regime.

Democratisation was never likely to bring such upsurges of politicised mass religion in the secularised developed West and the communist regions. Even in the nineteenth century, the Church in the numerous mono-confessional Roman Catholic countries of southern Europe and Latin America was a force of opposition, not of potential, let alone actual, power, keeping at bay the advance of liberalism and reason. Its embattled forces mobilised to protect the control of education, morality and the great rituals of life as part of a pluri-party political system, though not a democratic one. In pluri-religious countries, the Catholic Church was inevitably integrated into a political system that left room for trading votes for concessions. This is as evident in India as it has been in Germany and the USA. The crisis in Roman Catholicism since the 1960s has severely reduced the political potential of mass Catholicism. The politics of the era when the Church no longer embodies national resistance is not the politics of religious parties, though, as in Italy and perhaps Poland and Croatia, the hostility of Catholicism towards the political left remains very influential. I can only speculate about the potential impact of democratisation on countries populated by Buddhists. In the sole Buddhist constitutional monarchy, Thailand, Buddhism does not seem to play any detectable role in politics.

Nevertheless, the major cause for alarm about the rise of politicised religion is not the emergence of a mass religious electorate in a world of effective universal suffrage. It is the rise of radical but predominantly right-wing ideologies within religion: notably

Protestant Christianity and traditionalist Islam. Both are missionary and radical, even potentially revolutionary, in the traditional 'fundamentalist' mode of the 'religions of the book', namely by a return to the simple text of their scriptures, thus purifying the faith from its accumulated accretions and corruptions. Their future appears as a reconstructed past. In Europe we have the precedent within Christianity of the sixteenth-century Reformation. Within Islam we have the repeated cycle out of which Ibn Khaldun formulated a theory of historic development: Bedouin fighters with the austere monotheism of the desert periodically conquer the rich, cultured and decadent cities before being in turn corrupted by them. Another technique of public religious radicalism, secession from the main body of the faith, culminating in the setting-up of separate godly communities, also plays some part in the current Christian versions of religious radicalisation, but seems to be of scant importance in the Islamic ones.

The Islamic radical revival is complicated by several political factors, notably the presence on its territory of Mecca and its pilgrimages, which have made the Saudi Arabian monarchy in effect the focus of global Islam, a sort of Muslim Rome. Historically this monarchy has long been identified with the Bedouin puritanism of the Wahhabi version of Islam, which today provides what is now a far from austere desert regime with the religious bona fides that maintain its political stability. Its immense oil wealth has been used to finance the vast expansion of the Mecca pilgrimages and the mosques as well as religious schools and colleges all over the world, logically enough, for the benefit of the intransigent Wahhabite (Salafite) fundamentalism that looks back to the founding generations of Islam. To an unknown extent the USA's Cold War backing of the Muslim anti-communist fighters in the USSR's Afghan War probably also helped to establish the most effective of the new global jihadi organisations, Osama Bin Laden's Al Qaeda. Its popular basis is impossible to assess, but a useful and visible sign of the rise of fundamentalist Islam is the growing and, in the new century, probably increasing tendency of women to wear the all-covering black garments of this orthodoxy. And not always by domestic compulsion. This is very noticeable in the students in the great Indian Muslim university of Aligarh, as it is in some British universities, as well as on the streets of British and, until officially banned, French cities with large Muslim populations. Nevertheless, with or without an independent popular basis, the new Islamic fundamentalism can be regarded as a modernising movement of reform in the face of the communally or tribally based religious practices of traditional grass-roots Islam with its folkloric local cults, saints, holy leaders and Sufi mysteries. However, unlike the Protestant Reformations of the sixteenth century, it lacked the powerful frame of vernacular translations of the holy book. Islamic fundamentalism remained anchored to the Arabic language of the Koran (which raised problems with the Berber populations of the Maghreb) as well as to the ecumenism of the global Islamic *umma*. In terms of modern political discourse, Islamic fundamentalism is plainly reactionary.

In this respect it is profoundly unlike the explosion of fundamentalist evangelicalism or, rather, charismatic and Pentecostal Protestantism, which is probably the most dramatic form of religious transformation today. Like Islam, this movement has widened or even created a cultural gap in countries of the older industrial revolution in Europe (though not the less secular USA), as well as those of South-East and East Asia and the regions of Africa, Latin America and west-central Asia.

Its most spectacular growth has taken place in large parts of Latin America and across most of Africa, where Protestant charismatics are now more numerous and dynamic than the Catholics. On the other hand, its impact in the Islamic world has been negligible and, in the rest of Asia, insignificant (except in the Philippines and perhaps South Korea and post-Maoist China). It has benefited from no significant political patronage, except possibly from occasional ventures of the CIA type to mobilise it in central America against communism. However, the largely North American missionaries who pioneered its expansion, brought with them much of the economic and political assumptions of the USA. While they are patently and militantly moved by the conviction that the word of God and the values of fundamentalist biblical texts must be shared by the world as a whole, charismatics, especially in Pentecostalism, should be seen essentially as a separatist and sectarian rather than a universalist phenomenon.

Evangelicalism is at bottom an ensemble of autonomous congregations. It is, or began chiefly as, a grass-roots movement of the poor, oppressed, marginal or socially disoriented, and its main constituents are women, who also occupy positions of leadership,[11] as is sometimes the case in radical Christian sects. Its rooted hostility to the liberalising of sexual relations (divorce, abortion and homosexuality, as well as the use of alcohol) may surprise contemporary feminists, but should be seen as a defence of traditional stability against uncontrollable and unsettling change. Nevertheless, in terms of contemporary public discourse, evangelicalism gives the charismatic movement a conservative tilt. So does its propagation of the values of personal enterprise and economic advancement, which is reinforced by the conviction that the born-again Christian is destined to succeed. This seems to have greatly impressed the Chinese authorities, who have consequently found Pentecostalists economically acceptable. An unnamed Chinese minister is even reported as saying that the economy would be even more dynamic if all Chinese were evangelicals (*si non è vero, è ben trovato*).

Yet these are not movements centrally concerned with the politics of their societies, but with the creation or re-creation of communities on the basis of the collective recognition of 'rebirth' by powerful, individual spiritual experiences and emotionally satisfying, often ecstatic, rituals. Healing and protection against evil are essential to them. A study of Pentecostals in ten countries showed that 77–79 per cent in Latin America and up to 87 per cent in Africa have witnessed divine healings, while 80 per cent in Brazil and 86 per cent in Kenya have experienced or witnessed exorcism.[12] 'Speaking in tongues', a sign of direct divine inspiration, is practised by only a minority, but generally approved. Such communities seek to contract out of rather than to transform an essentially unsatisfactory society, though, being a large and spectacularly expanding body of citizens, they become important elements in the politics of their countries. However, unlike in the nineteenth century, when the Mormons showed that an actual exodus was feasible, at least in the huge open spaces of the Americas, charismatic Protestantism today seeks to convert their countries. The desire to leave the wider society and found self-contained communities outside it is exceptional.

Evangelicalism has less of a built-in bias to political conservatism than the current politics of the US bible belt would suggest. Its cultural conservatism can be combined with a wide variety of attitudes to politics. In the USA, the bible belt of backwood whites – let alone African-Americans and Latinos – was once aligned with social radicalism, even in pre-1914 Oklahoma with socialism.[13] William Jennings Bryan, whose oratory had mobilised people in the prairies and mountains in the largest rural movement of the late nineteenth century against those who wanted 'to crucify mankind on a cross of gold', also defended the literal truth of Genesis against the theory of evolution in the famous 'Monkey trial' of 1925. Elsewhere the politics of charismatic and Pentecostalist Protestantism range from a marked passivity in apartheid South Africa to the passionate communism of the Lota mining communities in pre-Pinochet Chile; from the massacre of guerrillas in Guatemala by Pentecostal generals to the leftist sympathies of Brazilian 'Evangelicals', who may by now represent some 20 per cent of their population, with or without the admixture of numerous other cults for propitiating the next world. In Africa we find Mr Chiluba, elected President of Zambia in 1991, dedicating his country to the Lordship of Jesus Christ, a process initiated by a team of Pentecostal ministers cleansing the presidential palace of evil spirits. The politics of the African combinations of Pentecostalism with old beliefs are too complex to fit into Western categories.

The term 'charismatic' Protestantism was coined in 1962 by a clergyman in the USA. This is not accidental. It was in the 1960s that movements of this kind, notably the Pentecostals, began their great expansion. (They had existed since the mid-1900s, without any very striking effect, though in Italy their few congregations were held in great respect in the countryside during the aftermath of the Second World War. This was also the case during the great peasant unrest, possibly because of their superior literacy, but more probably because they were against the Catholic Church. That some rural branches of the Communist Party proposed Seventh Day Adventists or Pentecostals as branch secretaries puzzled its national leaders, who did what they could to discourage this tendency.) The 1960s, more precisely from 1965 onwards, was also the decade when the decline in vocations for the Catholic priesthood became evident, and attendance at mass fell from 80 per cent to 20 per cent in that traditional stronghold of Catholicism, Quebec in French Canada.[14] Indeed, 1965 was the year in which the French fashion industry for the first time produced more trousers than skirts. It was also the era of mass decolonisation, notably in Africa. In short, it was the time when a visible decline in old certainties provided a strong incentive to look for new ones. Charismatic evangelicalism claimed to have found them.

In what was then called the 'Third World', unprecedented social change, especially massive migration from country to city, provided suitable conditions for such conversions. Most of the Latino Pentecostals in the USA seem to have converted only after their arrival in the country.[15] In some countries, war and the pervasive violence of the immigrants' new environment, often shanty towns (such as the favelas of Brazilian cities) gave them a powerful impetus. Thus among the Igbo in Nigeria, Pentecostalism took off during the appalling Biafran civil war of 1967–70,[16] and in Peru, the insurrection of the Shining Path Maoists and its brutal suppression led to a wave of conversions among the Quechua Indians in the stricken areas. This process has been superbly described and analysed by an anthropologist with local connections.[17]

In short, as many of the old ways were battered by the hurricanes bringing dramatic economic transformation and crisis to the later twentieth and early twenty-first centuries, the need to recover lost certainties became more urgent. Globalisation dismantled all lesser boundaries and the secular theology created a void, a worldwide aggregate of purely individual agents maximising their benefits in a free market (as in Mrs Thatcher's 'there is no such thing as society'). What was our place in this social darkness, too vast for the nineteenth-century sociologists' concepts of 'community' or 'society', let alone for institutions consisting of people as distinct from statistical groups? Where did we belong, on a human scale and in real time and real space? Whom or what did we belong to? Who were we? It is characteristic that sometime from the 1960s onwards the phrase 'identity crisis', originally coined by a psychologist to encapsulate the uncertainties of teenage development in North America, broadened into the general assertion, even the invention, of a group identity in a universe of shifting human relations. To be more exact, the demand was for a primary identity among the plethora of ways in which we can all describe ourselves, ideally one that included and subsumed all of them under a single heading. Personal religious rebirth was a way of answering these questions.

It should by now be clear that the rise of politics based on religious radicalism and the actual revival of personal religion were both phenomena of the late twentieth and early twenty-first centuries. Few would have paid attention to them before 1960, but few could have overlooked them in the 1970s. They are plainly the progeny of the spectacular transformation of the world economy in that decade, which continues to accelerate.[18] They have penetrated deeply into the politics of large parts of the globe, notably the Islamic world, Africa, South and South-East Asia, and the USA. In those regions, and possibly elsewhere, their aggressive assertion of values that they present as traditional morality, family and gender relations in the face of what they call 'liberalism' or 'Western corruption' now plays a prominent role in public discourse. As usual, some of their traditions are invented (for example, the Islamic fundamentalists' homophobia in a region where sex between men has been traditionally widespread and quietly tolerated, or the limitation of births in some Christian peasant societies). They have been hostile to, or at least sceptical of, learning that is critical of sacred texts and scientific research that undermines them. However, on balance they have been less successful in their endeavours, except in slowing down the emancipation of women with the aid of theocratic state power or tradition.

For it is the paradox of revived religious fundamentalism that it sprang from a world where human existence rests on techno-scientific foundations that are incompatible with it, but remain indispensable even to the pious. If contemporary fundamentalists followed the logic of their Anabaptist ancestors, they should forgo any technological innovation produced since their foundation, like the Pennsylvania Amish with their horses and buggies. But the new Pentecostal converts do not shy away from the world of Google and the iPhone: they flourish in it. The literal truth of Genesis is propagated on the internet. The theocratic authorities in Iran base their country's future on nuclear power, while their nuclear scientists are assassinated with the most sophisticated technology, wielded from war-rooms in Nebraska, very likely by born-again Christians. Who can tell on what terms reason and revived anti-reason will coexist in the ongoing earthquakes and tsunamis of the twenty-first century?

18

Art and Revolution

There is no necessary or logical connection between Europe's artistic and cultural avant-gardes – the term came into use around 1880 – and the nineteenth- and twentieth-century parties of the extreme left, though both regarded themselves as representatives of 'progress' and 'modernity', and both were transnational in their range and ambitions. In the 1880s and 1890s, the new (generally Marxist) social democrats and the radical left were sympathetic to the avant-garde art movements: naturalist, symbolist, arts and crafts, even post-Impressionist. In return, these artists were drawn into social and even political statements by their sympathy with factions devoted to the poor and oppressed. This was also true of established artists like Sir Hubert Herkomer (*On Strike,*1890) or, as in the new exhibition, Ilya Repin (*24th October 1905*). In Russia, the artists of the 'world of art' group probably represent a similar phase of the avant-garde before Diaghilev's move to the West. The years 1905–7 demonstrated the political commitment of the eminent portraitist Serov.

In the decade before 1914, the rise of new and radically subversive avant-gardes in Paris, Munich and the Habsburg capitals
divided the political and the artistic branches of modernity and
revolution. A little later, this group was joined by a uniquely
large component of women artists in Russia, who were well
represented in the new exhibition.

Under varying and overlapping labels – Cubist, Futurist,
Cubo-futurist, Suprematist, etc. – these radical innovators, subversive in their views on art, or cosmic and (in Russia) mystical
in their aspirations, took no interest in the politics of the left and
had few contacts with them. After 1910, even the young
Bolshevik poet and playwright Vladimir Mayakovsky dropped
out of politics for a while. If avant-garde artists before 1914
read any thinker, it was not Marx but the philosopher Nietzsche,
whose political implications favoured elites and 'superman'
rather than the masses. Only one of the artists appointed to
responsible posts by the new Soviet government in 1917 seems
to have been a member of any socialist party: the Bundist David
Shterenberg (1881–1938).

On the other hand, the socialists distrusted the incomprehensible innovations of the new avant-gardes, being committed
to bringing the arts – by which they generally understood the
high culture of the educated bourgeoisie – to the labouring
masses. At most they contained one or two leading figures, such
as the Bolshevik journalist Anatoly Lunacharsky, who, while
unconvinced themselves, were sufficiently sensitive to the intellectual and artistic currents of the time to recognise that even
apolitical or antipolitical artistic revolutionaries might have
some bearing on the future.

In 1917–22, the central and east European avant-gardes,
which were to form a close cross-border web, converted en
masse to the revolutionary left. Perhaps this was more surprising
in Germany than in Russia, a *Titanic* on which people were
conscious of waiting for the iceberg of revolution. Unlike in
Germany and the Habsburg lands, revulsion against the Great

War does not seem to have been a major element in Russia. Two icons of the avant-garde, the poet Vladimir Mayakovsky and the painter Kasimir Malevich, had actually produced popular patriotic broadsheets in 1914. It was the revolution itself that inspired and politicised them, as it would in Germany and Hungary. It also gave them an international visibility, which until the 1930s made Russia the centre of modernism.

The revolution put the new Russian avant-gardes in a unique position of power and influence under the benevolent supervision of the new Commissar for Enlightenment, Anatoly Lunacharsky. Their reach was limited solely by the regime's insistence on maintaining the heritage and institutions of high culture, which most of them, notably the Futurists had wanted to raze. (In 1921 the Bolshoi only just escaped closure.) Few other artists were committed to the Soviets. ('Are there no reliable Anti-Futurists?' asked Lenin.) Chagall, Malevich and Lissitzky headed art schools, the architect Vladimir Tatlin and the theatre director Vsevolod Meyerhold ministerial arts departments. The past was dead. Art and society could be made anew. Everything seemed possible. The dream of life and art, creator and public, as no longer separate or separable but unified by revolutionising both, might now be realised every day on the street, in city squares, by men and women who were themselves creators, as was to be demonstrated in Soviet films, with their (early) suspicion of professional actors. The avant-garde writer and critic Osip Brik encapsulated this when he wrote, 'Every man should be an artist. Everything can become fine art.'

The 'Futurists', a blanket term, and those later called Constructivists (Tatlin, Rodchenko, Popova, Stepanova, Lissitzky, Naum Gabo, Pevsner) pursued this aim most consistently. It is chiefly through this group, also influential in film (Dziga Vertov and Eisenstein), theatre (Meyerhold), and via Tatlin's architectural ideas, that the Russian avant-garde made its extraordinary impact on the rest of the world. It was the leading partner in the closely intertwined Russo-German movements that were to remain the major international influences on the modern arts between 1917 and the Cold War.

The legacy of these radical views still forms part of the basic know-how of everyone concerned with film editing, layout, photography and design. And it is almost impossible not to be excited by their triumphs: Tatlin's projected Monument to the Communist International, Lissitzky's 'Red Wedge', Rodchenko's montages and photographs, or Eisenstein's *Battleship Potemkin*.

Little survived of their work in the first years after the revolution. There was no building. As a pragmatist, Lenin recognised the propagandist potential of films, but the blockade kept practically all film stock out of Soviet-Russian territory during the civil war, although the students at the new State Film Institute in Moscow (established in 1919) under Lev Kuleshov honed their skills at the new art of montage by cutting and recutting the content of surviving cans. An early decree in March 1918 ordered the dismantling of the monuments of the old regime and their replacement by statues of inspirational revolutionary and progressive figures from all parts of the world for the benefit of an illiterate people. Some forty went up in Moscow and Petrograd, but since they were quickly built, mostly in plaster, few have lasted. Perhaps this is fortunate.

The avant-garde itself plunged with gusto into street art, painting slogans and images on walls and squares, railway stations 'and the ever-speeding trains', as well as providing artwork for revolutionary celebrations. These were temporary by their very nature, though one organised in Vitebsk by Marc Chagall was deemed insufficiently political; and Lenin protested against another, which coloured the trees outside the Kremlin with blue paint that was difficult to remove. They have left little behind except a few photos and stunning designs for portable orators' platforms, kiosks, ceremonial installations and the like, including a picture of Tatlin's famous Comintern tower. During the civil war probably the only fully realised creative visual projects were in theatre, which continued throughout, but stage performance is itself evanescent, even if stage designs occasionally survived.

After the civil war ended the market-friendly New Economic Policy of 1921–8 gave much more scope for the new artists to realise their plans, and moved the avant-garde from a utopian outlook to one that was more practically oriented, though at the cost of growing fragmentation. The Communist Party ultras insisting on a wholly working-class *Proletkult* attacked the avant-garde. Within it, the champions of a spiritually pure and totally revolutionary art, like Naum Gabo and Antoine Pevsner, denounced the 'Productivists' who wanted an art applied to industrial production and an end to easel painting. This led to further personal and professional conflicts such as those that ousted Chagall and Kandinsky from the Vitebsk school for the benefit of Malevich.

Links between Soviet Russia and the West – mostly via Germany – multiplied, and for some years several avant-garde artists moved easily to and fro across Europe's frontiers. Some (Kandinsky, Chagall, Julius Exter) were to remain in the West with the pre-revolutionary exiles gathered around Diaghilev, like Goncharova and Larionov. On the whole, the major lasting creative achievements of the Russian avant-garde occurred in the mid-1920s, notably the first triumphs of the new Russian 'montage' cinema, Dziga Vertov's *Kino-Eye* and Eisenstein's *Battleship Potemkin*, Rodchenko's portrait photographs and some of the (unrealised) architectural designs.

Until the late 1920s there was no serious attack on the avant-garde, although the Soviet Communist Party disapproved of it, among other reasons because its appeal to 'the masses' was indisputably negligible. It was protected not only by the open-minded Lunacharsky, who stayed in his ministry from 1917 to 1929, and by cultured Bolshevik leaders like Trotsky and Bukharin, but also by the need of the new Soviet regime to placate the indispensable 'bourgeois specialists', the educated but largely unconverted intelligentsia, who also made up the core public for the arts, including the avant-garde arts. Between 1929 and 1935, Stalin, while maintaining their relatively favoured material conditions, forced them to accept total submission to power. This ruthless cultural revolution meant the end of the 1917 avant-garde; socialist realism became mandatory. Shterenberg and Malevich fell silent; Tatlin, banned from exhibition, retreated to the theatre; Lissitzky and Rodchenko found a haven in the photo-journal *USSR in Construction*; Dziga Vertov ended up as little more than a newsreel editor. Unlike most of the Bolsheviks of 1917 who had given them their chance, most of the visual avant-garde survived Stalin's terror, but their work, buried in Russian museums and private collections, seemed forgotten.

And yet today we all still live in a visual world that was largely devised by them in the ten years after the revolution.

19

Art and Power

Art has been used to reinforce the power of political rulers and states since the ancient Egyptians, though the relationship between power and art has not always been smooth. The present exhibition illustrates probably the least happy episode in the twentieth century, in what has been called the 'Europe of the Dictators', between 1930 and 1945.

For a century before the First World War it had been confidently assumed that Europe was moving in the direction of political liberalism, civil rights and constitutional government by elected authorities, though not necessarily republics. Shortly before 1914 even democracy – government by the vote of all adult males, though not yet of females – was making rapid progress. The Great War seemed to accelerate this development dramatically. After it ended Europe consisted of parliamentary regimes of one kind or another, except for war-torn and revolutionary Soviet Russia. However, almost immediately, the direction of political development was reversed. Europe, and indeed most parts of the globe, moved away from political liberalism. By the middle of the Second World War no more than twelve out of the sixty-five sovereign states of the inter-war period had anything like constitutional elected governments. The regimes of the political right, which took over everywhere except in Russia, were hostile to democracy in principle. Communism, still confined to Russia, claimed to be democratic in theory and nomenclature, but was in practice an unlimited dictatorship.

Most of the regimes with which this exhibition is concerned consciously and deliberately broke with the immediate past. Whether this radical break was made from the political right or left – outside Europe, as in Kemal Atatürk's Turkey, these labels were sometimes beside the point – is less important than that such regimes saw their role, not as maintaining or restoring or even improving their society but as transforming and reconstructing it. They were not landlords of old buildings but architects of new ones. Equally to the point, they were ruled, or came to be ruled, by absolute leaders whose command was law. Moreover, although these were the opposite of democratic, they all claimed to derive from and operate through 'the people' and to lead and shape them. These common characteristics distinguished both Fascist and communist regimes in this period from the older states, in spite of their fundamental differences and mutual hostility. In them, power not only made enormous demands on art, but art found it difficult or even impossible to escape the demands and controls of political authority. Not surprisingly, an exhibition on art and power in this period is dominated by the arts in Hitler's Germany (1933–45), Stalin's USSR (*c.*1930–53) and Mussolini's Italy (1922–45).

However, it cannot overlook the public arts of the states whose governments were being subverted. Appropriately, therefore, this exhibition begins with the one occasion when all states and their arts were in public confrontation: the Paris International Exhibition of 1937, the last before the Second

World War of a series of such displays that began in London in 1851. They had been perhaps the most characteristic form in which art and power collaborated during the era of bourgeois liberalism. While providing prestige for the countries that organised them, rather as the Olympic Games do today, what they had celebrated was not the state but civil society, not political power but economic, technical and cultural achievement, not conflict but the coexistence of nations. Descended from fairs (the American ones were even called 'World Fairs'), they were not designed as permanent structures, though they left some monuments behind, notably the Eiffel Tower.

Small 'national' pavilions had first appeared in 1867, but became increasingly prominent in what developed into public competitions between states. In 1937 they dominated the exhibition totally. The thirty-eight rival displays – more than in any previous exhibition – represented a higher proportion of the world's sovereign states than ever before or since. All, or almost all, made political statements, if only by advertising the virtues of their 'way of life' and arts. The show itself was designed to bring glory to France, then governed by a Popular Front of the left under its first socialist prime minister, and its most permanent memorial is probably Picasso's *Guernica*, first shown in the pavilion of the embattled Spanish Republic. Yet the 1937 Exhibition was clearly then, and is still in retrospect, dominated by the German and Soviet pavilions, huge and deliberately symbolic, which confronted each other across the mall.

There are three primary demands that power usually makes on art, and which absolute power makes on a larger scale than more limited authorities. The first is to demonstrate the glory and triumph of power itself, as in the great arches and columns celebrating victories in war ever since the Roman Empire, the major model for Western public art. Rather than by single constructions, the dimensions and ambitions of power in the age of the great leaders were to be demonstrated by the sheer scale of the structures they planned or realised and, typically, not so much by single buildings and monuments as by giant ensembles – replanned cities or even regions – for example, the motorways pioneered in an Italy with few cars. These could best express the planned reshaping of countries and societies. Pomp and gigantism were the face of power they wished the arts to present.

The second major function of art under power was to organise it as public drama. Ritual and ceremony are essential to the political process, and with the democratisation of politics, power increasingly became public theatre, with the people as audience and – this was the specific innovation of the era of dictators – as organised participants. The construction of wide rectilinear processional avenues for secular political display belongs essentially to the nineteenth century. The Mall in London (1911), with its vista from the Admiralty Arch to Buckingham Palace, is a characteristic late example. Increasingly, national monuments, built to stimulate or provide expression for mass patriotism, also included planned spaces for special ceremonies. The Piazza Venezia in Rome was as essential to the awful Vittorio Emanuele monument as it was, later, to Mussolini's harangues. The rise of public mass entertainment, and above all mass sport, provided an additional supply of public terrains and structures custom-built for the expression of mass emotion, notably stadiums. These could be and were used for the purposes of power. Hitler both spoke at the Berlin Sportpalast and also discovered the political potential of the Olympic Games of 1936.

The importance of art for power in this field lay not so much in the buildings and spaces themselves, but in what took place inside or between them. What power required was performance art in the enclosed spaces, elaborate ceremonies (the British became particularly adept at inventing royal rituals of this kind from the late nineteenth century onwards); and, in the open spaces, processions or mass choreography. The leaders' theatre

of power, combining military and civilian components, preferred open spaces. The contribution to crowd choreography of
labour demonstrations, stage spectacles and the new cinema
epics pioneered before 1914 by the young Italian cinema
remains to be adequately investigated.

A third service that art could render power was educational
or propagandist: it could teach, inform and inculcate the state's
value system. Before the era of popular participation in politics,
these functions had been left mainly to churches and other religious bodies, but in the nineteenth century they were
increasingly undertaken by secular governments, most obviously through public elementary education. The dictatorships
did not innovate in this field, except by banning dissident voices
and making state orthodoxy compulsory.

However, one traditional form of political art requires some
comment, if only because it was rapidly on the way to extinc-
tion: monumental public statuary. Before the French Revolution,
it had been confined to princes and allegorical figures; in the
nineteenth century, however, it became a sort of open-air
museum of national history as seen through great men. (Unless
they were royal or symbolic, women were absent.) Its educational value was patent. Not for nothing did the arts in
nineteenth-century France come under the Ministry of Public
Instruction. Thus, in order to educate a largely illiterate people
after the 1917 revolution, Lenin proposed to put up monuments
to suitable persons – Danton, Garibaldi, Marx, Engels, Herzen,
assorted poets and others – in conspicuous spots in cities, especially where soldiers could see them.

What has been called 'statuemania' reached its peak
between 1870 and 1914, when 150 statues were erected in
Paris, as against only twenty-six from 1815 to 1870 – and those
primarily military figures, which had almost all been removed
after 1870. (Under the German occupation in 1940–4 a further
seventy-five of these glories of culture, progress and republican
identity were removed by the Vichy government.) Yet after the

Great War, with the exception of the now universal war memorials, bronze and marble statuary went distinctly out of fashion. The elaborate visual language of symbolism and allegory became as incomprehensible in the twentieth century as the classical myths had become for most people. In France the Paris municipal council of 1937 feared that 'the tyranny of commemorative statuary rests like a heavy weight in projects that might be proposed by gifted artists and administrators with good taste.' Only the USSR, true to Lenin's example, maintained its unqualified attachment to public statuary, including giant symbolic monuments surrounded by workers, peasants, soldiers and arms.

Power clearly needed art. But what kind of art? The major problem arose out of the 'modernist' revolution in the arts in the last years before the Great War, which produced styles and works designed to be unacceptable to anyone whose tastes were, like most people's, rooted in the nineteenth century. They were therefore unacceptable to conservative and even to conventional liberal governments. One might have expected regimes dedicated to breaking with the past and hailing the future to be more at ease with the avant-garde. However, there were two difficulties, which were to prove insurmountable.

The first was that the avant-garde in the arts was not necessarily marching in the same direction as the political radicals of right or left. The Soviet revolution and general revulsion against the war may have attracted many to the radical left, although in literature some of the most talented writers can only be described as men of the extreme right. The German Nazis were not entirely wrong to describe the modernism of the Weimar Republic as 'cultural Bolshevism'. National Socialism was therefore a priori hostile to the avant-garde. In Russia, most of the pre-1917 avant-garde had been non-political or doubtful about the October Revolution, which, unlike the 1905 Revolution, made no great appeal to Russian intellectuals. However, thanks to a sympathetic minister, Anatoly Lunacharsky, the avant-garde was given its head, so long as artists were not actively hostile to the revolution, and it dominated the scene for several years, although several of its less politically committed stars gradually drifted westwards. The 1920s in Soviet Russia were desperately poor, but culturally vibrant. Under Stalin this changed dramatically.

The only dictatorship relatively at ease with modernism was Mussolini's (one of whose mistresses saw herself as a patroness of contemporary art). Important branches of the local avant-garde (for example the Futurists) actually favoured Fascism, while most Italian intellectuals not already strongly committed to the left did not find it unacceptable, at least until the Spanish Civil War and Mussolini's adoption of Hitler's racism. It is true that the Italian avant-garde, like most of the Italian arts at that time, formed a somewhat provincial backwater. Even so, it can hardly be said to have dominated. The brilliance of Italian architecture, later discovered by the rest of the world, had little chance of emerging. As in Hitler's Germany and Stalin's Soviet Union, the mood of the official Fascist architecture was not adventure, but pompous rhetoric.

The second difficulty was that modernism appealed to a minority, whereas the governments were populist. On ideological and practical grounds they preferred arts that would appeal to the public, or at least be readily understood by it. This was rarely a top priority for creative talents who lived by innovation, experiment and quite often by provoking those who admired the art displayed in official salons and academies. Power and art disagreed most obviously over painting, since the regimes encouraged works in older, academic, or at any rate realistic, styles, preferably blown up to a large size and filled with heroic and sentimental clichés – even, in Germany, adding a little male erotic fantasy. Even in broad-minded Italy official prizes like the Premio Cremona of 1939 (with seventy-nine contestants) were won by what could almost serve as a photofit portrait of public painting in any dictatorial country. This is perhaps not surprising, since its subject was 'Listening to a speech by Il Duce on the radio'.

Architecture did not produce equally dramatic conflicts between power and art, since it did not raise the problem of how to represent any reality other than itself. Nevertheless, in one important respect, power and modernist architecture (did not Adolf Loos proclaim 'Ornament is Crime'?) remained part of the artistic instrumentarium both of populist regimes and commercial producers for the mass market. Consider the London and the Moscow Undergrounds – the Metro being probably the largest artistic enterprise undertaken in Stalin's Soviet Union. The London Tube, thanks to the patronage and decisions of an enlightened manager, became the largest show-case of a stripped, simple, lucid and functional modernism in inter-war Britain, running far ahead of public taste. The stations of the Moscow Metro, though initially still sometimes designed by surviving Constructivists, increasingly became sub-terranean palaces full of marble, malachite and grandiose decoration. They were, in a sense, a far more ambitious coun-terpart to the gigantic art deco and neo-baroque movie palaces that went up in Western cities during the 1920s and 1930s with the same object: to give men and women who had no access to individual luxury the experience that, for a collective moment, it was theirs.

One might even argue that the less sophisticated the mass public, the greater the appeal of decoration. It probably reached its peak in the architecture of post-war Stalinism, from which the surviving vestiges of early Soviet modernism had finally been expunged, to produce a sort of echo of nineteenth-century taste.

How are we to judge the art of the dictators? The years of Stalin's rule in the USSR and of the Third Reich in Germany show a sharp decline in the cultural achievement of these two countries, compared to the Weimar Republic (1919–33) and the Soviet period before 1930. In Italy the contrast is not so

great, since the pre-Fascist period had not been one of such creative brilliance – nor, unlike Germany and Russia in the 1920s,
had the country been a major international style-setter.
Admittedly, unlike Nazi Germany, Stalin's Russia and Franco's
Spain, Fascist Italy did not drive out its creative talents en masse,
force them into silence at home or, as in the worst years of
Stalin, kill them. Nevertheless, compared to the cultural
achievements and international influence of post-1945 Italy,
the Fascist era does not look impressive.

Hence, what power destroyed or stifled in the era of the dictators is more evident than what it achieved. These regimes
were better at stopping undesirable artists creating undesirable
works than at finding good art to express their aspirations. They
were not the first to want buildings and monuments to celebrate
their power and glory, nor did they add much to the traditional
ways of achieving these objects. And yet it does not look as
though the era of the dictators produced official buildings,
spaces and vistas to compare with, say, the Paris of the two
Napoleons, eighteenth-century St Petersburg or that great song
of triumph to mid-nineteenth-century bourgeois liberalism, the
Vienna Ringstrasse.

It was harder for art to demonstrate the dictators' intention
and ability to change the shape of their countries. The antiq-
uity of European civilisation deprived them of the most
obvious way of doing so: the building of entirely new capital
cities like nineteenth-century Washington and twentieth-
century Brasilia. (The only dictator who had this opportunity
was Kemal Atatürk in Ankara.) Engineers symbolised this
better than architects and sculptors. The real symbol of the
Soviet planned world-change was 'Dneprostroi', the much pho-
tographed great Dnieper Dam. The most lasting stone
memorial to the Soviet era (other than the distinctly pre-
Stalinist Lenin Mausoleum, which has survived on Red Square)
is, almost certainly, the Moscow Metro. As for the arts, their
most impressive contribution to expressing this aspiration was

the (pre-Stalinist) Soviet cinema of the 1920s – the films of Eisenstein and Pudovkin, and V. Turin's unjustly neglected *Turksib*, the epic of railway building.

However, dictators also wanted art to express their ideal of 'the people', preferably at moments of devotion to, or enthusiasm for, the regime. This produced a spectacular quantity of terrible paintings, distinguished from each other chiefly by the face and costume of the national leader. In literature the results were less disastrous, though seldom worth turning back to. However, photography and, above all, film lent themselves rather successfully to the aims of power in this respect.

Lastly, the dictators wished to mobilise the national past on their behalf, mythologising or inventing it where necessary. For Italian Fascism, the point of reference was ancient Rome; for Hitler's Germany, a combination of radically pure barbarians of the Teutonic forests and medieval knighthood; for Franco's Spain, the age of the triumphant Catholic rulers who expelled unbelievers and resisted Luther. The Soviet Union had more trouble taking up the heritage of the tsars which the revolution had, after all, been made to destroy, but eventually Stalin also found it convenient to mobilise it, especially against the Germans. However, the appeal to historic continuity across the imagined centuries never came as naturally as in the dictatorships of the right.

How much of the art of power has survived in these countries? Surprisingly little in Germany, more in Italy, perhaps most (including the magnificent post-war restoration of St Petersburg) in Russia. Only one thing has gone from all of them: power mobilising art and people as public theatre. This, the most serious impact of power on art between 1930 and 1945, disappeared with the regimes that had guaranteed its survival through the regular repetition of public ritual. The Nuremberg rallies, the May Day and revolution anniversaries on Red Square, were the heart of what power expected from art. They died for ever, along with that power. States that realised themselves as show-politics demonstrated their and its impertinence. If the theatre-state is to live, the show must go on. In the end it did not. The curtain is down and will not be raised again.

20

The Avant-Garde Fails

The fundamental assumption behind the various movements of the avant-garde in the arts which dominate the past century was that relations between art and society had changed fundamentally, that old ways of looking at the world were inadequate and new ways must be found. This assumption was correct. What is more, the ways in which we look at and mentally apprehend the world *have* been revolutionised. However, and this is the core of my argument, in the visual arts this had not been achieved, and could not have been achieved, by the projects of the avant-garde.

Why, among all the arts, the visual ones have been particularly handicapped, I shall discuss in a little while. Anyway, they have patently failed. Indeed, after half a century of experiments in the revolutionary rethinking of art – say from 1905 to the middle 1960s – the project was abandoned, leaving behind avant-gardes which became a subdepartment of marketing, or, if I may quote what I wrote in my short history of the twentieth century, *Age of Extremes*, 'the smell of impending death'. In that book I also considered whether this meant just the death of the avant-gardes or of the visual arts as conventionally recognised and practised since the Renaissance. However, I will leave the wider question aside here.

To avoid misunderstanding, let me at the outset say one thing. This essay is not about aesthetic judgments on the twentieth-century avant-gardes, whatever that means, or about assessing skill and talent. It is not about my own tastes and preferences in the arts. It is about the historic failure in our century of the sort of visual art which Moholy-Nagy of the Bauhaus once described as 'confined to picture-frame and pedestal'.[1]

We are talking about a double failure. It was a failure of 'modernity', a term which comes into use around the middle of the nineteenth century, and which held programmatically that contemporary art must be, as Proudhon said of Courbet, 'an expression of the times'. Or, to put it in the words of the Vienna Sezession, 'Der Zeit ihre Kunst, der Kunst ihre Freiheit' [Each age needs its art, Art needs its freedom][2] – for the liberty of artists to do what they and not necessarily anybody else want, was as central to the avant-garde as its modernity. The demand for modernity affected the arts equally: the art of each era had to be *different* from its predecessors, which, in an age which assumed continuous progress, seemed to suggest on the false analogy of science and technology that each new way of expressing the times was likely to be *superior* to what went before; which is patently not always the case. There was, of course, no consensus about what 'expressing the times' meant, or how to express them. Even when artists agreed that the century was essentially a 'machine age', or even – I am quoting Picabia in New York in 1915 – that 'through machinery art ought to find a most vivid expression'[3] or that 'the new art movements can exist only in a society that has absorbed the tempo of the big city, the metallic quality of industry' (Malevich),[4] most of the answers are trivial or rhetorical. Did it mean more to the

Cubists than preferring, as Ortega y Gasset complained, the geometric scheme to the soft lines of living bodies? Or sticking artefacts of industrial society onto easel paintings? Did it mean more to the Dadaists, than the satirical construction by John Heartfield called *Electromechanical Tatlin Shape*, made out of industrial components, which they exhibited, inspired by news of a new 'machine art' of the Russian Constructivists?[5] Did it mean just making pictures inspired by machinery, as Léger did so splendidly? The Futurists were smart enough to leave real machines out and concentrate on trying to create the impression of rhythm and speed; the opposite of Jean Cocteau, who talked of the rhythm of machinery in terms of the metre and rhyme of poetry.[6] In short, the numerous ways of expressing machine-modernity in painting or non-utilitarian constructions had absolutely nothing in common except the word 'machine' and possibly, though not always, a preference for straight lines over undulating ones. There was no compelling logic to the new forms of expression, which is why varying schools and styles could coexist, none lasted, and the same artists could change styles like shirts. The 'modernity' lay in the changing times, not in the arts which tried to express them.

The second failure was much more acute in the visual arts than elsewhere: it was the increasingly evident technical inability of the main medium of painting since the Renaissance – the easel picture – to 'express the times', or indeed to compete with new ways of carrying out many of its traditional functions. The history of the visual avant-gardes in the present century is the struggle against technological obsolescence.

Could we also say that painting and sculpture found themselves at a disadvantage in another respect? They were the least important or prominent components in the great multiple or collective movement-filled presentations which have become increasingly typical of twentieth-century cultural experience: from grand opera at one pole to film, video and rock concerts at the other. No one was more aware of this than the avant-gardes which, ever since art nouveau, and with impassioned conviction since the Futurists, believed in breaking down the walls between colour, sound, shape and words, that is in the unification of the arts. As in Wagner's *Gesamtkunstwerk*, music, word, gesture, lighting carry the action; the static image is background. Films depended on books from the start, and imported writers who had made a literary reputation – Faulkner, Hemingway – though rarely to good effect. The impact of twentieth-century painting on the movies (other than on specific avant-garde films) is limited: some Expressionism in the Weimar cinema, the influence of Edward Hopper's pictures of American houses on Hollywood set designers. It is no accident that the index of the recent *Oxford History of World Cinema* contains a heading *music*, but none relevant to painting except *animation* (which, in turn, does not figure in Robert Hughes's *American Visions*, 'the epic history of art in America'). Unlike literary writers and classical composers, no painter known to mainstream art history has ever been in the running for an Oscar. The only form of collective art in which the painter, and especially, since Diaghilev, the avant-garde painter, really acted as a partner rather than a subordinate, was the ballet.

However, apart from this possible disadvantage, what were the special difficulties of the visual arts?

Any study of non-utilitarian visual arts in the twentieth century – I mean painting and sculpture – must start from the observation that they are a minority interest. In 1994 21 per cent of people in this country had visited a museum or art gallery at least once in the last quarter, 60 per cent read books at least once a week, 58 per cent listened to records and tapes at least once a week, and almost all the 96 per cent of televiewers presumably saw films or their equivalent regularly.[7] As for practising them, in 1974 only 4.4 per cent of French people claimed to paint or sculpt as a hobby against 15.4 per cent who said they played a musical instrument.[8] The problems of painting and sculpture are, of course, rather different. The demand for pictures is essentially for private consumption. Public painting such as murals has been prominent only occasionally in our century, notably in Mexico. This has restricted the market for works of visual art, unless they are attached to something for which there is a larger public, such as record-sleeves, periodicals and book-jackets. Still, as the population grew and people became richer, there was no a priori reason for this market to shrink. As against this demand for the *plastic* arts was public. Their problem was that the market for its major product collapsed in our century, namely the public monument and the decorated building or space, which modernist architecture rejected. Remember Adolf Loos's phrase: 'Ornament is Crime.' Since the peak era before 1914, when an average of about thirty-five new monuments were erected in Paris every decade, there has actually been a holocaust of statuary: seventy-five disappeared from Paris during the war, and in so doing changed the face of the city.[9] The enormous demand for war memorials after 1918, the temporary rise of sculpture-happy dictatorships, have not halted the secular decline. So the crisis of the plastic arts is somewhat different from that of painting, and I will, reluctantly, say no more about them. Nor, indeed, except incidentally, about architecture, which has been largely immune to the problems that have beset the other visual arts.

But we must also start from another observation. More than any other form of creative art, the visual arts have suffered from technological obsolescence. They, and in particular painting, have been unable to come to terms with what Walter Benjamin called 'the age of technological reproducibility'. From the middle of the nineteenth century – that is, from the time when we can recognise conscious movements of the avant-garde in painting – though the word itself had not yet entered current discourse on the arts – they have been aware both of the competition of technology, in the form of the camera, and of their inability to survive this competition. A conservative critic of photography pointed out as early as 1850 that it must seriously jeopardise 'entire branches of art such as engravings, lithography, genre pictures and portraiture'.[10] Some sixty years later, the Italian Futurist Boccioni argued that contemporary art must be expressed in abstract terms, or rather by a spiritualisation of the objective, because 'traditional representation has now been taken over by mechanical means' ['in luogo della riproduzione tradizionale ormai conquistata dai mezzi meccanini'].[11] Dada, or so at least Wieland Herzfelde proclaimed, would not try to compete with the camera, or even try to be a camera with soul, like the Impressionists, trusting as they had done to the least reliable of lenses, the human eye.[12] Jackson Pollock, in 1950, said art had to express feelings, because making pictures of things was now done with cameras.[13] Similar examples could be quoted from almost any decade of the century up to the present. As the president of the Pompidou Centre observed in 1998: 'The twentieth century belongs to photography, not painting.'[14]

Statements of this kind are familiar to everyone who has even glanced at the literature of the arts – at least in the Western tradition since the Renaissance – since they can plainly not apply to arts which are not concerned with mimesis or other modes of representation, or which pursue other ends. There is obvious truth in them. However, there is, in my view, another equally powerful reason for the losing battle the traditional arts have waged against technology in our century. It is the mode of production to which the visual artist was committed, and from which he or she found it difficult or even impossible to escape. This was the production by manual labour of unique works, which could not be literally copied except by the same method. Indeed, the ideal work of art is deemed to be completely uncopiable, since its uniqueness is authenticated by signature and provenance. There was, of course, much potential, including much economic potential, in works designed for technical reproduction, but the one-off product, ascribable to one and only one maker, remained the foundation of the status of high-class visual art and the high-status 'artist', as distinct from the journeyman artisan or 'hack'. And avant-garde painters also insisted on their special status as artists. Until almost this day the stature of painters has tended to be proportional to the size of the frames surrounding their pictures. Such a mode of production belongs typically to a society of patronage or of small groups competing in conspicuous expenditure, and indeed these are still the foundation of the really lucrative art trade. But it is profoundly unsuited to an economy which relies on the demand not of single individuals or a few dozens or scores, but of thousands or even millions; in short, to the mass economy of this century.

None of the other arts suffered so severely from this problem. Architecture, as we know, continues as an art to rely on patronage, which is why it continues happily to produce jumbo-sized one-off prodigies, with or without modern technology. For obvious reasons it is also immune to forgery, the bane of painting. The arts of the stage, though technically pretty antediluvian, have by their nature relied on repeated performance before a large public, that is to say on reproducibility. The same is true of music even before the modern technology of sound reproduction made it accessible beyond the range of mouth-to-ear communication. The standard version of the musical work is expressed in a code of symbols whose essential function is to make possible repeated performance. Of course *invariant* repetition was neither possible nor highly appreciated in these arts, before the twentieth century, when accurate mechanical reproduction became feasible. Literature, finally, had solved the problem of art in the age of reproducibility centuries ago. Printing emancipated it from the calligraphers and their underclass, the copyists. The brilliant invention of the pocket-sized bound volume in the sixteenth century gave it the universally portable and multipliable form which has so far seen off all the challenges of modern technology which were supposed to replace the book – film, radio, television, audio-book and, except for special purposes, CD-Rom and computer-screen.

The crisis of the visual arts is therefore different in kind from the twentieth-century crisis so far undergone by the other arts. Literature never gave up the traditional use of language, or even, in poetry, the constraints of metre. The brief and isolated experiments to break with these, like *Finnegans Wake*, remain peripheral, or are not treated as literature at all, like the Dada 'phonetic poem-poster' of the Dadaist Raoul Hausmann. Here modernist revolution was compatible with technical continuity. In music the avant-garde of composers broke more dramatically with the nineteenth-century idiom, but the bulk of the musical public remained loyal to the classics, supplemented by assimilated nineteenth-century post-Wagnerian innovators. They retained and still retain a virtual monopoly of the popular performance repertoire. This therefore comes almost entirely from the graveyard. Only in the visual arts, and especially in painting, did the then conventional form of mimesis, the salon art of the nineteenth century, virtually disappear from sight, as witness the almost vertical fall in its price on the art market between the wars. Nor, in spite of all the efforts of the art-traders, has it been rehabilitated even today. The good news for avant-garde painting was therefore that it was the only live game in town. The bad news was that the public didn't like it. Abstract painting did not begin to sell at serious prices until the Cold War when, by the way, it benefited from Hitler and Stalin's hostility to it. It therefore became a sort of official art of the Free World against Totalitarianism – a curious destiny for the enemies of bourgeois convention.

So long as the essence of traditional visual art, namely representation, was not abandoned, this was not a major problem. In fact, until the end of the nineteenth century both musical and visual avant-gardes – Impressionists, Symbolists, post-Impressionists, art nouveau and the like – extended rather than abandoned the old language, as well as widening the range of subjects that could be treated by artists. Paradoxically, here the competition of photography proved stimulating. Painters still had exclusive rights to colour, and it is hardly an accident that, from the Impressionists through the Fauves, colour becomes increasingly vivid, if not strident. They also seemed to retain the monopoly of 'Expressionism' in the most general sense, and thus exploited the ability to infuse reality with emotion – all the more powerfully once the bonds of naturalism were relaxed, as witness Van Gogh and Munch. Actually, film technology was later to demonstrate an ability to compete.

Again, artists could still try, or at least claim, to get closer to perceived reality than the machine could, by appealing to science against technology. At least that is what artists like Cézanne, Seurat and Pissarro said or propagandists like Zola or Apollinaire said for them.[15] The drawback of this procedure was that it removed painting from what the eye saw – that is the physical perception of ever-changing light on objects, or the relations of planes and shapes or geological structure – to the conventional codes of what skies, trees, people were *supposed* to look like. Still, until the Cubists, the distance was not too great: the avant-gardes of the late nineteenth century, up to and including post-Impressionism, have become part of the accepted corpus of art. In fact, their artists acquired genuine mass popularity, insofar as this term applies to painting. In Bourdieu's enquiry on French taste in the 1970s, Renoir and Van Gogh emerge as by far the most popular artists at all socioprofessional levels, except academics and 'producteurs artistiques'. (There Goya and Brueghel beat Renoir into fourth place.[16]) The real break between public and artist came with the new century. In Bourdieu's sample, for instance, Van Gogh remained about four times as popular as Braque even among the most highbrow group, in spite of the social cachet of abstract art, which 43 per cent of the group claimed to like. For every one who chose the eminent and thoroughly French Cubist in the so-called 'popular classes', ten chose the Dutchman; in the middle classes seven did so, and even in the upper classes Van Gogh beat Braque easily by five to one.

Why, between say 1905 and 1915, the avant-garde deliberately broke this continuity with the past is a question I can't
answer adequately. But once it had done so, it was necessarily
on the way to nowhere. What could painting do once it abandoned the traditional language of representation, or moved
sufficiently far from its conventional idiom to make it incomprehensible? What could it communicate? Where was the new
art going? The half-century from the Fauves to Pop Art was
filled with desperate attempts to answer this question by means
of an endless succession of new styles and their associated and
often impenetrable manifestos. Contrary to the conventional
belief, they had nothing in common except the conviction that
it was important to be an artist and, once representation was left
to cameras, that anything was legitimate as art, so long as the
artist claimed it as a personal creation. Except for brief periods
it is not even possible to define a general trend, such as one away
from representation to abstraction, or from content to form and
colour. *Neue Sachlichkeit* and Surrealism did not come before but
after Cubism. A perceptive critic has said of Jackson Pollock, the
Abstract Expressionist par excellence, that 'perhaps if he had
lived to seventy ... he would now be seen as a basically imagis-
tic artist who had one abstract phase in his early middle age'.[17]

This uncertainty gives the history of the avant-gardes an air
of particular desperation. They were constantly torn between
the conviction that there could be no future to the art of the
past – even yesterday's past, or even to any kind of art in the old
definition – and the conviction that what they were doing in the
old social role of 'artists' and 'geniuses' was important, and
rooted in the great tradition of the past. The Cubists very naturally, but to Marinetti's displeasure, 'adore the traditionalism
of Poussin, Ingres and Corot'.[18] More absurdly, the late Yves
Klein, who coloured all his canvases and other objects a uniform blue in the manner of a house-painter, may be regarded
as a *reductio ad absurdum* of the artist's activity, but he justified this
by saying that the intention of Giotto and Cimabue had been

'monochromatic'.[19] The recent 'Sensation' exhibition catalogue tried to mobilise the status of Géricault, Manet, Goya and Bosch in favour of the likes of Jake and Dinos Chapman.

Nevertheless, the new freedom enormously increased the range of what could be done in the visual arts. It was both inspiring and liberating, especially for people who believed an unprecedented century needed to be expressed in unprecedented ways. It is almost impossible not to share the sheer excitement and exhilaration radiated by such records of an heroic age in the arts as the great *Berlin-Moskau* exhibition of 1996–7. Nevertheless, it could not conceal two things. First, much less could be communicated in the impoverished new languages of painting than in the old ones. This actually made it harder, or even impossible, to 'express the times' in a communicable way. Anything more than exercises in 'significant form' – the famous Bloomsbury phrase – or than the expression of subjective feeling, needed subtitles and commentators more than ever. That is to say it needed words, which still had conventional meanings. As a poet W. B. Yeats had no trouble in communicating his odd and somewhat esoteric views, but without words it is impossible to discover in Mondrian and Kandinsky that these artists wished to express very strongly held and equally eccentric views about the world. Second, the new century could be much more effectively expressed by its own novel media. In short, whatever the avant-garde tried to do was either impossible or done better in some other medium. For this reason most of the revolutionary claims of the avant-garde were rhetoric or metaphor.

Let us consider Cubism, the avant-garde which has been described, more than once, as 'the most revolutionary and influential of the twentieth century'.[20] This may be true as far as other painters are concerned, at least for the period from 1907 to the First World War; though I think that, so far as the arts as a whole are concerned, Surrealism was to be more influential, possibly because its inspiration was not primarily visual. And yet, was it Cubism that revolutionised the way we all – and not just professional painters – see the world? For instance, Cubism claimed to present different aspects of objects simultaneously, giving, as it were, a multidimensional view of what would otherwise be, say, a still life or the human face. (Actually, when we look at the paintings of the analytical phase of Cubism, we still have to be told that this is what they are supposed to do.) Yet almost simultaneously with Cubism, that is from 1907 on, the movies began to develop those techniques of multiple perspective, varying focus and tricks of cutting, which really familiarised a huge public – indeed all of us – with apprehending reality through simultaneous, or almost simultaneous, perceptions of its different aspects; and this without the need for commentary. Moreover, even when the inspiration was directly Cubist, as, presumably, in Rodchenko's photo,* it is the photograph which, plainly, communicates the sense of the innovation more effectively than a comparable painting by Picasso.† That is why photomontage was to prove so powerful a tool for propaganda. I am not, of course, comparing the aesthetic value of the Picasso and the Rodchenko.

In short, it is impossible to deny that the real revolution in the twentieth-century arts was achieved not by the avant-gardes of modernism, but outside the range of the area formally recognised as 'art'. It was achieved by the combined logic of technology and the mass market, that is to say the democratisation of aesthetic consumption. And chiefly, of course, by the cinema, child of photography and the central art of the twentieth century. Picasso's *Guernica* is incomparably more expressive as art, but, speaking technically, Selznick's *Gone with the Wind* is a more revolutionary work. For that matter Disney's animations, however inferior to the austere beauty of Mondrian, were

* Alexander Rodchenko, *Portrait of the Artist Alexander Svenchenko*, 1924, uses double exposure to achieve a multi-dimensional effect.
† Pablo Picasso, *Cubist Portrait of Daniel-Henry Kahnweiler*, 1910.

both more revolutionary than oil-painting, and better at passing on their message. Advertisements and movies, developed by hucksters, hacks and technicians, not only drenched everyday life in aesthetic experience, but converted the masses to daring innovations in visual perception, which left the revolutionaries of the easel far behind, isolated and largely irrelevant. A camera on a footplate can communicate the sensation of speed better than a Futurist canvas by Balla. The point about the real revolutionary arts is that they were accepted by the masses because they *had* to communicate with them. Only in avant-garde art was the medium the message. In real life, the medium was revolutionised for the sake of the message.

It took the triumph of modernist consumer society in the 1950s to make the avant-garde recognise this. Once they did so their justification was gone.

The avant-garde schools since the 1960s – since Pop Art – were no longer in the business of revolutionising art, but of declaring its bankruptcy. Hence the curious reversion to conceptual art and Dadaism. In the original versions of 1914 and after, these were not supposed to be ways of revolutionising art but of abolishing it, or at least declaring its irrelevance, for instance by painting a moustache on the Mona Lisa and treating a bicycle wheel as a 'work of art' as Marcel Duchamp did. When the public didn't get the point, he exhibited his urinal with an invented artist's signature. Duchamp was lucky enough to do this in New York, where he became a great name, and not in Paris, where he was just one very bright intellectual joker among many, and had no standing as an artist. (As Cartier-Bresson says: he was 'not a good artist at all'.) Dada was serious even in its most desperate jokes: nothing cool, ironic and shoulder-shrugging about it. It wanted to destroy art together with the bourgeoisie, as part of the world which had brought about the Great War. Dada did not accept the world. When George Grosz moved to the USA and there found a world he did not abominate, he lost his power as an artist.

Warhol and the Pop Artists did not want to destroy or revolutionise anything, let alone any world. On the contrary, they accepted, even liked it. They simply recognised that there was no longer a place for traditional artist-produced visual art in the consumer society, except, of course, as a way of earning money. A real world, flooding every waking hour with a chaos of sounds, images, symbols, presumptions of a common experience, had put art as a special activity out of business. Warhol's significance – I might even say the greatness of his strange and disagreeable figure – lies in the consistency of his refusal to do anything but make himself the passive, accepting conduit for the world experienced through media saturation. Nothing is shaped. There are no winks and nudges, no ironies, no sentimentality, no ostensible commentary at all, except by implication in the choice of his mechanically repeated icons – Mao, Marilyn, Campbell's Soup tins – and perhaps in his deep preoccupation with death. Paradoxically, in the ensemble of this troubling oeuvre – though not in any single work – we actually come closer to an 'expression of the times' in which contemporary Americans lived. But it was not achieved by creating works of art in the traditional sense.

Effectively, since then there has been nothing left for avant-garde painting to do. Dadaism has returned, but this time not as a desperate protest against an intolerable world, but just as the old Dadaist gift for publicity stunts. Easel painting itself is in retreat. Conceptualism is the flavour of the day, because it is easy and it is something that even unskilled humans can do and camcorders can't, namely having ideas, especially if they need not be good or interesting ideas. I note in passing that actual painting disappeared from this year's Turner Prize altogether.

So, has the history of the twentieth-century avant-gardes then been entirely esoteric? Have its effects been entirely confined to a self-contained art-world? Did they entirely fail in their project of expressing and transforming the twentieth century? Not entirely. There was a way in which they could break with the crippling tradition of art as the production of irreproducible artefacts by artists pleasing only themselves. It was by recognising the logic of life and production in industrial society. For, of course, industrial society could recognise the need for aesthetic as well as technical innovation, if only because production and marketing/propaganda needed both. 'Modernist' criteria had practical value for industrial design and mechanised mass production. Avant-garde techniques were effective in advertising. To the extent that these ideas came from the avant-gardes of the early twentieth century we live in a visual environment shaped by them. Often they did, though not always and necessarily. The most original work of avant-garde art in Britain between the wars was not produced as a work of art at all, but as an efficient technical solution for a problem of how to present information: it is the map of the London underground system. Incidentally, the bankruptcy of the avant-garde is vividly demonstrated in the pointless adaptation of this by Simon Patterson* in this year's 'Sensation' show.

One avant-garde tradition did make the junction between the nineteenth- and twentieth-century worlds. This was the tradition which – as Nikolaus Pevsner rightly recognised[21] – led from William Morris, arts and crafts and art nouveau to the Bauhaus, at least once it had shaken off the original hostility to industrial production, engineering and distribution. John Willett has shown how the Bauhaus did this in the early 1920s. The strength of this tradition – reinforced as it was in the Bauhaus by Russian Constructivism – was that it was fuelled not by the concerns of artists as individual genius-creators with esoteric technical problems, but as builders of a better society. As Moholy-Nagy, an exile from Hungary after the defeat of the short-lived Hungarian Soviet republic, put it: 'Constructivism is the socialism of vision.' This kind of post-1917 avant-garde

---

* Simon Patterson, *The Great Bear*, lithograph, 1992.

leaped back across the non-political or even anti-political avant-gardes of 1905–1914 to the socially committed movements of the 1880s and early 1890s. New art was once again inseparable from building a new, or at least an improved society. Its impetus was social as well as aesthetic. Hence the centrality of building – the German word which gave the Bauhaus its name – to this project.

Here the aesthetics of the 'machine age' made more than rhetorical sense. In the 1920s the programme for changing the way humans lived that appealed to the artists who could contribute directly to this object tended to be a combination of public planning and technological utopia. It was a marriage between Henry Ford, who wanted to provide cars where there had been none, and the aspirations of socialist municipalities to provide bathrooms where there had been none. Both in their different ways claimed to be experts who knew best; both aimed at universal improvement; neither gave priority to personal choice ('You can have my cars in any colour so long as it's black'). Houses and even cities, like the cars which Le Corbusier regarded as the model for constructing houses,[22] were conceived as products of the universal logic of industrial production. The basic principle of the 'machine age' could be applied to human environments and human dwellings ('a machine for living in') by finding the solution for the combined problem of optimising the human use of limited space, ergonomics and cost-effectiveness. It was a good ideal, which made the lives of a lot of people better, even if the utopian aspirations of its Cité Radieuse belong to an era, even in the world's rich countries, of modest needs and restricted means, far from the super-abundance, and hence the possible consumer choice, of our times.

Nevertheless, as even the Bauhaus discovered, changing society is more than schools of art and design alone can achieve. And it was not achieved. Let me conclude by quoting the last and sad sentences of Paul Klee's lecture 'On Modern Art', given not far from the Bauhaus, then at its creative peak (1924):

'We don't have the support of a people. But we are looking for a people. That is how we began, over there at the Bauhaus. We started with a community to which we gave all we had. We can't do more than that.'[23] And it wasn't enough.

Part IV

FROM ART TO MYTH

21

Pop Goes the Artist:
Our Exploding Culture

The social history of that noble animal, the horse, is not without its relevance to the student of the arts. Its function in the world was once assured: so much so that to this day it provides the notional measure of all its power. It transported men and pulled things, and its less obvious role in human life – to be a status symbol for the landed rich, an excuse for gambling and holidays for the unlanded poor, an object of admiration for painters and sculptors, etc. – derived essentially from its practical indispensability in ordinary life. Today this has gone. Outside a few underdeveloped countries and special areas, it has been entirely and satisfactorily replaced by the automobile, which runs much faster, and the tractor, which pulls heavier loads. It survives entirely as a luxury. In consequence human thinking both about the problems of transport and about the functions of the horse has had to be not merely revised but fundamentally changed, for most of the horse-age thinking on these subjects has become irrelevant or otiose.

The situation of the arts in the twentieth century is analogous. They also have been made redundant by technological progress, and the first task of criticism ought to discover how this has come about and what precisely has replaced them. So far most of those who practise and write about the arts have been reluctant to face this situation frankly, partly because they have the excuse that novels – even thrillers – are not yet actually written by computers, but mainly because no class of people is enthusiastic about writing its own obituary. Moreover, old-fashioned handicraft or artisan art continues to thrive as a luxury, like the ex-urban pony; and old-fashioned, handicraft-type artists have been more successful in adapting themselves to mechanised mass production than the horse. Yet the economic facts are conclusive. The professional writer of books is in the position of the hand-loom weaver after the intervention of the power loom: two thirds or three quarters of his profession can earn less than a typist's income, and the number of writers who can live entirely by the sales of their books would fit into a single, not excessively large room. As every advertising agent and editor knows, it is the photographer and not the 'artist' who today commands the high fees.

The industrial revolution that has taken place in the productions of the mind, like that of material productions, has two causes: technical progress, which replaces manual skills, and mass demand, which makes them inadequate. Its crucial aspect is not simply the capacity to reproduce individual creations in large quantity – the various forms of printing have long done so without essentially changing the character of writing, and the gramophone has not substantially altered music – but the capacity to replace creation. The visual arts have been so transformed by photography, still and moving; music has more recently entered the realm of artificial sound (comparable perhaps to the artificial fibre in textiles); though writing still resists genuine mechanisation, in spite of the scientists' intensive search for effective translating machines. In fact, however, it is not the adoption of actual mechanical devices that determines the 'industrial' character of an art, but the break-up of the process of individual creation into specialised segments, as in Adam Smith's famous pin manufactory. It is the dissolution of the individual producer into a collective, coordinated by a director or manager. The novel has an author, the newspaper has not. In the case of the paper whose 'stories' are subbed, rewritten or compiled from raw or semi-processed material, it may not even have anything that can be described as a plurality of authors.

Such industrial methods are essential to supply the entirely unprecedented demand of a mass public that is accustomed to entertainment or art, not as an occasional activity but as an unbroken flow, like water, as in the most logical product of technological culture, broadcasting. In certain branches of literature, such as utilitarian fiction, craft productions can persist, not only because the demand for it is smaller, more lasting and more intermittent, but also because the market can rely on large quantities of casual part-time labour and on the readiness of professional writers to turn themselves into hacks. Still, the individual artisan who genuinely attempts to produce books at an industrial pace either kills himself with overwork, like Edgar Wallace, or abandons the attempt after a while, like Simenon. The arts that are the new products of the industrial age – films, broadcasting, popular music – adopt an elaborate division of labour from the start, as indeed certain essentially collective or cooperative arts have always done, notably those of architecture and stage performance.

What emerges from such industrial or semi-industrial production is obviously something very different from the 'works of art' of the traditional handmade type and cannot be judged in the same way. There may still be identifiable 'works' of a revolutionary type, but capable of being judged in the old way, like major films, though it is not clear that this is the best way to judge them. There may be old-fashioned works of art, as it were by accident, as when writers of individual literary talent – a Hammett or a Simenon – emerge from an essentially hack genre; but the modern crime novel asks to be judged not by Sam Spade but by Perry Mason, who presents traditional criticism with a total blank. In the extreme and increasingly familiar cases of the newspaper, the television series, the cartoon strip, the oeuvre of some pop music manufacturer, there may not even be this reminiscence of the past. It would be ridiculous to judge *Gunsmoke* by the tests we apply to Hemingway, Andy Capp by those of Hogarth, or the Rolling Stones by those fit for Hugo Wolf or even Cole Porter. Conversely, the achievement of the western is unaffected by the observation that no single novel or film about the West has ever been made an undeniable 'great' work of art in the conventional sense. The fact is that the old-fashioned critic has been made redundant by industrialisation to the same extent as the old-fashioned artist.

The first thing to be done about this situation is to accept – which does not mean to approve – it. To wish it away is a natural but fruitless reaction. Umberto Eco has put the matter with Latin lucidity:

> The problem is not how to return, i.e., to a pre-industrial state, but to ask ourselves under what circumstances the relation of man to the productive cycle subordinates man to the system, and conversely, how we ought to elaborate a new image of man in relation to the system which conditions him: an image not of humanity free *from* the machine, but free *in relation to the machine.*[1]

Neither the refusal to accept the world of the mass media nor its uncritical acceptance will do, though of the two attitudes the latter is a shade less useless, for it implies at least the capacity to recognise the need to make a new analysis of an unprecedented situation.

Among those who have attempted to come to intellectual terms with industrial culture there have been, speaking broadly, three main approaches. The Americans have discovered, described and measured; the continentals – especially the French and Italians – have analysed and theorised; the British have moralised. American work in the field, mainly sociological, is fairly well known. Italo-French work, with the possible exception of Edgar Morin's brilliant *The Stars*, is virtually unknown. Morin's own *L'Esprit du Temps*, though published over two years ago, has passed virtually unperceived in Britain, and such attempts as Roland Barthes's to analyse the meaning of the jargon of women's fashions or Evelyn Sullerot's to explore *La presse féminine* (Paris, 1963) are entirely unknown. Umberto Eco's own *Apocalittici e integrati* – an unnecessarily Mandarin title – with its elaborate close analyses of Steve Canyon, Superman and Charlie Brown, the pop song industry and television, may introduce the reader to the intellectual effort that Italian critics have devoted to mass culture in the past five years or so. The greater part of this remarkably able book consists of reprints or already published studies.

British criticism in the field has long been the virtual monopoly of the local new left: that is to say, it reflects a lot of Leavis (but without the Leavisite rejection of post-industrial culture), a much smaller quantity of Marx, a good deal of nostalgia for 'working-class culture', a pervasive passion for democracy, a strong pedagogic urge and an equally strong urge to do good. It is in fact very British. That is why our studies in mass culture, though intellectually unsystematic and sometimes amateurish, make up in practical strength for their theoretical deficiencies. Not only have we actually done something to improve our mass media, as a comparison of British with foreign television will make clear, but also our observers have been aware earlier and more sensitively of certain trends – for example, in teenage tastes – than the academically weightier but less with-it sociologists of France and the United States.

The Popular Arts by Stuart Hall and Paddy Whannel[2] – one of the first publications in Hall's notable career as a cultural theorist – has the virtues of this tradition. It is essentially critical and pedagogical, supplementing the 'Topics for Study' that are its core with practical teaching material. The main topics include studies of 'good' popular forms and artists (the blues, the western, Billie Holiday), of the treatment of violence, private eyes, romance, love, 'people', the adolescent public and that familiar subject of such researches, the advertising industry. There is a bibliography and a particularly useful list of good films and jazz records. The authors' hearts are in the right place, their arguments and conclusions are admirable, their taste excellent and their sensitiveness to social developments great. Yet, like so many British discussions of mass culture, they rarely quite face the question whether 'standards' of the traditional kind really fit the subject. At one extreme they tend to search for that crock at the end of the rainbow, good as distinct from bad mass art, sometimes with the question-begging qualification 'good of its kind'.

But while the teacher in undemanding comprehensive schools who is the ideal reader of *The Popular Arts* may welcome advice on how to show his charges that Anita O'Day is better than Helen Shapiro, who in turn is superior to Susan Maughan, or that *Z-Cars* ought to be preferred to *Compact*, such advice obscures the reality, that a Billie Holiday in the world of pop music today is a greater freak than a Rimbaud among the writers of greeting-card verse, and that bad mass art may be as effective as good (where 'bad' and 'good' are equally irrelevant categories), or more effective than good (when they are not).

At the other extreme, British studies of mass culture may tend towards an uncritical acceptance of what mirrors the 'people', which is by definition good. Richard Hoggart in his famous *The Uses of Literacy* has sometimes come close to this, as in his discovery of the overriding interest in the close details of the human condition in *Peg's Paper*.[3] One might say as much of some detergent commercials. The essential weakness of both these approaches to the mass art is a determination to discover the values of humanity before mass production in a situation in which they are at best marginal. There is no horse trying to look out from under the engine bonnet.

But if there is no horse, what is there? The flow of industrial culture produces not (or only incidentally) the 'work' that calls for individual and concentrated attention, but the continuing artificial world of the newspaper, the cartoon strip, or the endless succession of western or criminal episodes. It produces not the specific occasion of the formal ballet, but the constant flux of the ballroom, not the passion but the mood, not the good building but the city, not even the exclusive and specific experience, but simultaneous multiplicity: the juxtaposition of heterogeneous headlines, the jukebox in the café, the drama interspersed with shampoo ads. This is not entirely new – Walter Benjamin once pointed out that this is the traditional way in which architecture is experienced, namely, as a general environment of life rather than a sum of individual buildings – but today it is dominant. Traditional aesthetic criticism is irrelevant to it, because the products of cultural industrialisation bypass the techniques of art and proceed directly to a heightened stylisation of life. Not for nothing is the 'personality' the characteristic protagonist of the endless daily epic that press and broadcasting unroll before us, and 'star quality' a more important asset in the popular performer than talent or technique. The television series 'based on' some character or traditional fiction illustrates this process.

Paradoxically enough this ultra-modern development takes us back to the most archaic function of the arts, the elaboration of myth and morality. As Morin has put it somewhere in *Les Stars*:[4]

> The structure of imagination follows archetypes; there are patterns of the human spirit which orders its dreams, and especially those rationalized dreams, the themes of myth and romance ... What the cultural industry does is to standardize the great romantic themes by turning the archetypes into stereotypes.

The term 'art' may be applied to this process, or it may not. For practical purposes the new Olympus may consist of the cast of characters presented to us daily in the press. They may step from moving picture to paper, like the stars who enter the gossip column. They may also, like the now forgotten ex-queen Soraya or, for that matter, much later Princess Diana, move in the opposite direction.

Two crucial questions arise out of this analysis: how are we to judge, and perhaps improve, the output of the cultural flow? And what room does it leave for the values of art, or individual creation? Those who contrast 'good' and 'bad' popular films, who ask for pop songs to be 'good of their kind', or who comment on the defective style or layout of newspapers tend to confuse these two questions. In the first question it is the content, and especially the moral content, of mass culture that is at issue. A bad comic strip does not become better if it is drawn by a master-draughtsman; it merely becomes more acceptable to critics. The fundamental criticism of Pop Art is that of the ideal and quality of life it endorses. As Hall and Whannel show, the objection to the forgotten television series *The Third Man* is not its mediocrity but its idealisation of acquisitiveness; nor would this be any less so if suitably agreeable morals – for instance, about the need for racial toleration – were tacked on to it. And the real danger of industrialised culture, which eliminates all its competitors to become the only spiritual communication to reach the majority of people, is that it leaves no alternative to the mass-production world, which is an undesirable world. Even when its products do not accept the prevailing official ethos totally, like the American strip *Superman*, of which Signor Eco provides a blood-curdling and brilliant analysis, they cannot escape from it. *Li'l Abner*, praised for its dissent and critical spirit by American intellectuals who have trouble in finding much else to praise, is, as Signor Eco points out, 'The best and most enlightened of Stevensonian radicals, and so is his author. In his search for purity the only thing he never suspects is that purity might take the form of total subversion, the negation of the system.'[5] The major charge against mass culture is that it creates a closed world, and in doing so removes that essential element in humanity, the desire for a perfect and good world – the great hope of man.

That hope is not eliminated, but in mass culture it takes the negative and evasive form of fantasy, in general of nihilist fantasy. The Dadaists and Surrealists anticipated this, making them probably the only representatives of the traditional line of development in the arts to make a central contribution to modern mass culture. In spite of the Marx Brothers and the Goons, of some (but not all) animated cartoons and other institutionalisations of this ethereal kind of revolutionism, the mass arts have not yet adequately reflected the growing element of sheer reality-negating fantasy that has become so obvious a part of popular life, especially in the specialised subcultures of the young. The advertisers alone have already set about the process of castration by incorporating it in their commercials.

The fantastic, the unpredictable, the partly irrational have also provided the most obvious refuge within mass culture for old-fashioned 'art'. It has, logically enough, tended to retreat to those activities that cannot yet be mechanised. The jazz musicians who set their improvisation against the machine of 'Micky Mouse music' were the first explorers of this realm. They are today being followed by the hand-held cameras, the unscripted discussions and unplanned programmes of television, and above all by the improvisations of the stage. Indeed, the striking revival of stage-arts in the 1950s is in many ways the artist's deliberate response to the triumph of industrialisation. For on the stage, as in the jazz session, the creator cannot be reduced to the cog, because no effect can be precisely repeated, nor the relation between artist and public deprived of its dangerous, exciting and unpredictable immediacy.

And yet, improvisation can provide no solution, but only a palliative. Its relation to industrialised culture is that of leisure to industrialised life, an enclave of (sometimes factitious) free-dom in the vast territory of compulsion and routine. The ancient resources of the artist, craft skill and craft pride, are more satisfactory, because they can operate within industri-alised culture. But the best available solution for the artist lies in the need of the industry itself for what Morin calls 'a negative electrode in order to function positively': that is, a certain margin for genuine creation, which can alone provide the raw material that it can process. This applies especially to the sup-plies of new material, which give the artist very little scope within the actual productive process, but its most successful genres, notably the cinema, have always – even in Hollywood – allowed for a certain marginal freedom, while the financial structure of other film industries has provided even greater lat-itude for creation.

Nevertheless, in the last analysis the pop arts cannot be judged by the scope they provide for the traditional arts. The western is not important because John Ford has made good films within its conventions. These are secondary consequences of its vogue. Its achievement is a landscape of the mind, a mythology and a moral universe, which were created by hun-dreds of bad stories, films and television episodes, and survive not because of them but through them. It is the strength of books like that by Hall and Whannel that they recognised such facts; their weakness that – at least in the 1960s – they hesitated before their implications. They remained guides to what is 'good' and 'bad' in the pop arts. They had not yet come to terms with them.

22

The American Cowboy: An International Myth?

I shall begin my reflections on that well-known American invented tradition, the cowboy, with one, or rather two, linked questions that go a long way beyond Texas. Why is it that populations of mounted men herding livestock generally – but not always – become the subject of powerful and typically of heroic myth? And why, among the many myths of this kind, did the one generated by a socially and economically marginal group of rootless proletarian drifters who rose and fell in the course of a couple of decades of the nineteenth-century USA have such an extraordinary, indeed unique, global fortune?

I am unable to answer the first of these questions, for it takes us, I fancy, into some very profound Jungian archetypal undergrowth in which I should certainly lose my way. The capacity of mounted herders to generate such heroic images, by the way, is not quite universal. I doubt whether it usually extends to pastoral nomads, such as the Huns, the Mongols or the Bedouin. For the sedentary populations with whom such pastoral nomads must coexist as separate communities, they are likely to appear primarily as a public danger: necessary but menacing. The groups that generate the heroic myth most easily, I suggest, are populations specialising in horsemanship but, in some sense, still linked to the rest of society; at any rate in the sense that a peasant or city lad can conceive of himself becoming a cowboy or gaucho or Cossack. Is a dude ranch in which Chinese imperial mandarins behaved like Mongol horsemen conceivable? Probably not.

But why the myth? What is the role of the horse in it, clearly an animal carrying a powerful emotional and symbolic charge? Or of the centaur, whom the man living on horseback represents? One thing, however, is clear. The myth is essentially macho. Though cowgirls appeared, and had a certain vogue, in the Wild West shows and rodeos of the inter-war years – presumably on the analogy of circus acrobats, since the combination of femininity and daring has some box-office appeal – they have since evaporated. Rodeo has become very macho indeed. Upper-class women who knew all about horses and rode to hounds with as much bravery as men – indeed, with more bravery since they had to ride side-saddle – were familiar enough in Victorian Britain, and especially in Ireland where the prevailing style of fox-hunting was particularly suicidal. Nobody questioned their femininity. One might even, if malicious, suggest that an association with horses was a selling point for femininity in an island in which men to this day are said to develop more passion for horses and drink than for sex. Still, the rider's myth is essentially macho, and even the fair horsewomen were admiringly compared to the martial Amazons. The myth tends to represent the warrior on show, the aggressor, the barbarian, the raper rather than the raped. It is highly characteristic that the designs of European cavalry uniforms in the eighteenth and nineteenth centuries, mainly the work of aristocratic officers or princes, were frequently inspired by the clothing of semi-barbarian horsemen who, indeed, formed irregular auxiliary units for many such armies: Cossacks, hussars, pandurs.

Today, populations of such wild horse-riders and herdsmen exist in a large number of regions all round the world. Some of them are strictly analogous to cowboys, such as gauchos on the plains of the southern cone of Latin America; the *llaneros* on the plains of Colombia and Venezuela; possibly the *vaqueiros* of the Brazilian north-east; certainly the Mexican *vaqueros* from whom indeed, as everyone knows, both the costume of the modern cowboy myth and most of the vocabulary of the cowboy's trade are directly derived: mustang, lasso, lariat, *remuda* (a herd of horses or 'remount'), sombrero, chaps (*chaparro*), a cinch, bronco, wrangler (or *caballerango* = horse herdsman), rodeo or even buckaroo (= *vaquero*). There are similar populations in Europe, such as the *csikos* on the Hungarian plain, or *puszta*, the Andalusian horsemen in the cattle-raising zone whose flamboyant behaviour probably gave the earliest meaning of the word 'flamenco', and the various Cossack communities of the south Russian and Ukrainian plains. I leave aside various other forms of unmounted herdsmen, or smaller communities of cattlemen, or even the important European populations of cattle-drovers whose function is exactly analogous to that of the cowboys: namely, to get the cattle from the remote places they are raised to the market. In the sixteenth century there were the exact equivalents of the Chisholm trail leading from the Hungarian plains to the market cities of Augsburg, Nuremberg or Venice. And I do not have to tell you about the great Australian outback, which is essentially ranching country, though for sheep more than cattle.

There is thus no shortage of potential cowboy myths in the Western world. And, in fact, practically all the groups I have mentioned have generated macho and heroic semi-barbarian myths of one kind or another in their own countries and sometimes even beyond. I suspect that even in Colombia, the last country that could be described as a gigantic and variegated

Wild West, the horsemen of the eastern plains will – especially now that they are disappearing – inspire the writers and movie producers. Their major literary monument so far is a magnificent account of their guerrilla war under Liberal Party ranchers during the *violencia* of 1948–53 by their chieftain, a fine, short, barrel-chested and bow-legged gentleman who, with his bodyguard, attended last year's learned conference on the *violencia* in Bogotá: Eduardo Franco Isaza's *Los guerrilleros del llano*.[1]

What is more, whereas the real cowboys were of no political significance whatever in the history of the USA – which is why the towns that figure in the myth of the Wild West are not real cities or even state capitals, but holes in a lost corner, like Abilene or Dodge City – the wild horsemen of other countries were crucial and sometimes decisive elements in their national development. The great Russian peasant risings of the seventeenth and eighteenth centuries began on the Cossack frontier; and conversely the Cossacks became the praetorian guard of the later tsarism. The omnipresent Balkan *haiduks*, outlaw robbers and national guerrillas about whom I've written elsewhere, took their name from a Hungarian word meaning 'cattle-drover', or cowboy.

In Argentina the gauchos, organised as rough-riding armies under their great chieftain Rosas, controlled the country for a generation after independence. Turning Argentina into a modern, civilised country was essentially seen as a struggle of city against prairie, of the educated and commercial elite against the gauchos, of culture against barbarism. As in Walter Scott's Scotland, so in the Argentina of Sarmiento, the tragic element in this struggle was clearly seen: for the progress of civilisation implied the destruction of values that were recognised as noble, heroic and admirable, but historically doomed. Gain was paid for by loss. Uruguay, as a country, was actually formed by a cowboy revolution under Artigas, and acquired from these origins that bent for democratic freedom and popular welfare that was to make it into what was called 'the

Switzerland of Latin America' until the generals put an end to all that in the 1970s. Similarly, the horsemen of Pancho Villa's revolutionary army came from the cattle and mining frontier.

Australia, like Argentina and Uruguay, rapidly became an urbanised society – in fact probably the most urbanised society outside small areas of Europe in the nineteenth century. Yet in terms of sheer area it consisted of a Wild West with a couple of big cities attached to one end; and in terms of its economy, it rested on the products of livestock ranches to a far greater extent than the USA ever did. It is therefore not surprising that such groups generated myths: for instance, the Australian out-back, with its migratory proletarian cattlemen, sheep-shearers and other hobos, still provides the essential Australian national myth. And indeed, 'Waltzing Matilda', which is about one such drifter, is the Australian national song. But none of them has generated a myth with serious international popularity, let alone one that can compare, even faintly, with the fortunes of the North American cowboy. Why?

Before speculating about the answer, let me briefly say a word or two about these other cowboy myths. This is partly to draw attention to what they all have in common, but chiefly to remind you of the ideological and political flexibility of such myths or 'invented traditions' to which I shall return in a moment in the American context. What they have in common is obvious: toughness, bravery, the bearing of arms, the readiness to inflict or undergo hardship, indiscipline, and a strong dose of barbarism, or at least lack of surface polish, which shades over into the status of noble savage. Probably also that contempt of the man on a horse for the footslogger, of the herdsman for the farmer, and that swaggering style and costume by which he indicates his superiority. To this must be added a distinct non-intellectuality, or even anti-intellectuality. All of which has turned on more than one sophisticated middle-class son of the city. Cowboys – even midnight cowboys – are rough trade. But beyond this, they reflect the myths and realities of their societies. Cossacks, for instance, are wild men but socially rooted and 'placed'. A Cossack 'Shane' is not conceivable. The Australian outback myth – and reality – is that of a class-conscious and organised proletariat: as it were, of a Wild West as it might have been if it had been organised by the Wobblies. Cattlemen might well be Aborigines rather than whites, but the local equivalent of the cowboy, the migratory sheep-shearers, were union men. When a bunch of them had been – this is still so – hired from among a bunch of apparent bums moving across the hinterland on horse, mule or jalopy, the first thing they'd do would be to organise a union meeting and elect a spokesman to negotiate with the boss. That's not the way they did things in and around the OK Corral. They were not, I would like to add, ideological leftists. When in 1917 a large number of such characters in the hinterland of Queensland organised a meeting to hail the October Revolution and demand soviets, a number were arrested – with some trouble – and frisked for subversive literature. The authorities did not find any subversive literature, or in fact any literature, on these men, except a leaflet which a number of them had in their pockets. It contained the following message: 'If water rots your boots, what will it do to your stomach?'

In short, a cowboy myth provides plenty of scope for variation. John Wayne is only one special version. As we shall see, even in the USA he is just one special version of the local myth.

How are we to discover why the US cowboy myth has been so much more powerful than the others? We can only speculate. Our starting point is the fact that, in and outside Europe, the 'western' in its modern sense – that is, the myth of the cowboy – is a late variant of a very early and deep-rooted image: that of the Wild West in general. Fenimore Cooper, whose popularity in Europe followed immediately upon his first publication – Victor Hugo thought he was 'the American Walter Scott' – is the most familiar version of this. Nor is he dead. Without the memory of Leatherstocking, would English punks have invented Mohican hairstyles?

The original image of the Wild West, I suggest, contains two elements: the confrontation of nature and civilisation, and of freedom with social constraint. Civilisation is what threatens nature; and (as we can see, but this is not so clear initially) their move from bondage or constraint into independence, which constitutes the essence of America as a radical European ideal in the eighteenth and early nineteenth centuries, is actually what brings civilisation into the Wild West and so destroys it. The plough that broke the plains is the end of the buffalo and the Indian. Now I suggest that the original European image of the Wild West pays virtually no real attention to the collective search for freedom, that is, to the settlement frontier. The Mormons, for instance, come into the story mainly as villains – at least in Europe. (Think of Sherlock Holmes.)

It is clear that many white protagonists of the original Wild West epic are in some sense misfits in, or refugees from, 'civilisation', but that is not, I think, the main essence of their situation. Basically they are of two types: explorers or visitors seeking something that cannot be found elsewhere – and money is the very last thing they seek; and men who have established a symbiosis with nature, as it exists in its human and non-human shape, in these wilds. They are not bringing with them the modern world, except in the sense that they come with its self-consciousness and equipment. The most dramatic example of a visiting searcher is that young Jacobinical Welshman who set out in the 1790s to check whether the Mandan Indians really spoke Welsh and were thus descendants of Prince Madoc, who had discovered America long before Columbus. (This was a story, beautifully analysed by Gwyn Williams, that was widely believed, including by Jefferson.) John Evans made his way up the Mississippi and Missouri alone, found – alas – that those noble-looking people whose portraits we all know didn't speak Welsh, and died of drink on his return to New Orleans at the age of twenty-nine.

The original myth of the West, as of America itself, was

thus utopian – but in the case of the West the utopia was that of the re-creation of the lost state of nature. The real heroes of the West were Indians, and hunters who learned to live with and like Indians – in fact, Leatherstocking and Chingachgook. It was an ecological utopia. Cowboys, of course, couldn't enter it so long as the West was that of the old North-West, the future Midwest. But even when the cowboy had joined the cast of the western stage-spectacle, he was merely one of the figures on the stage, together with the miner, the buffalo hunter, the US cavalry, the railroad builder and the rest. The basic themes of the international western myth are well exemplified in the novels of Karl May, on which every German-speaking boy has been brought up since the 1890s, when he published his massive trilogy *Winnetou.* I mention Karl May because he was and is by far the most influential of the European versions of the Wild West. It was, incidentally, the enormous success of the movies made of *Winnetou* in the early 1960s in Germany (or rather on Yugoslav locations) that gave Italian and Spanish producers the idea of mass-producing spaghetti westerns, thereby making the fortunes of Clint Eastwood and transforming the image of the West yet again.

May's West is entirely derived from literature, including serious travel and ethnological literature that he read when he was a prison librarian; for he was a highly talented fantasist whose romancing led him into fraud before it took him into creative literature. Fundamentally it is about the affinity of the perceptive educated European who learns to find his way in the West with the noble savage – pitted against the Yankee who desecrates and destroys the ecological paradise he cannot understand. The German hero and the Apache warrior become blood brothers. The story cannot but end in tragedy. The noble and extremely handsome Winnetou must die, because the West itself is doomed: that much the European myth has in common with the later versions of the American western. But in this version of the myth, the true barbarians are not red but white. Karl May, of course, did not set foot in America until long after writing about it. There is no analogous theme in his writings about adventurers in other parts of the world, notably the Islamic zone to which he devoted numerous volumes.

As it happens, the enormous vogue of *Winnetou* (volume I was written in 1893) coincided almost exactly with the discovery or construction of the idealised cowboy of the American ruling class – the cowboy as seen by Owen Wister, Frederick Remington and Theodore Roosevelt. But the two have nothing in common. At most one might link both with imperialism, for like other European practitioners of such genres, Karl May (who, in spite of his vaguely pacifist inclinations, was greatly admired by Hitler) gloried in exotic locales and, brother to the red man or not, he unquestionably took for granted a certain superiority of the white man, or rather the German.

If there is any link between the western vogue of the different continents in the 1890s, it is almost certainly provided by Buffalo Bill, whose Wild West show began its international travels in 1887 and sharply increased the public interest in cowboys, Indians and the rest wherever it went. Karl May is simply the most successful representative of a familiar genre, most of whose products have long been forgotten, such as the novels of the Frenchman Gustave Aimard, with titles such as *Les Trappeurs de l'Arkansas*.[2] I mention them merely to underline that the European myth of the Wild West was not derived from the American, as a great deal of English popular music was derived from Broadway hits. It was contemporary with the American myth at least as far back as Fenimore Cooper and, in fact, even earlier. The European West did not become derivative until the early twentieth century, when it became parasitic on western sub-novels like those of Clarence Mulford, Max Brand and, above all, Zane Grey (1875–1939) as well as western movies. I suppose an early and distinguished example of such derivation is the first and only work that genuinely deserves the title of

horse opera, namely Puccini's *La Fanciulla del West* (1907), based
on a Belasco spectacular.

What of the invented tradition of the American cowboy,
which, as we have seen, emerged in the 1890s and which eventually – at least for a half-century or so – swamped and
absorbed the original native international tradition of the
West? Or rather, what of the invented traditions of the cowboy,
for this particular literary or sub-literary topos proved enormously malleable and flexible. I do not need to establish this
emergence at a crucial moment in American history, drama-
tised, if you like, by the coincidence at the Chicago Expo of
1893, of Turner reading his frontier thesis to the infant
American Historical Association while, outside, Buffalo Bill
displayed his safari park of western fauna no longer freely
roaming under natural conditions.

The cowboy did indeed become a standard theme of dime-
novels and popular media in the 1870s and 1880s; but, as Lonn
Taylor makes quite clear, his image, while it did not exclude
heroism, was mixed. In the 1880s it became, if anything, rather
antisocial: 'rowdy, dangerous, lawless, reckless, individualist'[3] –
at any rate when he impinged on the settled town population.
The new image was made by the Eastern middle classes who
were heavily involved in ranching and it was profoundly literary;
that is clear not just from the comparisons of cowpunchers to
Thomas Malory's medieval chivalrous knights, and perhaps
from the popularity of the showdown at high noon between two
single champions – a sort of knightly duel – but from the actual
European origin of several western topoi. The noble and lonely
gunfighter, arriving from nowhere with a mysterious past behind
him, was already being exploited by the Irish novelist Mayne
Reid. The idea that 'a man's got to do what a man's got to do'
has its classical Victorian expression in Tennyson's now no
longer famous poem 'The Revenge', about Sir Richard
Grenville fighting a Spanish fleet single-handed.

In terms of literary pedigree, the invented cowboy was a

late romantic creation. But in terms of social content, he had a double function: he represented the ideal of individualist freedom pushed into a sort of inescapable jail by the closing of the frontier and the coming of the big corporations. As a reviewer said of Remington's articles, illustrated by himself in 1895, the cowboy roamed 'where the American may still revel in the great red-shirted freedom which has been pushed so far to the mountain wall that it threatens soon to expire some-where near the top'. In hindsight the West could seem thus, as it seemed to that sentimentalist and first great star of movie westerns William S. Hart, for whom the cattle and mining frontier 'to this country . . . means the very essence of national life . . . It is but a generation or so since virtually all this coun-try was frontier. Consequently its spirit is bound up in American citizenship.'[4] As a quantitative statement this is absurd, but its significance is symbolic. And the invented tra-dition of the West is entirely symbolic, inasmuch as it generalises the experience of a comparative handful of mar-ginal people. Who, after all, cares that the total number of deaths by gunshot in all the major cattle towns put together between 1870 and 1885 – in Wichita plus Abilene plus Dodge City plus Ellsworth – was forty-five, or an average of 1.5 per cattle-trading season,[5] or that local western newspapers were not filled with stories about bar-room fights, but about prop-erty values and business opportunities?

But the cowboy also represented a more dangerous ideal: the defence of the native Waspish American ways against the mil-lions of encroaching immigrants from lower races. Hence the quiet dropping of the Mexican, Indian and Black elements, which still appear in the original non-ideological westerns – for instance, Buffalo Bill's show. It is at this stage and in this manner that the cowboy becomes the lanky, tall Aryan. In other words, the invented cowboy tradition is part of the rise of both segre-gation and anti-immigrant racism; this is a dangerous heritage. The Aryan cowboy is not, of course, entirely mythical. Probably the percentage of Mexicans, Indians and Blacks did diminish as the Wild West ceased to be essentially a south-western, even a Texan, phenomenon, and at the peak of the boom it extended into areas like Montana, Wyoming and the Dakotas. In the later periods of the cattle boom the cowboys were also joined by a fair number of European dudes, mainly Englishmen, with Eastern-bred college-men following them. 'It may be safely said that nine tenths of those engaged in the stock business in the far west are gentlemen.'[6] For, incidentally, one aspect of the reality of the cattle economy, which does not get much into the invented tradition of the cowboy, is that a substantial amount of British Victorian investment went into western cattle-ranching.

The Aryan cowboy had, initially, no special appeal to the Europeans, even though westerns were enormously popular. A fair number were indeed made in Europe. Europeans were still into Indians rather than just cowboys, and you may recall that the Germans produced a film version of *The Last of the Mohicans* before 1914 with the Indian hero, surprisingly, played by Bela Lugosi.

The new cowboy tradition made its way into the wider world by two routes: the western movie and the much underrated western novel or sub-novel, which was to many foreigners what the private eye thriller was to become in our own times. It emerged with the invention of the new West. I will say nothing about it, except to quote the example of the militant and Methodist leader of the British miners' union who died in 1930, leaving behind him little money but a large collection of the novels of Zane Grey. By the way Grey's *Riders of the Purple Sage*[7] was turned into four movies between 1918 and 1941. As for the movies, we know that the genre of the western was firmly established by about 1909. Show business for a mass public being what it is, it will surprise nobody that the celluloid cowboy tended to develop two subspecies: the romantic, strong, shy, silent man of action of exemplified by W. S. Hart, Gary Cooper and John Wayne, and the cowboy entertainer of the Buffalo Bill type – heroic, no doubt, but essentially showing off his tricks and, as such, usually associated with a particular horse. Tom Mix was no doubt the prototype and much the most successful of these. Let me observe once again, in passing, that the literary influences on the ambitious western – as against the Hoot Gibson type of western – are clearly to be found in popular sentimental nineteenth-century writing. This is fairly evident in *The Covered Wagon* of 1923, the first Hollywood epic other than those of Griffiths, and it is very clear in *Stagecoach*, which is, of course, based on de Maupassant's *Boule de Suif.*[8]

But I don't want to give you yet another rundown on the development of the western movie, nor even to trace, however briefly, the transformation of the horse opera into a sort of national epic, which it originally was not. Westerns obviously did not seriously tempt D. W. Griffith, but *The Covered Wagon* was patently treated as something more than mere entertainment: it was, for instance, very carefully researched. And in the 1930s when the Europeans turned to a classical western theme which they interpreted in an anti-capitalist spirit, as in *Sutter's Gold*, Hollywood was moved to get the author of *The Covered Wagon* to make a more patriotic version of the same subject, released in 1936.

What I want, instead, is to draw your attention at the conclusion of this survey to a curious fact: the reinvention of the cowboy tradition in our times, as the established myth of Reagan's America. This is really very recent. For instance, cowboys did not become a serious medium for selling things until the 1960s, surprising though this seems: Marlboro country really revealed the enormous potential in American male identification with cow-punchers, who, of course, are increasingly seen not as riding herd but as gunslingers. Who said: 'I've always acted alone like the cowboy... the cowboy entering the village or city alone on his horse ... He acts, that's all'? Henry Kissinger to Oriana Fallaci in 1972, that's who.[9] Can we imagine a boss before the 1970s being described as 'riding herd' by the people he commands? Let me quote you the *reductio ad absurdum* of this myth, which dates back to 1979:

> The West. It's not just stage-coaches and sagebrush. It's an image of men who are real and proud. Of the freedom and independence we all would like to feel. Now Ralph Lauren has expressed all this in Chaps, his new men's cologne. Chaps is a cologne a man can put on as naturally as a worn leather jacket or a pair of jeans. Chaps. It's the West. The West you would like to feel inside yourself.[10]

The real invented tradition of the West, as a mass phenomenon that dominates American policy, is the product of the eras of Kennedy, Johnson, Nixon and Reagan. And, of course, Reagan, the first president since Teddy Roosevelt whose image is deliberately western and on horseback, knew what he was doing. To what extent Reaganite cowboys reflect the shift of American wealth to the south-west, I must leave others to judge.

Is this Reaganite myth of the West an international tradition? I think not. In the first place because the major American medium by which the invented West was propagated has died out. The western novel or sub-novel, as I have already suggested, is no longer an international phenomenon as it was in the days of Zane Grey. The private eye has killed the Virginian. Larry McMurtry and his like, whatever their place in American literature, are virtually unknown outside their native country. As for the western movie, it was killed by TV; and the western TV series, which was probably the last genuinely international mass triumph of the invented West, became a mere adjunct to children's hour, and in turn it has faded away. Where are the Hopalong Cassidys, Lone Rangers, Roy Rogers, *Laramies*, *Gunsmokes* and the rest on which the kids of the 1950s thrived? The real western movie became deliberately highbrow, a carrier of social, moral and political significance in the 1950s, until it in turn collapsed under their weight as well as the advancing age of the makers and stars – of Ford and Wayne and Cooper. I'm not criticising them. On the contrary, practically all the westerns that any of us would wish to see again date from after *Stagecoach* (which was released in 1939). But what carried the West into the hearts and homes of five continents was not movies that aimed at winning Oscars or critical applause. What is more, once the late western movie had itself become infected by Reaganism – or by John Wayne as an ideologist – it became so American that most of the rest of the world didn't get the point, or, if it did, didn't like it.

In Britain, at least, the word 'cowboy' today has a secondary meaning, which is much more familiar than the primary meaning of a fellow in the Marlboro ads. It means chiefly a fellow who comes in from nowhere offering a service, such as to repair your roof, but who doesn't know what he's doing or doesn't care except about ripping you off: a 'cowboy plumber' or a 'cowboy bricklayer'. I leave you to speculate (a) how this secondary meaning derives from the Shane or John Wayne stereotype and (b) how much it reflects the reality of the Reaganite wearers of dude Stetsons in the sunbelt. I don't know when the term first appears in British usage, but certainly it was not before the mid-1960s. In this version, what a man's got to do is to fleece us and disappear into the sunset.

There is, in fact, a European backlash against the John Wayne image of the West, and that is the revived genre of the western movie. Whatever the spaghetti westerns mean, they certainly were deeply critical of the US western myth, and in being so, paradoxically, they showed how much demand there still was among adults in both Europe and the USA for the old gunslingers. The western was revived via Sergio Leone, or for that matter via Kurosawa, that is, via non-American intellectuals steeped in the lore and the films of the West, but sceptical of the American invented tradition.

In the second place foreigners simply do not recognise the

associations of the western myth for the American right or indeed for ordinary Americans. Everyone wears jeans, but without that spontaneous even if faint urge that so many young Americans feel, once they wear them, to slouch against an imagined hitching post, narrowing their eyes against the sun. Even their aspiring rich don't ever feel tempted to wear Texan-type hats. They can watch Schlesinger's *Midnight Cowboy* without a sense of desecration. In short, only Americans live in Marlboro country. Gary Cooper was never a joke, but JR and the other platinum-plated inhabitants of the great dude ranch in *Dallas* are. In this sense the West is no longer an international tradition.

But it once was. And at the end of these brief reflections I return to the question, why? What was so special about cowboys? First, clearly, that they occurred in a country that was universally visible and central to the nineteenth-century world, of which it constituted, as it were, the utopian dimension – at least in the pre-1917 period, whatever your utopia was: the living dream. Anything that happened in America seemed bigger, more extreme, more dramatic and unlimited even when it wasn't – and of course often it was, though not in the case of the cowboys. Second, because the purely local vogue for western myth was magnified and internationalised by means of the global influence of American popular culture, the most original and creative in the industrial and urban world, and the mass media that carried it and which the USA dominated. And let me observe in passing that it made its way in the world not only directly, but also indirectly, via the European intellectuals it attracted to the USA, or at a distance.

This would certainly explain why cowboys are better known than *vaqueros* or gauchos, but not, I think, the full range of the international vibrations they set up, or used to set up. This, I suggest, is due to the in-built anarchism of American capitalism. I mean not only the anarchism of the market, but the ideal of an individual uncontrolled by any constraints of state authority.

In many ways the nineteenth-century USA was a stateless society. Compare the myths of the American and the Canadian
West: the one is a myth of a Hobbesian state of nature miti-
gated only by individual and collective self-help: licensed or
unlicensed gunmen, posses of vigilantes and occasional cavalry
charges. The other is the myth of the imposition of government
and public order as symbolised by the uniforms of the
Canadian version of the horseman-hero, the Royal Canadian
Mounted Police.

Individualist anarchism had two faces. For the rich and powerful it represents the superiority of profit over law and state.
Not just because law and the state can be bought, but because
even when they can't, they have no moral legitimacy compared
to selfishness and profit. For those who have neither wealth nor
power, it represents independence, and the little man's right to
make himself respected and show what he can do. I don't think
that it was an accident that the ideal-typical cowboy hero of the
classic invented West was a *loner*, not beholden to anyone; nor, I
think, that money was *not* important for him. As Tom Mix put
it: 'I ride into a place owning my own horse, saddle and bridle.
It isn't my quarrel, but I get into trouble doing the right thing for
somebody else. When it's all ironed out, I never get any money
reward.'[11] I don't want to discuss the more recent westerns,
which are the apotheosis not of the lone individual but of the
macho gang. Whatever they signify – and one wouldn't exclude
the homosexual element – they mark a transformation of the
genre.

In a way the loner lent himself to imaginary self-identification
just because he was a loner. To be Gary Cooper at high noon or
Sam Spade, you just have to imagine you are one man, whereas
to be Don Corleone or Rico, let alone Hitler, you have to imagine a collective of people who follow and obey you, which is less
plausible. I suggest that the cowboy, just because he was a myth
of an ultra-individualist society, the only society of the bourgeois era without real pre-bourgeois roots, was an unusually

effective vehicle for dreaming – which is all that most of us get in the way of unlimited opportunities. To ride alone is less implausible than to wait until that marshal's baton in your knapsack becomes reality.

Notes

PART I: THE PREDICAMENT OF
'HIGH CULTURE' TODAY

3: A Century of Cultural Symbiosis?

1   See Jean-Pierre Vernant, *La volonté de comprendre* (La Tour d'Aigues: Édi-
     tions de l'Aube, 1999), pp. 37–8.
2   Ian Buruma,'Tibet disenchanted', *New York Review of Books* (July 2000),
     24.
3   The British experience in the Olympic Games of 2012 would make this
     point with even greater force.

PART II: THE CULTURE OF THE
BOURGEOIS WORLD

6: Enlightenment and Achievement: The Emancipation of Jewish Talent since 1800

1   J. Katz, *Out of the Ghetto: The Social Background of Jewish Emancipation
     1770–1870* (Cambridge, MA: Harvard University Press, 1973), p. 26.
2   Ibid, p. 34.

3 Simon Dubnow, *Die neueste Geschichte des jüdischen Volkes*, vol. IX (Berlin: Jüdischer Verlag, 1929), pp. 253ff.

4 Simon Dubnow, *Die neueste Geschichte des jüdischen Volkes*, vol. VIII (Berlin: Jüdischer Verlag, 1930), p. 402; vol. IX, pp. 170ff.

5 Stephan Thernstrom (ed.), *Harvard Encyclopaedia of American Ethnic Groups*, 'Jews' (Cambridge, MA: Belknap Press, 1980), p. 573ii.

6 Dubnow, *Die neueste Geschichte des jüdischen Volkes*, vol. VIII, pp. 263–4.

7 Peter Pukzer, 'What about the Jewish non-intellectuals in Germany?', in S. Feiner (ed.), *Braun Lectures in the History of the Jews in Prussia* (Ramat Gan: Bar-Ilan University Press, 2001), no. 7, p. 10.

8 Oskar Ansull, quoting Theodor Fontane, in *Ossietzky*, Zweiwochenschrift, 24 (2004).

9 Karl Emil Franzos, *Vom Don zur Donau* (Berlin: Rütten & Loening, 1970), pp. 383–95.

10 Dubnow, *Die neueste Geschichte des jüdischen Volkes*, vol. VIII, p. 405.

11 Arthur Schnitzler, *Gesammelte Werke*, Erzählende Schriften Band III (Berlin, 1918), p. 82.

12 Shulamit Volkov, 'The dynamics of dissimilation: Ostjuden and German Jews', in J. Reinharz and W. Schatzberg (eds), *The Jewish Response to German Culture from the Enlightenment to the Second World War* (Hanover, NH and London: University Press of New England, 1985). For a good example (relations between German émigrés and Hollywood), see Michael Kater, 'Die vertriebenen Musen', in H. Lehmann and O. G. Oexle (eds), *Nationalsozialismus in den Kulturwissenschaften Bd 2* (Göttingen: Vandenhoeck & Ruprecht, 2004), pp. 505–6.

13 Gerald Stourzh, 'Galten die Juden als Nationalität Altösterreichs?', *Studia Judaica Austriaca X* (Eisenstadt, 1984), 83–5, esp. 84. See also 94, n. 29.

14 Yuri Slezkine, *The Jewish Century* (Princeton: Princeton University Press, 2004).

15 A list of 300 eminent Americans drawn up in 1953 (Richard B. Morris, *Encyclopedia of American History*, New York: Harper) contains twelve Jews (4 per cent) although all but three of these (marked *) belong to the pre-1880s immigration. They include four scientists (Boas, Cohn*, Michelson, Rabi*), two jurists (Brandeis, Cardozo), two newspaper editors (Ochs, Pulitzer), one 'educator' (Flexner), one labour leader (Gompers), one business tycoon (Guggenheim) and one composer (Gershwin*). Would such a list, fifty years later, have omitted all Jews from the list of politicians, state servants, writers and artists?

16 Cf. Dr A. v. Guttry, *Galizien, Land und Leute* (Munich and Leipzig: G. Müller, 1916), p. 93: 'die juedische Intelligenz ist voellig im Polentum

aufgegangen, ist von der polnischen Gesellschaft aufgenommen worden und gehört heute zum grossen Teil zu den geachtesten Mitgliedern derselben'.

17 Corrado Vivanti (ed.), *Einaudi Storia d'Italia, Annali 11, Gli ebrei in Italia* (Turin: Grandi Opere, 1997), pp. 1190, 1625.

18 Daniel Snowman, *The Hitler Émigrés: The Cultural Impact on Britain of Refugees from Nazism* (London: Pimlico, 2002), p. 326.

19 Gerd Hohorst, Jürgen Kocka and Gerhard A. Ritter, *Sozialgeschichtliches Arbeitsbuch: Materialien zur Statistik des Kaiserreichs 1870–1914* (Munich: Beck, 1975), p. 164; H. U. Wehler, *Deutsche Sozialgeschichte Bd 3 1849–1914* (Munich: Beck, 1995), p. 419.

20 Wehler, *Deutsche Sozialgeschichte Bd 3 1849–1914*, p. 615.

21 Before then there were only seven in physics and chemistry, compared with something like twenty-five to thirty in the next thirty years.

22 Educational discrimination (the numerous clauses) was abandoned in practice after the 1905 revolution, but even before then 13.4 per cent of the students at Kiev University and 14.5 per cent of those at Odessa University were Jewish. G. L. Shetilina in *Istoriya SSSR* (1979), vol. 5, p. 114.

8: Mitteleuropean Destinies

1 John C. Bartholomew, *The Edinburgh World Atlas* (7th edn, Edinburgh: J. Bartholomew, 1970).

2 Ivan T. Berend and Györgi Ránki, *Economic Development in East Central Europe in the 19th and 20th Centuries* (New York: Columbia University Press, 1974).

3 Austria, Hungary, the Czech Republic, Slovakia, Poland, Ukraine, Romania, Italy, Slovenia, Croatia, Bosnia, Serbia.

4 Since Franz Joseph ruled as emperor in the Austrian but as king in the Hungarian part of his realm.

5 Karl Emil Franzos, *Aus Halb-Asien: Culturbilder aus Galizien, der Bukowina, Südrussland und Rumänien*, vol. 1 (Leipzig, 1876).

6 Gregor von Rezzori, *Maghrebinische Geschichten* (Hamburg: Rowohlt, 1953); *Ein Hermelin in Tschernopol: Ein maghrebinischer Roman* (Hamburg: Rowohlt, 1958).

7 See Gerald Stourzh, 'Galten die Juden als Nationalität Altösterreichs?', *Studia Judaica Austriaca*, vol. X (Eisenstadt, 1984), 74–9.

8 Carl E. Schorske, *Fin-de-Siècle Vienna: Politics and Culture* (London: Vintage, 1980), p. 31.

9: Culture and Gender in European Bourgeois Society 1870–1914

1 In this chapter, the word 'culture' is used in the sense usually given to it in nineteenth-century bourgeois discourse: namely, the body of achievements in the various creative arts assumed to have moral and aesthetic value (as distinct from mere 'entertainment'), their proper appreciation, and the body of knowledge necessary for their proper appreciation.

2 Jihang Park, 'Women of their time: the growing recognition of the second sex in Victorian and Edwardian England', *Journal of Social History*, 21 (September 1987), 49–67.

3 Ibid.

4 Edmée Charrier, *L'Évolution intellectuelle féminine* (Paris: A. Mechelinck, 1937).

5 Anne Sayre, *Rosalind Franklin and DNA* (New York: Norton, 1975).

6 Martha Vicinus, *Independent Women: Work and Community for Single Women, 1850–1920* (London: University of Chicago Press, 1986).

7 David Marsh, *The Changing Social Structure of England and Wales, 1871–1961* (London: Routledge & Kegan Paul, 1965).

8 Jihang Park, 'The British suffrage archivists of 1913: an analysis', *Past and Present*, 120 (August 1988), 147–63.

9 The best introductions to this much-publicised secret society can be found in Paul Levy, *Moore: G. E. Moore and the Cambridge Apostles* (Toronto: Oxford University Press, 1981); and in Robert Skidelsky, *John Maynard Keynes: Hopes Betrayed 1883–1920*, vol. I (London: Macmillan, 1983).

10 Theodore Zeldin, *France 1848–1975*, vol. I (Oxford: Oxford University Press, 1977).

11 *The Englishwoman's Handbook* (1905).

12 Skidelsky, *John Maynard Keynes*.

13 Norman MacKenzie and Jeanne MacKenzie (eds), *The Diaries of Beatrice Webb* (London: Virago, 1983)

14 The period 1900–1914 is probably the only one in English literature since 1800 when the list of major novelists – say, Thomas Hardy, Joseph Conrad, H. G. Wells, Arnold Bennett, Rudyard Kipling, E. M. Forster and George Gissing – contains no obvious woman.

10: Art Nouveau

1 Rosemary Hill, '"Gorgeous, and a wee bit vulgar": from *Gesamtkunstwerk* to "lifestyle": the consumable daring of Art Nouveau', *Times Literary Supplement* (5 May 2000), 18.

2 Eric Hobsbawm, *Workers: Worlds of Labour* (New York: Pantheon, 1985), p. 136.
3 Stephen Escritt, *Art Nouveau* (London: Phaidon, 2000), p. 77.
4 Schorske, *Fin-de-Siècle Vienna: Politics and Culture*, p. 304.
5 Debora L. Silverman, *Art Nouveau in Fin-de-Siècle France* (Berkeley: University of California Press, 1989), pp. 138–9.
6 Eric Hobsbawm, *Age of Empire* (London: Weidenfeld & Nicolson, 1987), p. 165.
7 Escritt, *Art Nouveau*, p. 70.
8 Ibid, p. 72.
9 Silverman, *Art Nouveau in Fin-de-Siècle France*, p. 189.
10 Hobsbawm, *Age of Empire*, p. 169.
11 Escritt, *Art Nouveau*, p. 329.
12 'La Barcelona del 1900', *L'Avenc* (October 1978), 22.
13 Ibid, p. 36.

PART III: UNCERTAINTIES, SCIENCE, RELIGION

13: Worrying about the Future

1 Richard Overy, *The Morbid Age: Britain Between the Wars* (London: Allen Lane, 2009), p. 376.
2 Ibid, p. 92.

14: Science: Social Function and World Change

1 Andrew Brown, *J. D. Bernal: The Sage of Science* (Oxford: Oxford University Press, 2006).
2 Fred Steward, 'Political Formation', in Brenda Swann and Francis Aprahamian (eds), *J. D. Bernal: A Life in Science and Politics* (London: Verso, 1999).
3 Cf. the present writer's preface to Swann and Aprahamian (eds), *J. D. Bernal*, esp. pp. xv–xviii.
4 Brown, *J. D. Bernal*, p. 19.
5 J. D. Bernal, *The Social Function of Science* (Cambridge, MA: MIT Press, 1967).
6 J. D. Bernal, *Science in History* (Cambridge, MA: MIT Press, 1971).
7 Georges Friedmann, *La Crise du Progrès: esquisse d'histoire des idées, 1895–1935* (Paris: Gallimard, 1936).

8 Yoram Gorlicki and Oleg Khlebniuk, *Cold Peace: Stalin and the Soviet Ruling Circle, 1945–53* (New York: Oxford University Press, 2004), p. 39.

9 C. P. Snow, 'J. D. Bernal: a personal portrait', in M. Goldsmith and A. Mackay (eds), *The Science of Science* (London: Penguin, 1964).

15: Mandarin in a Phrygian Cap: Joseph Needham

1 Only one other brief biography exists, published under the auspices of UNESCO shortly after his death: Maurice Goldsmith, *Joseph Needham, Twentieth Century Renaissance Man* (Paris: UNESCO, 1995).

2 Joseph Needham, *Chemical Embryology* (Cambridge: Cambridge University Press, 1931).

3 Joseph Needham (ed.), *The Chemistry of Life: Lectures on the History of Biochemistry* (Cambridge: Cambridge University Press, 1961).

4 T. E. B. Howarth, *Cambridge Between Two Wars* (London: Collins, 1978), p. 190.

5 Ibid, p. 209.

6 Peter J. Bowles, *Reconciling Science and Religion: The Debate in Early Twentieth-Century Britain* (Chicago: University of Chicago Press, 2001), p. 39.

7 Obituary in *Current Science*, 69, no. 6 (25 September 1995).

8 Joseph Needham, *Within the Four Seas: The Dialogue of East and West* (London: Routledge, 2005), pp. 189–91.

9 F. R. Leavis (ed.), *Scrutiny* (May 1932), 36–9.

10 *Science and Society*, vol. 23 (1959), 58–65, from which the above quotes are taken.

11 Ibid, 64.

17: The Prospect of Public Religion

1 Robert W. Hefner, *Civic Islam: Muslims and Democratization in Indonesia* (Princeton: Princeton University Press, 2000), p. 17.

2 CIA World Factbook, at https://www.cia.gov/library/publications/the-world-factbook/index.html.

3 J. D. Long-Garcia, 'Admission deferred: modern barriers to vocation', *The US Catholic*, 76: 9 (16 August 2011), 30–5; at http://www.uscatholic.org/church/2011/07/admission-deferred-modern-barriers-vocations.

4 CIA, *World Fact Book*, 'Field Listing: Religions' ('Orthodox churches are highly nationalist and ethnic').

5 *The Jewish Week*, New York (2 November 2001); Judaism 101, an online

encyclopaedia: 'Movements of Judaism' at http://www.jewfaq.org/movement.htm.

6 Sami Zubaida, 'The "Arab Spring" in historical perspective' (21 October 2011), at http://www.opendemocracy.net/sami-zubaida/arab-spring-in-historical-perspective.

7 YouGov/Daybreak poll, Religion + school + churches, September 2010, at http://d25d2506sfb94s.cloudfront.net/today_uk_import/YG-Archives-Life-YouGov-DaybreakReligion-130910.pdf.

8 Office for National Statistics, *Social Trends*, no. 40 (2010 edn), table 2.12, p. 20.

9 David E. Eagle, 'Changing patterns of attendance at religious services in Canada 1986–2008', *Journal for the Scientific Study of Religion*, 50: 1 (March 2011), 187–200.

10 P. Brenner, 'Exceptional behavior or exceptional identity?: overreporting of church attendance in the U.S.', *Public Opinion Quarterly*, 75: 1 (February 2011), 19–41; C. Kirk Hadaway and P. L. Marler, 'How many Americans attend worship each week?', *Journal for the Scientific Study of Religion*, 44: 3 (August 2005), 307–22.

11 Andrea Althoff, 'Religious identities of Latin American immigrants in Chicago: preliminary findings from field research' (University of Chicago, Divinity School, Religion Cultural Web Forum, June 2006), at http://divinity.uchicago.edu/martycenter/publications/webforum/062006/.

12 Pew Forum, 'Spirit and power: a 10-country survey of Pentecostals', at http://www.pewforum.org/Christian/Evangelical-Protestant-Churches/Spirit-and-Power.aspx.

13 James R. Green, *Grass-Roots Socialism: Radical Movements in the Southwest 1895–1943* (Baton Rouge and London: Louisiana State University Press, 1978), pp. 170–3.

14 Gérard Bernier, Robert Boily and Daniel Salée, *Le Québec en chiffres de 1850 à nos jours* (Montreal: ACFAS, 1986), p. 228.

15 Althoff, 'Religious identities'.

16 Richard Hugh Burgess, 'The civil war revival and its Pentecostal progeny: a religious movement among the Igbo people of eastern Nigeria', Ph.D. thesis, University of Birmingham (2004).

17 Billie Jean Isbell, *Finding Cholita* (Champaign: University of Illinois Press, 2009).

18 These were discussed in Eric Hobsbawm, *The Age of Extremes: A History of the World, 1914–91* (London: Pantheon Books, 1995), chapters 9–11.

20: The Avant-Garde Fails

1   Cited in John Willett, *The New Sobriety: Art and Politics in the Weimar Period 1917–1933* (London: Thames and Hudson, 1978), p. 76.

2   Cited in Linda Nochlin (ed.), *Realism and Tradition in Art, 1848–1900: Sources and Documents* (Englewood Cliffs: Prentice-Hall, 1996), p. 53.

3   'French Artists Spur on American Art', *New York Tribune*, 24 October 1915.

4   Cited in L. Brion-Guerry (ed.), *L'Année 1913: Les forms esthétiques de l'oeuvre d'art à la vielle de la première guerre mondiale* (Paris: Éditions Klinksieck, 1971), p. 89 n. 34.

5   Catalogue of Exhibition *Berlin-Moskau 1900–1950*, pp. 118 (fig. 1), 120–1.

6   Brion-Guerry (ed.), *L'Année 1913*, p. 86 n. 27.

7   The Economist, *Pocket Britain in Figures: 1997 Edition* (London: Profile Books, 1996), pp. 194, 195.

8   Theodore Zeldin, *France 1848–1945: Intellect, Taste and Anxiety* (Oxford: Clarendon, 1977), p. 446.

9   Pierre Nora (ed.), *Les lieux de mémoire II: La Nation* (Paris: Gallimard, 1986), vol. III, p. 256.

10   Gisèle Freund, *Photographie und bürgerliche Gesellschaft* (Munich: Verlag Rogner & Bernhard, 1968), p. 92.

11   Cited in Brion-Guerry (ed.), *L'Année 1913*.

12   Catalogue *Paris-Berlin. 1900–1933* (Pompidou Centre, 1978), pp. 170–1.

13   Cited in Charles Harrison and Paul Wood (eds), *Art in Theory 1900–1990: An Anthology of Changing Ideas* (Oxford: Blackwell, 1992), p. 576.

14   Cited in Suzy Menkes, 'Man Ray, Designer behind the Camera', *International Herald Tribune*, 5 May 1998.

15   Zeldin, *France 1848–1945*, pp. 480, 481.

16   P. Bourdieu, *La Distinction: critique sociale du jugement* (Paris: Éditions de Minuit, 1979), p. 615. Respondents were asked to choose among the following artists: Raphael, Buffet, Utrillo, Vlaminck, Watteau, Renoir, Van Gogh, Dalí, Braque, Goya, Brueghel, Kandinsky.

17   Robert Hughes, *American Visions: The Epic History of Art in America* (London: Harvill, 1997), pp. 487–8.

18   Brion-Guerry (ed.), *L'Année 1913*, p. 297 n. 29.

19   Harrison and Wood (eds, *Art in Theory 1900–1990*, p. 804.

20   Alan Bullock and Oliver Stallybrass (eds), *The Fontana Dictionary of Modern Thought* (London: Fontana, 1977), entry: 'Cubism'.

21   Nikolaus Pevsner, *Pioneers of Modern Design: From William Morris to Walter Gropius* (1936; London: Penguin, 1991, revised edn).

22 Brion-Guerry (ed.), *L'Année 1913*, p. 86 n. 27.

23 Paul Klee, *Uber die moderne Kunst* (Bern: Verlag Benteli, 1945), p. 53.

PART IV: FROM ART TO MYTH

21: Pop Goes the Artist: Our Exploding Culture

1 Umberto Eco, *Apocalittici e integrati: comunicazioni di massa e teorie della cultura di massa* (Milan: Bompiani, 1964).

2 Stuart Hall and Paddy Whannel, *The Popular Arts* (London: Hutchinson, 1964).

3 Richard Hoggart, *The Uses of Literacy: Aspects of Working Class Life* (London: Chatto and Windus, 1957), pp. 86–7.

4 Edgar Morin, *Les Stars* (Paris: Éditions de Minuit, 1957).

5 Eco, *Apocalittici e integrati*, pp. 180–1.

22: The American Cowboy: An International Myth?

1 Eduardo Franco Isaza, *Los guerrilleros del llano* (Bogotá: Mundial, 1959).

2 Gustave Aimard, *Les Trappeurs de l'Arkansas* (Paris: Amyot, 1858).

3 Lonn Taylor and Ingrid Maar (eds), *The American Cowboy*, vol. 39, issue 2 of *American Studies in Folklife* (Library of Congress: American Folklife Centre, 1983), p. 88.

4 William S. Hart, 1916, quoted in George Fenin and William Everson, *The Western: From Silents to the Seventies* (Harmondsworth: Penguin, 1977).

5 Robert A. Dykstra, *The Cattle Towns* (New York: Alfred A. Knopf, 1968), p. 144.

6 Robert Taft, *Artists and Illustrators of the Old West 1850–1900* (New York: Scribners, 1953), pp. 194–5, quoting 'Ranching and ranchers of the Far West', *Lippincotts Magazine*, 29 (1882), 435.

7 Zane Grey, *Riders of the Purple Sage* (New York: Harpers & Brothers, 1912).

8 Guy de Maupassant, 'Boule de Suif', first published in *Les Soirées de Médan* (1880).

9 The full text of the passage is 'riding ahead alone on his horse, the cowboy who rides all alone into the town, the village, with his horse and nothing else. Maybe even without a pistol, since he doesn't shoot. He acts, that's all ... This amazing, romantic character suits me precisely

because to be alone has always been part of my style or, if you like, my technique.' See special section: 'Chagrined Cowboy', *Time Magazine* (8 October 1979).

10 This advertisement appeared in various periodicals including *New York Magazine* and *Texas Monthly.*

11 Fenin and Everson, *The Western*, p. 117.

Dates and Sources of Original Publication

1 Manifestos
Originally given as a contribution to the Serpentine Gallery Manifesto Marathon, conceived by Hans Ulrich Obrist, in 2008.

2 Where Are the Arts Going?
Originally given as a lecture in German at the Festival of Dialogues, Salzburg, 1996. Translation by Christine Shuttleworth.

3 A Century of Cultural Symbiosis?
Originally given as a lecture in German at the Salzburg Music Festival, 2000. Translation by Christine Shuttleworth.

4 Why Hold Festivals in the Twenty-First Century?
Originally given as a lecture in German at the Salzburg Music Festival, 2006. Translation by Christine Shuttleworth.

5 Politics and Culture in the New Century
Originally given as the Hesse Lecture, Aldeburgh Festival, 2002.

6 Enlightenment and Achievement: The Emancipation of Jewish Talent since 1800
Original title of a lecture given on 10 May 2005 on the fiftieth anniversary of the Leo Baeck Institute. First published as 'Benefits of Diaspora', *London Review of Books*, vol. 27 no. 20, 20 October 2005.

7 The Jews and Germany
Written as a review of Peter Pulzer, *Jews and the German State: The Political History of a Minority, 1848–1933* (Blackwell, 1992) and Ruth Gay, *The Jews of Germany: A Historical Portrait* (Yale University Press, 1992) and published as 'Homesickness', *London Review of Books*, vol. 15 no. 7, 8 April 1993.

8 Mitteleuropean Destinies
First published in *COMPARARE: Comparative European History Review*, by Association international des musées d'histoire, Paris, 2003.

9 Culture and Gender in European Bourgeois Society 1870–1914
First published in David Olson and Michael Cole (eds), *Technology, Literacy and the Evolution of Society: Implications of the Work of Jack Goody* (Lawrence Erlbaum Associates, 2006).

10 Art Nouveau
First publication. Originally given as a lecture at the Victoria and Albert Museum, 25 June 2000.

11 The Last Days of Mankind
Not previously published in English. Translation by Christine Shuttleworth.

12 Heritage
First publication. Written in 2011–12.

13 Worrying About the Future
First published as 'C for Crisis', *London Review of Books*, vol. 31 no. 15, 6 August 2009, as a review of Richard Overy, *The Morbid Age: Britain between the Wars* (Allen Lane, 2009).

14 Science: Social Function and World Change
First published as 'Red Science', *London Review of Books*, vol. 28 no. 5, 9 March 2006, as a review of Andrew Brown, *J. D. Bernal: The Sage of Science* (Oxford University Press, 2005).

15 Mandarin in a Phrygian Cap: Joseph Needham
First published as 'Era of Wonders', *London Review of Books*, vol. 31 no. 4, 26 February 2009 as a review of Simon Winchester, *Bomb, Book and Compass: Joseph Needham and the Great Secrets of China* (Viking, 2008).

16 The Intellectuals: Role, Function and Paradox
Not previously published in English. Based on a German contribution to Ilse Fischer and Ingeborg Schrems (eds), *Der Intellektuelle: Festschrift für Michael Fischer zum 65. Geburtstag* (Peter Lang, 2010). Author's own translation.

17 The Prospect of Public Religion
First publication.

18 Art and Revolution
First published as 'Changing of the avant-garde', *RA Magazine*, no. 97, winter 2007.

19 Art and Power
    First published as the foreword to Dawn Ades, David Elliott, Tim
    Benton and Iain Boyd Whyte (eds), *Art and Power: Europe under the Dictators
    1930–45* (Thames and Hudson, 1995).

20 The Avant-Garde Fails
    Eric Hobsbawm, *Behind the Times: The Decline and Fall of the Twentieth-Century
    Avant-Gardes* (Thames and Hudson, 1998), © 1998 Eric Hobsbawm.

21 Pop Goes the Artist: Our Exploding Culture
    First published as 'Pop Goes the Artist', *Times Literary Supplement*, no.
    3277, 17 December 1964.

22 The American Cowboy: An International Myth?
    First publication. Based on a lecture.

Index

To buy any of our books and to find out
more about Abacus and Little, Brown, our authors
and titles, as well as events and book clubs,
visit our website

www.littlebrown.co.uk

and follow us on Twitter

@AbacusBooks
@LittleBrownUK

To order any Abacus titles p & p free in the UK,
please contact our mail order supplier on:

+ 44 (0)1832 737525

Customers not based in the UK should contact
the same number for appropriate postage
and packing costs.